Thinking Twice

Thinking Twice
Two minds in one brain

Jonathan St B T Evans

Emeritus Professor of Psychology
University of Plymouth, UK

OXFORD
UNIVERSITY PRESS

OXFORD
UNIVERSITY PRESS

Great Clarendon Street, Oxford OX2 6DP

Oxford University Press is a department of the University of Oxford.
It furthers the University's objective of excellence in research, scholarship,
and education by publishing worldwide in

Oxford New York

Auckland Cape Town Dar es Salaam Hong Kong Karachi
Kuala Lumpur Madrid Melbourne Mexico City Nairobi
New Delhi Shanghai Taipei Toronto

With offices in

Argentina Austria Brazil Chile Czech Republic France Greece
Guatemala Hungary Italy Japan Poland Portugal Singapore
South Korea Switzerland Thailand Turkey Ukraine Vietnam

Oxford is a registered trade mark of Oxford University Press
in the UK and in certain other countries

Published in the United States
by Oxford University Press Inc., New York

British Library Cataloguing in Publication Data
Data available

Library of Congress Cataloging-in-Publication Data
Data available

Typeset by Glyph International, Bangalore, India
Printed in Great Britain
on acid-free paper by
CPI Antony Rowe, Chippenham, Wiltshire

ISBN 978–0–19–954729–6

10 9 8 7 6 5 4 3 2 1

Preface

We all feel as though we—conscious persons—are in charge of our own behaviour, carrying out our conscious wishes and intentions. But psychologists have shown that what we do is often a matter of intuition or habit and the reasons we give ourselves for our actions can be invented. It seems that while we feel as though we have but a single mind, we actually have two. One is an old intuitive mind which evolved early and shares many its features with other animals. We also have a new, reflective mind which evolved much later and makes us distinctively human. These are not the conscious and unconscious minds of Freudian theory. Although the old mind often seems to work in an automatic way and the new mind corresponds more with the conscious person, both minds have conscious and unconscious aspects. The two minds hypothesis, explored in this book, is that the new mind was *added* to the old mind, which continues to influence much of our behaviour. The two usually co-operate but can also conflict.

The case for the two minds hypothesis is scattered across a wide range of psychological literature. Most academics, including me for most of my career, work within relatively narrow research fields, rarely looking over the tall metaphorical hedges that separate them from the concerns of other researchers. In my case, I mostly studied the experimental psychology of human reasoning, while also dabbling in the related fields of judgement and decision making. This work started in the early 1970's and quickly led me to the view there are two kinds of thinking. I started out by discovering and documenting a number of cognitive biases that afflict and deflect the reasoning of the university students on whom we mostly test our problems. I soon discovered that they were quite unaware of these biases and instead gave us rational sounding accounts of their often erroneous inferences. Over the next twenty years, I developed a number of so-called 'dual process' accounts of reasoning and judgement.

During this time I was blissfully unaware of parallel developments in other fields of psychology. Arthur Reber, with a programme of work that started in the 1960's, proposed a theory that were two kinds of learning: implicit (reflected only in the behaviour) and explicit (with conscious knowledge of what had been learned). He later developed this into a broader two system theory of the mind, in which the implicit system was regarded as evolutionarily older and more closely linked with animal cognition. I was equally unaware of developments in social psychology, from the early 1980's onwards, in which a number of dual-process theories were developed. Social psychologists realised that people could hold attitudes and beliefs at an implicit as well as an explicit level. While people were not aware of the nature of these beliefs, or even that they held them, their influence was detectable in their social behaviour. It also became apparent that implicit processes were involved in many other phenomena studied by social psychologists: how we are persuaded to change our views, how we form impressions of people we meet, how we are influenced by the behaviour and norms of the people around us, and so on. These influences were often seen to conflict and compete with people's conscious beliefs and intentions.

By the early 1990's I was starting to take a broader view. I read Reber and realised that there was an important connection between dual-process theories of learning and reasoning. In 1996, I published, with the philosopher David Over, a book called *Rationality and Reasoning* (Psychology Press) in which we proposed a two system theory that could also account for reasoning and decision making. Our ideas in turn were taken up and developed by the psychologist Keith Stanovich, who explored the idea that explicit processing is related to general intelligence, while implicit processing is not. By the early 2000's, I was starting to take seriously the idea that we might have two minds that underlie all the dual-process accounts that had appeared in various fields of psychology. However, I was well aware that proper examination of this hypothesis would require a single scholar to study a very wide range of scientific literature, well beyond my current familiarity with reasoning and decision making. There was relevant work also to be examined in the study of learning and memory, in evolutionary psychology, social psychology, consciousness studies and neuroscience. The task was enormous and daunting.

In the end, I decided that someone needed to take this on, and that I was as well placed to do it as anyone. I hence applied for and was granted a personal fellowship by the Economic and Research Council of the United Kingdom (RES-00-27-0184). This gave me, on paper, 30 months of full-time research to devote to the project, free of all normal university duties. In effect, this was extended to a full three year period, courtesy of my employer, the University of Plymouth. While a number of journal articles and two other scholarly books emerged from this period of work, it was always my intention also to write a book for the general reader on the topic. It took a couple of further years to complete, but would have been quite impossible without the funding from ESRC.

In the first six months of working on the ESRC fellowship, I wondered why on earth I had taken this on. Everything I read seemed to add complexity, detail and new issues to the problem and I came close to despair. But as is the nature of such scholarship, eventually links were found, and insights emerged. I was helped by an unanticipated collaboration with the philosopher Keith Frankish who was keen to organize an international conference on dual-process theory involving psychologists, philosophers and anthropologists. We pooled our resources and were able to hold a large meeting of international experts at the University of Cambridge in the summer of 2006, with a number of the papers being published in a book that we later edited (*In two minds*, Oxford University Press). My fellowship also provided me with funds for travel and discussion with a number of other scholars who helped me with the project. These include Keith Stanovich, Robin Dunbar, Max Velmans, Peter Carruthers, Tim Wilson and Elliot Smith. In addition to these I must acknowledge the help of my close research collaborators in the psychology of reasoning, especially David Over and Simon Handley, with whom I developed a number of more specific dual-process accounts.

The actual writing of the book was assisted in no small part by regular, chapter by chapter (and draft by draft) readings by both Shira Elqayam and Jane Evans, who detected my frequent lapses into the more familiar academic writing style, as well as commenting on the coherence of the emerging story. Keith Frankish also read parts of the manuscript and did his best to keep me on track while writing about philosophical issues, especially consciousness. In the time honoured tradition, I should hasten to add that the responsibility for any errors remaining in the book is entirely mine. Finally, I would like to acknowledge the contribution of my cat, Freddie, whose behaviour contributed to my understanding of the old mind, and my young grandchildren, Luca and Nina, whose emerging new minds were equally inspirational.

Jonathan Evans
Plymouth, March 2010

Contents

1 The two minds hypothesis *1*

2 Evolutionary foundations *23*

3 Two ways of knowing *53*

4 Two ways of deciding *79*

5 Reasoning and imagination *107*

6 Thinking about the social world *135*

7 Consciousness and control *159*

8 The two minds in action: conflict and co-operation *185*

Addendum: Some technical issues *215*

References *221*

Index *235*

Chapter 1

The two minds hypothesis

In the early 1980s, a resident of central Florida—a married man and regular commuter—set out to drive to work on a typical sunny, hot and steamy day. Everything was as normal except that his wife asked him to drop off their young child at a nursery on the way to work: something he rarely did. The child fell asleep in the back of the car and, preoccupied with his business problems, the man entirely forgot that she was there, parked his car in the Florida sunshine and went into his office. A couple of hours later, he realised what had happened and rushed to his car. Too late—the child was dead. This is a true story. I was on sabbatical leave at the University of Florida at the time and these events were reported in the local press.

How could such a tragedy happen? There was no reason to believe that this man was mentally disturbed in any way, nor any less caring than the average devoted parent. He had a normal human mind. Indeed, the really frightening aspect of this story is that it could have happened to any of us. We can all probably recall similar, but less costly, errors of this kind. For example, we may decide to drop off a letter on the way to work, which necessitates a change in route, but drive straight past the junction where we should have turned, as we plan our busy day ahead. On one occasion, some years ago, my wife asked me to drop her into town on my way in to the university, on a day when I was much preoccupied with the organization of a local conference. She waited at the front of the house while I fetched the car from the garage at the back. However, I never picked her up but drove straight into work, unable to keep track of my conscious intention even for a couple of minutes.

But surely such cognitive failures rarely lead to disastrous results? Not so. For example, the hot car story is far from an isolated incident. ABC News (July 2007) reported the following:

> Kevin Kelly is a law-abiding citizen who, much distracted, left his beloved 21-month-old daughter in a sweltering van for seven hours. Frances Kelly had probably been dead for more than four hours by the time a neighbour noticed her strapped in her car seat.

According to the same source 340 children died in hot cars in the previous 10 years in the United States alone. Paradoxically, safety legislation requiring

young children to be secured in the back seats of cars has exacerbated the problem, as they are then more easily forgotten. Sometimes the parents were pros-
ecuted but the cases engendered much debate about whether they were legally
responsible. No sane and loving parent would put their business problems
ahead of the life of their own child. And yet, on many occasions, this is exactly
what people appear to do.

In such cases, we may say that we are preoccupied or absent-minded. That
such absent-mindedness can have serious, even fatal, consequences gives us
some clues as to the divided nature of the normal human mind. Common
sense—or what is often described as 'folk psychology'—may tell us that we
have but a single mind, an 'I', that is in control, making rational decisions to
achieve our consciously held desires and intentions[1]. Most of the time, we can
maintain the illusion, and it most definitely is an illusion, that this is how our
minds and those of our fellow human beings actually work. But if we are
absent-minded, if our minds are *elsewhere* then exactly who or what is in control of our behaviour? When conscious attention is diverted, habitual behaviour takes over. But habits are part of our mind as well, just a *different* part.

The modern discipline of 'cognitive psychology' is concerned with the nature
of mental processes such as perception, attention, learning, memory, language,
reasoning and decision-making. The more one studies these topics, the more
apparent it becomes that the processes that underlie the bulk of these functions
must be partly or wholly unconscious. What is involved, for example, when we
understand a sentence spoken to us in conversation? The speaker vibrates air
molecules into wave patterns that are detected by the tympanic membranes of
our inner ears. These are then translated into electrical signals that are transmitted via the auditory nerve to primary reception areas in the brain and from
there to other regions for linguistic and semantic processing. Somewhere *en
route* to consciousness, phonemes, syllables and grammatical structure emerge
as does an analysis of meaning that ultimately takes into account all relevant
knowledge that the context evokes. All this takes place in 'real time', allowing
rapid and meaningful conversational exchanges to occur.

Now how much of all this amazing sequence of cognitive processing, which
we are as yet unable to reproduce in the world's most powerful computers, is
actually conscious? Can 'we', our conscious selves, congratulate ourselves on
the smartness of this operation? Not really; we cannot, for example, explain to
researchers in artificial intelligence how we actually do this, so that they can try
to program their computers with same methods. In fact, all we are really aware
of is the meaning of utterance we have heard and, if we attend to it, some characteristics of the sound, such as timbre and pitch of the voice, and gender of
the speaker. Even our ability to recall the actual words stated, as opposed to

their gist, or essential meaning, will be rapidly lost from our memories, especially if utterances are lengthy or followed by other statements from the speaker.

In this book, I am not concerned with *everything* that the brain does. There will be no discussion of the processes that control our digestion and blood sugar levels. The term 'mind' refers to those aspects of the brain that in some way *represent* the external world in which we find ourselves, and determine our behaviour within it. Even this definition is too broad for the current purposes, however. I will not, in fact, discuss in any detailed way how the brain processes visual information, or how it constructs the meaning of spoken sentences. To propose that such processes are automatic and unconscious is neither interesting nor controversial. I doubt that anyone would claim that they could explain the mechanism of the visual system by introspection. The focus here is instead on 'higher' functions of the brain that control our behaviour: everything from getting out of bed in the morning to learning to play a musical instrument; from putting on our shoes to writing a literary masterpiece. In essence, everything that defines us as biological, social and cultural creatures. Surely we are in control of these functions. Or are we?

The claim I shall explore is that there is no singular human mind in control of such higher functions. In the past 20 years, there has been a major growth of psychological research into the 'dual processes' that apparently underlie our learning, thinking, decision making and social judgements.[2] One kind of process (type 1) is described as fast, automatic and capable of processing large amounts of information at the same time. The other (type 2) is slow, sequential and limited in processing capacity but also appears to be under conscious control. What I am calling the 'two minds hypothesis' is based on the idea that there are two quite distinct cognitive systems underlying type 1 and 2 cognitive processes, in effect two minds within one brain.[3] On this basis, there are two ways of knowing, two ways of believing, two ways of thinking and two ways of acting. The mere observation that much working of the brain must be unconscious is beyond controversy. The two minds hypothesis is much stronger, however. It undermines our common sense belief that we (conscious people) are necessarily in control of our own behaviour.

The two minds hypothesis

Broadly, there are two ways that we can think about the fact that much of our mental function is unconscious. The first of these, the chief executive model, is compatible with common sense or folk psychology and the way we like to think about ourselves as conscious beings in control of our behaviour (see Figure 1.1). The philosophical position known as *dualism*, famously espoused

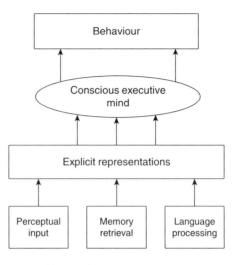

Fig. 1.1 The chief executive model.

by Decartes, is largely discredited in contemporary philosophy (see Chapter 7). Dualism involves the idea that the mind and body are separate, whereas the vast majority of cognitive scientists subscribe to the view of monism or materialism, in which the mind is simply considered to be the functioning of the brain. However, I contend that ordinary people think implicitly about minds and bodies in a dualistic manner, regardless of whether they hold explicit religious beliefs about souls or life after death. Essentially, we think of ourselves as conscious persons who inhabit our bodies and are in some way separate from them. Of course, there is no scientific foundation for this dualism at all; the conscious person is a construction of the brain, whose properties may be illusory. Part of this construct is the belief in intentional cognition or conscious will.[4] It appears to us that we freely chose our actions, after reflection on our beliefs, desires, goals and intentions. For example, I *chose* to write this book because I *believed* that this was an important scientific topic that deserved a wider audience and I *wanted* to be the one to communicate it.

It is easy to demonstrate that much of the information processing carried out by the brain is not accessible to the conscious person. However, this can easily be reconciled with our common sense intuition that the conscious person is in charge. I call this the chief executive model of the mind and illustrate it in Figure 1.1. Imagine that the chief executive of a large corporation sits in the penthouse suite of his skyscraper building, never visiting the lower floors in which his many subordinates work. His minions feed him the information he demands, wait for his decisions, and then carry out his instructions.

While all the hard work is done at the lower levels, he is still the boss, still calling the shots. This, I believe, is the way that our everyday folk psychology deals with the idea of unconscious processing in the brain. The conscious person is the executive mind, calling on various support systems within the brain to do its bidding. We are not aware, for example, of the means by which our brains construct images from perceptual input, retrieve knowledge from memory or extract the meaning of sentences. However, we see the purpose of such unconscious systems to be the creation of content for the executive mind, in the form of beliefs about the world. They are the workers who prepare and place the relevant papers in our in-tray. For example, if you make a tactless comment, you do not need access to the *processes* of social perception which enable you to see that you have upset your friend; you just need to know that she is, in fact, upset. The presence of this knowledge in your conscious mind is sufficient for you to make an appropriate decision for action, say, to apologise. Just as the chief executive of a large corporation does not need to know the detailed methods by which his or her subordinate staff work, neither does the conscious executive mind need to know the details of low level control processes. He or she is still the boss, still in charge of the big decisions.

The chief executive model is superficially attractive and I shall refer to it from time to time as an alternative to the two minds hypothesis. However, it cannot be right for a number of reasons that will become apparent in this book. By contrast, the two minds hypothesis (Figure 1.2) departs radically from common sense. Here we distinguish a *reflective mind* from an

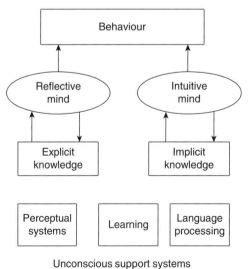

Fig. 1.2 The two minds model.

intuitive mind. The reflective mind does get to control some of our behaviour, but far less than folk psychology would lead us to believe. Most actions are controlled intuitively without any awareness of the cognitive processes involved. In this account, the reflective mind *feels like* the all-controlling executive mind to its owner, but this is largely illusory. In reality, it competes for control of behaviour with the intuitive mind, often unsuccessfully. Moreover, the two minds have access to different kinds of knowledge: explicit memory for the reflective mind and implicit memory for the intuitive mind. We still need unconscious support systems for learning, perception, etc. for both minds, but I have deliberately not drawn the links in Figure 1.2. As we shall see in Chapter 3, there is evidence that perceptual systems have both conscious and unconscious routes to behaviour, and that there are both explicit and implicit forms of learning and memory.

If the two minds hypothesis is right, then our common sense is wrong. The reflective mind does consciously control some of our behaviour, some of the time. However, when the intuitive mind takes charge, which it often does, then the reflective mind only *thinks* it is in control. In fact, one of the major functions of the reflective mind is confabulation. In other words, we (conscious beings) make up stories to maintain the illusion that we are the chief executive who is really in control. We may, for example, vote for a right wing political party because of unconscious motivations. Perhaps we aspire to be rich and powerful (even though we are not) and our intuitive minds have associated such people with right-wing politics. This association delivers an intuitive feeling of rightness in voting for the party but without any conscious awareness of its basis. When an opinion pollster (or a drinking partner) asks us to give reasons for our voting intentions, the reflective mind confabulates an answer. We say, for example, that we believe that they are more competent at handling the economy, a theory conveniently delivered by the newspaper we read. This argument may convince the pollsters, colleague and indeed ourselves, but it is not the actual reason for our voting behaviour.

Many psychologists try to capture the distinction between two minds in terms of actions that are controlled with and without conscious awareness and intention.[5] The issue of consciousness is important and will be discussed in detail in Chapter 7. However, the distinction between the reflective and intuitive minds cannot simply be termed as one between conscious and unconscious thinking. As indicated above, there must be unconscious support systems for *both* minds. The reflective mind cannot be wholly conscious, because many preconscious processes affect its content. What we are aware of at a given time depends, for example, on mechanisms which determine our attention. If a dog runs in front of our car while we are driving, our attention will immediately switch to the road and the dog, and away from the play we were listening to on the radio. Some mechanism, by definition preconscious, must be monitoring our routine driving behaviour and is able to alter us when conscious attention is required. The same is true of beliefs and memories that are evoked in particular contexts. If we meet an old friend, memories of our previous meeting or beliefs about her personality that come to mind may inform our decisions about what to say or do. But the mechanisms that identified and retrieved these memories cannot themselves be conscious.

If the reflective mind cannot be entirely conscious, then the intuitive mind cannot be entirely unconscious either. The latter has access to both emotions and what I call 'cognitive feelings', which result in conscious experiences. When we choose intuitively, we often have a feeling of confidence or rightness in the choice, even though we have no access to the underlying process. That is why we can usually tell the opinion pollster which party we will vote for, even though we are not conscious of the actual reasons for this 'intention'. There is also much psychological evidence, however, that our intuitive feelings of confidence or rightness can be unreliable. Such feelings may be based on poor grounds, such as stereotypes, that would be rejected by the reflective mind if it knew their basis. Say we are prejudiced against a male candidate for a job that is stereotypically considered female. Our reflective minds will seek and find conscious reasons to support our prejudice. Thus it will appear to us that his experience was less relevant or his interview performance less convincing than that of the female candidates. It is also hard to argue that the intuitive mind is wholly unconscious because we can become aware of conflict between the two minds. This is particularly true of compulsive behaviours that include behavioural addictions, such as gambling, and neurotic problems such as obsessive-compulsive disorder or phobias. The intuitive mind may compel us to continue gambling or to avoid flying, in spite of the reflective mind's explicit goals to the contrary. We can and often do become aware of such conflict.

So we can see that none of the brain processes that control our behaviour can be wholly conscious and few are wholly unconscious. We can say that brain processes are conscious only in the sense that some aspect of those processes registers consciously. For example, we may say that we have made a *conscious decision* to stay home this evening rather than go out to the pub to meet friends. We are certainly conscious *of* such a decision and can tell others what it is. That does not mean, however, that all the cognitive processes involved in the decision were conscious. Even when we reflect on a decision, the thoughts that come to our mind must be delivered by some preconscious mechanism. Memories and beliefs that appear relevant come to mind in reflective thinking but cannot be consciously willed to do so. We don't even know what we know. Similar problems attach to the idea of unconscious decision making. Suppose that we swerve our car when an unexpected hazard appears on the road, such as a driver unexpectedly overtaking towards us. Such actions can occur very rapidly without any time for conscious reflection, but we cannot say that they are wholly unconscious. We are certainly conscious of aspects of this process: an experience of fear, for example, and a visual perception of the hazard even if it *follows* our action of turning the wheel (see Chapter 3).

One apparent solution to this problem might be to distinguish mental processes that are *automatic* (in the intuitive mind) from those that are *controlled* (in the reflective mind). This terminology has also been popular with researchers in both cognitive and social psychology. However, these terms like unconscious and conscious again capture only part of the two minds hypothesis. The idea here is that behaviour is controlled if the conscious self is aware of and *intending* it; otherwise it is automatic. Now, it is true that we can assume conscious control of some actions while leaving others on automatic pilot. While I write this, for example, I am conscious of the meaning of what I want to say but not on the construction of the sentences (largely an unconscious process) and still less on the movements my fingers need to make to type the text in to my computer. But if I need to type in an unfamiliar symbol, the typing process will suddenly become conscious and controlled. Likewise, if I am having a conversation in a crowded room and someone across the room says my name, my attention will immediately switch to the other conversation, even though I was not consciously hearing it. So it was not 'I' who heard my name and it was not 'I' who decided to switch attention. So it cannot really be 'me' (the conscious self) who is in control!

The two minds hypothesis really concerns higher order control of behaviour such as that involved in decision-making. Decisions can be made intuitively and also reflectively (see Chapter 4). Intuitive decisions are made because they *feel* right, but without consciousness of their basis. Such decisions are quick and require little effort. Few people would reflect when offered a choice of tea or coffee, for example. They just go on habit or whim. Reflective decisions, on the other hand, are made with conscious thought about the options available and their likely consequences. We tend to decide reflectively when decisions are very important (whether to accept a job offer or make an offer to buy a house) but also when they are novel. When a choice is unfamiliar, intuition may not help us. This essentially is the basis for the terms 'intuitive' and 'reflective' minds. However, the two minds hypothesis involves a lot more than the proposal that there are two modes of decision-making, which might simply reflect one mind operating in two different ways. Two minds implies two distinct systems for knowing, thinking and acting within one brain. If this is true, then there must be neurologically distinct areas of the brain underlying the two minds. There must also be some evolutionarily plausible story about how this came about. The argument generally given is that the intuitive mind is old and animal-like, while the reflective mind is recently evolved and distinctively human (see Chapter 2). So I will also refer to them at times as the old and the new mind.

While neurological evidence and evolutionary arguments will be examined in this book, the bulk of the evidence for two minds comes from experimental psychology. For example, there is evidence for distinct systems of learning and memory (Chapter 3) and conflict within individuals in the ways in which they reason and make decisions (Chapters 4 and 5). These topics fall within the domain of 'cognitive psychology' discussed later in the chapter. Social psychology is a separate tradition that involves studying behaviour in a social context. But much research in this field also supports the two minds hypothesis: for example, people may hold implicit attitudes and stereotypes that conflict with their conscious beliefs (Chapter 6) and be completely lacking in insight into the causes of their behaviour (Chapter 7). I will draw on research from all of these areas in this book in my quest to explore and test the two minds hypothesis. First, we need some historical perspective.

Thinking about thinking

How should we define thinking? What stuff are thoughts made of and what purpose do they serve? The psychology of thinking has a long history.[6] For hundreds of years, psychology was part of the discipline of philosophy, only establishing a distinct identity in the mid-nineteenth century and thus sharing much common history with the contemporary philosophy of mind. We can trace the study of thought itself from the writings of Aristotle about 2,000 years ago. He clearly believed that thinking was the conscious activity of the mind, an idea that remained essentially unchallenged in philosophy and psychology until about the end of the nineteenth century. He also established a methodology for studying thought that has dominated until the past 100 years or so: the introspective method. After all, if the mind consists of conscious thoughts, who can study them but their owner? The mind must look inward for answers, it was thought, and for centuries it was the minds of the philosophers that studied themselves.

Aristotle developed a rudimentary but clearly psychological theory of thinking. He believed that thought was made of 'images'. For example, an image might be a mental picture of the face of someone who is not currently present. The image you can conjure up is in some ways similar to the experience you had when you looked at that person. It was viewed as reproduction of a past sensation (sensory experience). Aristotle supposed that you could store away the mental pictures you had when seeing an object, rather like a photograph in an album, and then recall them as images at a later time. These ideas were developed by the British Empiricist school of philosophers in the seventeenth and eighteenth centuries. They concerned themselves with describing the order and organisation of the images that make up our thoughts. Why, they wondered, did the particular images come to mind at particular times and why did one follow another? Their theory was based upon an *association of ideas*. One idea (image) follows another because they are associated in some way: by the fact that the two things are normally seen together, or due to some related meaning. Empiricist philosophy was based on the idea that all knowledge and thought was derived from experience and learning, starting out with the infamous *tabula rasa* or 'blank slate' proposed by the philosopher, John Locke[7]: a philosophical anticipation of the behaviourist psychology that later dominated early twentieth-century thinking. The alternative position known as *nativism* proposes that knowledge is innately present in human beings. This was espoused by Descartes and is echoed in much later twentieth-century thinking. Innate knowledge is a key idea in evolutionary psychology, as discussed in Chapter 2.

Association does indeed play an important role in thinking and remembering in a kind of thought known as 'daydreaming'. Daydreaming consists of thinking about matters not connected with your current situation: for example, planning your weekend instead of listening to a boring lecture: another form of absent-mindedness. Much of our time is taken up in daydreaming and this kind of thinking often involves what is known as *free association*. This means that one idea leads to another without any overall purpose or direction. For example, thinking about the trip you are planning at the weekend may remind you that the car needs a service. This may get you thinking about the fact that your previous car was less reliable; then you remember that awful occasion when you broke down on the motorway in pouring rain and so on. While such free associative thought may be common, it has received relatively little attention from experimental psychologists. The bulk of contemporary research instead concerns itself with thinking that is *directed* towards solving a problem or making a decision. Although association may play a part in directed thinking, it cannot account for it, as we shall see.

When the discipline of psychology emerged from philosophy in the mid-nineteenth century, the subject became an experimental science. I will describe many psychological experiments in the course of this book and an explanation of the language used is needed. Until quite recently, the volunteers who are tested in psychological experiments were described as 'subjects'. In recent years, however, this term has been banished by the great and the good who control publication in scientific psychology. In the modern era when all such research is regulated by strict ethical codes and the requirement of voluntary participation, the term 'participants' is now preferred. I will follow this convention here, when discussing research of any period. 'Participants' are hence the human subjects of the experiment, the volunteers who submit to testing.

The earliest psychological experiments continued initially to define thinking as the contents of consciousness and simply tried to refine the methodology of introspection by using trained observers operating in the laboratory. Such expert participants would be given tasks to perform and asked to report what was going on in their minds. Of particular interest is the work of a group of German psychologists at the University of Würzburg in the early 1900s.[8] The methodology used by the Würzburg psychologists was as follows: the participant (who was often one of the experimenters!) was asked to perform a specific task such as judging which of two weights was heavier or giving word associations. The task would be repeated many times or for a number of 'trials' as psychologists term it. After each trial, the participant would describe the thoughts of which they were conscious when performing the task.

What the psychologists expected when they started this research was that thoughts in the form of images would intervene between stimulus and response, in accordance with the then dominant associationist theory of thinking. For example, in a word association task if the experimenter says 'bacon' and the participant replies 'egg', then a report might be expected of the participant experiencing an image of a plate of eggs and bacon on a breakfast table. In some cases, this is what exactly they found, but more frequently such linking images were not reported. Some participants claimed not to be thinking at all. Others, more mysteriously, claimed that they had thoughts of an indescribable nature. This led to a major debate amongst psychologists at the time about whether there were 'imageless thoughts' in the mind.

If thinking is a conscious process that controls our actions, as folk psychology leads us to expect, then the results of these Würzburg experiments are indeed puzzling. There are actually many problems with the method of introspective report that have been identified in modern psychology (see Chapter 7). For example, can people attend to an external task and their own mental experiences at the same time? Will the contents of consciousness be remembered when a report is taken after the event? However, these were not the only early researchers to discoverer limitations of the introspective method. The great nineteenth-century British psychologist (also geneticist and statistician) Sir Francis Galton set out to study his own mind in a series of systematic introspective experiments. Galton was a flawed genius whose scientific, but not social thinking, was way ahead of its time. Sadly, he is best remembered now for founding the school of Eugenics that believed in selective breeding to improve human intelligence and other qualities. For all this, he was a man of exceptional brilliance who made many important scientific contributions.[9] It is most interesting that he discovered the limitations of introspection simply by trying to use the method himself, and without any of the evidence that has led modern psychologists to similar conclusions. Galton concluded that consciousness was no more than a 'helpless spectator', that most brainwork was automatic and only a fraction of it available to introspection.

The notion of thinking as consciousness was also called into question in the early part of the twentieth century by two contrasting movements: behaviourism and psychoanalysis. Each provided strong challenges to the traditional ways of thinking about the human mind. The school of behaviourism, founded by J. B. Watson, was a form of associationism, but with the association between a *stimulus* and a *response* replacing the association of ideas. The idea was to study human behaviour only in terms of what could be objectively observed: the environment to which people were exposed and the behaviours which they produced. Indeed, Watson decreed that the study of conscious thinking by introspection was 'mentalistic' and thoroughly unscientific. Watson had a point. Scientific method normally incorporates the principle that observations should be objective and capable of confirmation by independent and disinterested observers. How can this be so, if a person's mental states are the object of scientific enquiry and only observable to the person who experiences them? This problem remains for those who think consciousness is a proper subject of study for science. You don't have to be a dualist in order to recognise that mental events have a different character from physical ones. A brain viewed from the inside by its owner looks entirely different from the same brain as seen by an outside observer.[10]

According to Watson, all behaviour, including that which we describe as 'thinking', could be explained on the grounds that we learn to associate particular responses or behaviour with particular stimuli or situations, especially when some form of 'reinforcement' (reward) is also present to cement the bond. This kind of learning is known as classical conditioning. Watson's behaviourism was later developed by B. F. Skinner, who in his time was easily the most famous psychologist in the world and whose main emphasis was on operant conditioning. According to Skinner, our behaviour is shaped by our environment. We may generate behaviours initially at random, but those that get reinforced or rewarded will tend to be selected and strengthened whereas those that are not reinforced fade away. This was often demonstrated in animal experiments, such as those designed to show discrimination learning. If there is a black key and a white key in its cage, a pigeon will quickly learn to peck at the black one if that results in a food pellet, and where pecking the white one would have no reward. There are many experimental demonstrations that both classical and operant conditioning are real phenomena in people as well as animals. For radical behaviourists, this was sufficient to explain all behaviour: mental states were no more than descriptions of behavioural propensities. As the old joke goes, when one behaviourist meets another, he greets his friend with the comment, 'You are fine. How am I?'

Mentalism and behaviourism both ultimately failed as psychological theories because each concerned themselves only with a part (in this case, a different part) of the human mind. It is true, as common sense would have it, that we have conscious beliefs, desires and intentions, and that a psychological account of our behaviour in these terms may sometimes account successfully for what we do. It is also true, as behaviourism would have it, that we acquire many habits and low-level conditioned responses from our experiences in the world and that an analysis at *this* level can be successful in accounting for some of our behaviour. It is not true that either of these psychologies on their own can do the job. In essence, behaviourists were limiting their study to the intuitive mind. Mentalists, by contrast, were attempting to study only the reflective mind, but with the dubious method of introspection.

One strength of mentalism is also a fatal flaw for behaviourism. Behaviourists cannot account for the fact that much of what we do is driven by an *intention* or purpose. Consider again a commuter's habitual drive to work. At a particular road junction, say, our traveller normally turns left. A behaviourist would say that she has learnt an association linking the 'stimulus' of the road junction to the 'response' of turning left. Suppose that one day on her way to work, she needs to buy a newspaper. Such a deviation from established habits can have many causes. Let us say in this case that her daughter's photograph is to be published in a local newspaper that she would not normally buy. Visiting the newsagent requires a small diversion, in fact a *right* turn at the junction. To the watching behaviourist who does not know that she has the intention of buying a paper that day, her behaviour would be baffling. Everything would appear normal as she leaves her house, all responses being given in the usual way to stimuli, until she arrives at the junction. Suddenly, the behaviour reverses its normal pattern.

Of course, someone could have *told* the behaviourist that she was going to buy a newspaper on her way to work, but such mentalistic data are of no legitimate use to him as his theoretical system has no use for such concepts as goals, intentions, beliefs or desires. An account in terms of the conscious goals and intentions of the commuter would, of course, predict the change in routine.

However, there is much that could not be explained in this way. For example, why is the majority of the commuter's drive to work so automatic and effortless that she may be able to devote her conscious resources to entirely different matters, such as planning a holiday for the following month? And why, if she is not sufficiently alert, might she drive straight past the newsagents *in spite of* a conscious intention to buy the paper.

This example shows clearly that thinking is more than just learning associations and that much of a person's behaviour can only be understood if we know their intention or purpose. Behaviourism was, however, enormously successful in psychology, and was the dominant theory from the 1920s through to the late 1950s. It was also one of several influences which led to the loss of faith in introspection and the idea of thinking as a conscious act. Another, very different influence was that of the school of psychoanalysis associated with Sigmund Freud. In common with behaviourism, psychoanalysis questions the belief that our actions are caused by our conscious thoughts. Freud believed that much of our behaviour was caused by *unconscious* thinking. Freud's ideas about conscious and unconscious thinking were very different from those of a modern cognitive psychologist. However, his ideas were historically significant in undermining confidence in the traditional view that we need look no further than the contents of consciousness in order to understand human behaviour.

Freudian theory is regarded by most modern psychologists as unscientific because many of the proposals he made, for example, concerning the interpretation of dreams, cannot be tested by experiment. That is to say, one cannot see how the theory could be *disproved* by any observation that can be made. However, the ideas that Freud discussed have had a profound and lasting influence. Freudian theory includes the notion of an unconscious mind. He believed that much human behaviour was motivated by desires and fears that were *repressed*, i.e. kept out of consciousness because they were too painful or socially tabooed. Our conscious beliefs about the causes of our own actions are, according to this view, often *rationalisations*. For example, a man may cross the road to avoid passing a place where a traumatic incident took place such as a serious quarrel leading to the breakup of a relationship. When asked why he crossed the road, however, an explanation might be offered in terms unrelated to this incident. He may reply, for example, that he noticed an interesting display in a shop window and wanted to look at it. The notion of rationalisation or 'confabulation' in conscious thinking will be a key theme in this book (see especially, Chapter 7). However, in common with most modern psychologists there is much in Freudian theory that I would not accept. In particular, while most workings of the mind are unconscious, this is not (mostly) for reasons of motivation and emotion. There is simply far more computational work for the mind to achieve than can be performed by the highly limited flow of conscious thought.

In summary, although thinking was traditionally equated with consciousness from the time of Aristotle onwards, the work of psychologists from the late nineteenth century onwards led to serious questioning of this concept. For example, Freudian theory promoted the idea of unconscious thinking, and the experiments of early psychologists undermined confidence in the introspective method, used traditionally by philosophers to study thought. The behaviourist school, with all its inadequacies, dominated psychology from the early twentieth century well into the 1950s. Then came a major change: a revolution in psychological thinking. It was caused by the availability of a powerful new metaphor.

The emergence of cognitive psychology and cognitive science

In the 1960s, a new and important field of 'cognitive psychology' was identified, which has grown rapidly to become a major focus for current research in the subject.[11] The rise of cognitive psychology marked the fall of behaviourism and the development of a completely new way of regarding human thought. Cognitive psychology developed in parallel with the emergence of modern digital computers that provided a new metaphor for the human mind. The subject is founded essentially in the belief that the brain is a kind of computer and that mental activity is the 'software' or the many programs that it runs. Thus we see a return to the notion of thinking as an internal mental activity, but now without the assumption that this process is necessarily conscious and open to introspection.

Cognitive *science* is a more broadly based movement which includes cognitive psychology but also other disciplines, such as linguistics, artificial intelligence, aspects of neuroscience and much contemporary work in the philosophy of mind. Many contemporary philosophers now adopt a 'computational theory of mind'.[12] In this approach, we can talk of the mind as an information processing system, which *represents* percepts, concepts and objects in the external world. Like a computer, the brain has software, which can manipulate these representations and draw conclusions from them. In other words, human reasoning is simply computation. In fact, a key belief for most cognitive scientists is that intelligence lies in the software and not the hardware used for computation. In other words, the same intelligent functions may be implemented in biological systems (brains) or machines (computers). This does not, of course, prevent contemporary philosophers arguing about the *way* in which the mind is computational. There are, for example, debates about the extent to which knowledge may be innate or acquired and whether or not part or all of the traditional folk psychological concepts such as beliefs, desires and intentions can be retained in such an approach.[13]

What precisely is a computer? A generally accepted definition is that a computer is a general purpose, programmable, information-processing system. Let us break that down into its components. First of all an information processing system (IPS) is anything that processes input information by applying appropriate rules in order to produce an output. Many things qualify as IPS that are not computers. Consider, for example, a thermostat. The input information is that of ambient temperature and the output that of controlling a central heating boiler. The input is not wired directly to the output, as in a light switch, and some information processing takes place. The behaviour of the thermostat might be described by *rules* such as the following:

◆ If the temperature exceeds 21 degrees C and the boiler is on then switch the boiler off

◆ If the temperature is below 19 degrees C and the boiler is off then switch the boiler on

This is, of course, an extremely simple example of an IPS. A thermostat is not a computer because it is not general purpose and cannot be programmed to do anything else. Calculators are a more interesting case. Calculation is clearly a form of computation or information processing. An abacus, a mechanical calculator or a non-programmable electronic calculator are all clear examples of IPS that are not computers. Again the function of calculators can be described using rules. For example

If the number 4 is pressed then the "+" sign then the number 7 and then the "=" sign then display the answer 11

Of course you would need many thousands of rules of this type to describe the function of even the simplest of calculators; the actual internal design would consist of something much more efficient. However, the point is that all computation or information processing can be described using rules that relate inputs to outputs. A programmable calculator is closer to our idea of a computer, although we would discount it on the ground that it is not general purpose.

Any computer can be programmed, in principle, to perform any task of computation that can be devised subject only to limitations of speed and memory. A program consists of a set of instructions that in a computer of conventional design are processed in sequence, one after the other. A good way of describing what computers do is that of symbol processing, where symbols can stand for anything. The first major use of computers was for doing arithmetic, but numbers and arithmetic operators are just symbols of a particular kind. A computer does not need to understand what numbers are: it just needs a set of accurate rules that produce the right output symbols corresponding to the input symbols. In the same way, a word-processing program, one of the most used of modern computer applications, has no knowledge of language. A word is just a sequence of letters followed by a space; a paragraph a sequence of such 'words' followed by a carriage return. Most word processors now have the ability to check spelling by comparing your letter strings with an in-built library of words. Few can yet check grammar with great accuracy, and none (unfortunately) can extract the meaning of your text and comment on whether it makes sense.

At present, computers perform some tasks much better than we do, for example high-speed arithmetical calculations or accurate storage and fast retrieval of very large amounts of information. However, there are many tasks which computers are currently very poor at performing compared with human beings. A good example is that of understanding the meaning of language, and another that of recognising faces and other visual patterns regardless of distance, orientation, lighting and context. It is a tenet of faith among cognitive scientists that such functions are *in principle* 'computable'; that is they could be done by computers if only we had figured out how to write the programs. But we also know enough about the brain now to understand that it is organized in very different way from electronic computers.

Computers have to date been largely serial processing devices that carry out instructions in a sequential manner. By contrast, the brain is known to be massively *parallel* in design with large numbers of interconnections between brain cells. In other words, our brains can carry out many processes at the same time. Even a particular function, such as vision, involves many neurones that simultaneously process many different features of the environment that are represented in the light patterns that reach our eyes. Given enough time, a serial computer can compute anything that can be computed. However, some tasks (such as pattern recognition) can be solved much more quickly by parallel processing. This helps explain why brains, with their relatively slow biochemical means of transmitting information, can nevertheless rapidly perform complex tasks that currently defeat the world's most powerful computers.

A matter for great debate within cognitive science is the extent to which the mind acts like a general purpose computer that can be programmed for many tasks, and the extent to which it consists of dedicated computational systems with fixed programming, sometimes known as cognitive modules (see Chapter 2). Such modules are more analogous to a microprocessor than a computer: that is, a device which is special rather than general purpose and which comes with a fixed set of programs than cannot be re-written. For example, we might regard the visual system, at least at lower levels (detection of colours, contours, movement, etc.) to be 'hard-wired' with fixed programming in this sense. On the other hand, given the vast range of different things that people can learn to do, it seems most probable that our brains also contain general purpose systems that can be programmed by experience. What I will be arguing in this book is that the mind contains a number of different computational devices, both special and general purpose, which interact with each other in producing our behaviour.

Cognitive psychology as traditionally practised has its limitations. There is a tendency to talk of brains as though they were disembodied devices lying in vats, whereas they are actually integral parts of bodies capable of perception, action and emotional response. By neglecting emotion, in particular, cognitive psychology leaves out an essential part of what it is to be a sentient being. In recent years, there has been a reaction against this, with movements to study 'embodied' cognition and the relationship between emotion and thought. While I focus mostly on cognitive research in this book, I will acknowledge the importance of emotion, especially in the later chapters. Emotions, sensations and bodily experiences play an important role in the feelings arising from the intuitive mind, which often compete with the essentially cognitive processes of the reflective mind. As we shall see, it is often emotions and not thoughts that ultimately control our actions.

In my view, the computational approach of cognitive psychology provides a big advance on both the introspectionism and behaviourism that preceded it and will be the dominant metaphor used in this book. However, it has its limitations that we should recognise. While our brains do indeed seem to compute, they differ from electronic computers in many ways. If they were 'designed', it was by evolution not by another human being. They are made of soggy wet stuff that grew together with a body that they cannot do without. Through this body the brain is able to learn by an intense degree of interaction with the environment and to experience emotions through biochemical processes. Most of the functions of the brain seem not to involve consciousness, but if you take consciousness away (even through sleep) there is little behaviour of any interest to observe.

Questions and challenges for the two minds hypothesis

I have already indicated that it would be a mistaken simplification to describe the intuitive mind as unconscious and the reflective mind as conscious.

Nevertheless, the issue of consciousness provides a big challenge for the two minds hypothesis and I devote a whole chapter (Chapter 7) to this topic. Psychologists have, in fact, developed several different concepts of the unconscious mind. There is the *psychodynamic unconscious*, proposed by authors such as Freud and Jung. Then there is the *behavioural unconscious*, which refers to those aspects of our behaviour that are controlled by conditioning and other forms of learning that appear to take place without awareness. More recently fashionable is the notion of the *cognitive unconscious*, which refers to computational cognitive processes below the level of conscious awareness and control. But the cognitive unconscious covers a multitude of possibilities: processes that were innately present and provided by evolutionary mechanisms; processes that were acquired by experience without ever becoming conscious; processes that were once conscious but became rapid and automatic through habit and repetition. Some or all of these are parts of what I am calling the intuitive mind. But why is one part of the mind—the reflective mind—different? Why do we have any form of consciousness at all?

Another major issue that has exercised psychologists and philosophers is that of rationality.[14] One definition of rationality is that which compares our behaviour to what we *ought* to be doing, according to some predefined standard or 'normative' theory. Both academia and popular culture contain two contrasting notions of normative rationality which treat emotion in very different ways (see Chapter 8). One view pits rationality and emotionality as opposites. According to this view, we are rational if we reason in a logically correct and dispassionate manner. Another theory of rationality, however, is that it consists of acting in such a way as to be likely to achieve one's goals. This is the foundation of standard decision theory (see Chapter 4). But goals are only worth pursing if they bring satisfaction or pleasure or avoid pain, so it is inherent to this view that rationality *requires* emotion. This idea defines rationality through the decisions people make.

In the two minds theory, the notion of rationality becomes even more slippery. Typical cases of behaviour that are deemed irrational include those where someone vows to stop smoking, or reduce excessive consumption of alcohol or food and then manifestly fails to do so. If our consciously expressed beliefs and desires to live long and healthy lives, for example, are contradicted by our behaviour then we appear, in the decision theory sense, to be irrational. And indeed we would be so, if the reflective mind were the only level in operation. What such behaviours show is the power of other systems lurking in our brain to subvert our conscious rationality. Physical addictions can overcome our conscious desires as can strong innate drives such as hunger or sexual desire. But violations of decision-based rationality can also occur due to learnt habits, as when we forget our wish to buy a paper on the way to work, or due to acquired emotional responses such as phobias. A person with an earth-worm phobia, for example, may be unable to enjoy a walk in a garden or the countryside.

The two minds hypothesis has arisen from the proposal of numerous 'dual process' theories in cognitive and social psychology. As mentioned earlier, each appears to distinguish between type 1 processes that are fast, automatic and high in processing capacity from type 2 processes that are slow, intentional and limited in processing capacity. In fact, there are many different labels that have been given to type 1 and 2 processes, as indicated by the sample of theories listed in Table 1.1.[15] Just because there are lots of such theories, with many labels, it does not mean that the theories are necessarily very different.[16] Some of these authors are working in different fields of psychology that do not usually cross-reference each other. This is particularly true of cognitive and social psychology. Some are focussing on very specific kinds of tasks that they wish to explain. And, of course, scientists have career ambitions like everyone else. It is always good to sound as though you are saying something new!

What I am calling the two minds hypothesis does not belong to any one author. The essential ideas here have been proposed by a number of authors including Arthur Reber, Seymour Epstein, Keith Stanovich, David Over, and myself and will be further developed in this book. While the emphasis and detail differ somewhat between theorists, there is a broad consensus that the two systems (or minds) might include the set of features listed in Table 1.2. I will examine the case for most of these in the course of this book. For example, I will ask whether the intuitive mind is an *old* mind, which evolved early, and whether the reflective mind should be thought of as a *conscious* mind. I will look at much evidence suggesting that we have distinct forms of knowledge, both in the form of explicit memories and beliefs available to the reflective

Table 1.1 Some dual-process accounts of cognition

	Intuitive mind	**Reflective mind**
Reber	Implicit	Explicit
Epstein	Experiential	Rational
Chaiken	Heuristic	Systematic
Evans	Heuristic	Analytic
Sloman	Associative	Rule based
Various	Automatic	Controlled
Stanovich	System 1 (TASS)	System 2 (analytic)
Hammond	Intuitive	Analytic
Lieberman	Reflexive	Reflective
Nisbett	Holistic	Analytic
Wilson	Adaptive unconscious	Conscious

Table 1.2 Attributes often associated with dual system theories of cognition

Intuitive mind	Reflective mind
Evolutionarily old	Evolutionarily recent
Shared with animals	Unique to humans
Unconscious, preconscious	Conscious
High capacity	Low capacity
Fast	Slow
Automatic	Controlled or volitional
Low effort	High effort
Parallel	Sequential
Implicit knowledge	Explicit knowledge
Contextualised, belief based	Abstract, decontextualised
Linked with emotion	No direct link with emotion
Independent of individual differences in general intelligence and working memory capacity	Correlated with individual differences in intelligence and working memory capacity
Ecological or evolutionary rationality	Normative rationality

mind, and habits and procedures that affect our behaviour through the intuitive mind. I will show that our two minds give us two different ways of reasoning, making decisions and of understanding and acting in the social world. Finally, I will show that while our two minds often cooperate they can also come into serious conflict with each other.

Notes and references

1 Philosophers of mind tend to use the term 'folk psychology' in a narrow sense to refer to the idea that behaviour is controlled by mental states—beliefs and desires—without necessarily assuming that such states are conscious (Frankish, 2004). I use the term more broadly here to refer to the commonly-held—and quite possibility culturally influenced—sets of beliefs that people hold about human behaviour, at least in Western societies.

2 For a recent scholarly review of these theories see Evans (2008).

3 See Stanovich (2004).

4 Our belief in conscious will is illusory. See Wegner (2002) and the discussion in Chapter 7.

5 This is common in the writings of social psychologists. For example, Wilson (2002) distinguishes the conscious mind from the 'adaptive unconscious'.

6 For scholarly treatments of the history of the psychology of thinking see Reeves (1965) and Mandler and Mandler (1964).

7 Some evolutionary psychologists argue that belief in a blank slate persists in the social sciences to the present day, see Tooby and Cosmides (1992) and Pinker (2002). On this view, there is no innate knowledge and everything has to be learnt from scratch.

8 For detailed review of this work see Humphreys (1951).

9 One of Galton's greatest works was his *Enquiries into Human Faculty and its Development* (Galton, 1893).

10 There are many philosophical positions on consciousness and the one implied here is called 'double aspect monism'. For a detailed recent exposition of this approach, see Velmans (2000).

11 The field was identified in a brilliant review by Ulric Neisser (1967), the first of the now many books to be called *Cognitive Psychology*.

12 For an introduction to the philosophy of mind, including the computational approach as well as the problem of consciousness that is discussed in Chapter 7, see Ravenscroft (2005).

13 For examples of these arguments see Fodor (1983, 2001), Pinker (1997, 2002), Haselager (1997) and Frankish (2004).

14 See Manktelow and Over (1993), Evans and Over (1996) and Stanovich (1999) for relevant discussions.

15 For sources for the theories summarised in Table 1.1 see Chaiken and Trope (1999) Chen and Chaiken (1999), Epstein (1994), Epstein & Pacini (1999), Evans (2003, 2006b), Evans and Over (1996) , Hammond (1996), Lieberman (2003), Nisbett et al. (2001); Reber (1993), Sloman (1996), Stanovich (1999; 2004).

16 In fact, there are some important differences between these theories, which bear on the two minds hypothesis in somewhat different ways (see Evans, 2008a). Some theories propose competing implicit and explicit processes in manner that maps directly on to the two minds hypothesis. However, some deal with preconscious support processes for reflective thinking and others with different styles of reflective thought. The detail is not important at this stage and these different ideas will emerge in the course of the book.

Chapter 2

Evolutionary foundations

If we have two minds in one brain, how could such an arrangement have evolved? Let us start by considering the minds of higher (non-human, non-verbal) animals. Animals, like us, have brains, which are sophisticated computational devices. Like other organs in the body, their brains have been shaped by evolutionary processes that make them adaptive for the purposes of survival and reproduction. A key determinant of adaptation in animals resides in their *behaviour*, which is programmed by their brains. Predator species, for example, have to be highly skilled in stalking and hunting as well as having digestive systems that are adapted to a diet of meat. Prey species need to be adept at hiding and running away. Animals exhibit many other adaptive behaviours, some of which are extraordinarily complex. Female sea turtles, for example, may traverse hundreds or thousands of miles across oceans to return to precisely the beach on which they were born in order to lay their eggs, a quite incredible navigational feat. Many bird species have developed very precise usage of tools (e.g. twigs adjusted to the right length) in order to expose the worms and grubs that they wish to eat.

Whilst such complex adaptive behaviours are clearly purposive, they are not *intentional*. A bird using a stone to crack a snail is not like a man finding a hammer to break open a walnut. The bird's behaviour requires no explicit mental representation of a desire to eat and an intention to expose the flesh of the snail. It simply does what it was programmed by evolution to do. A man trying to open a walnut on the other hand can reason about the situation, taking into account multiple explicit goals. If he resorts to a hammer, in the absence of nutcrackers, he will move the nut off a glass table and on to a stone floor before striking it. His intention is to eat the nut, but also to avoid damaging valuable furniture and perhaps upsetting a host in the process. Such intentional processing of multiple goals plays no part in the mind of the hungry bird.

Many animal behaviours are instinctive. Biologically speaking, behaviour is instinctive if it is innate, fixed, and universal. We know that the hunting behaviour of cats is instinctive because they all do it in exactly the same way and without being taught. More fashionable than 'instinctive' these days, however, is the term *modular*. Many evolutionary biologists and psychologists would say that a cat has a hunting module, meaning a special purpose, innate, and self-contained component of their minds that has evolved to perform this one task. However, animal behaviour is not simply determined by instincts. Animals also learn to adapt to the particular environment in which they find themselves. A domestic dog may occasionally follow its ancient wolf instinct by chasing and killing a rabbit, but its strategy for obtaining food will mostly consist of begging it from humans, or reminding its owner to refill its bowl. Clearly, these are learnt behaviours.

During the period in which psychology was dominated by behaviourism, many experiments were carried out on animal learning. These experiments showed that similar principles may explain the learning of reptiles, birds, fish, and mammals. In particular, environments shape behaviour by selective reinforcement. Put simply, behaviours which are successful (rewarded) tend to be repeated and those which are not tend to be avoided. Hence, a fish, rat, or pigeon will quickly learn to choose a route in a maze, or to press or peck a key, which leads to a food reward. Exploratory behaviours may be random initially, but those that are non-reinforced tend to die out. This Skinnerian learning process involves a very similar method, or algorithm, to the Darwinian mechanism of evolution: random generation and selective retention. This kind of learning is also known to be associated with 'old' parts of the human brain.[1] This is indeed a form of cognition that is old and shared with other animals.

In the two minds hypothesis, the intuitive mind is regarded as old and animal-like, while the reflective mind is supposed to be uniquely—or at least, very distinctively—human. According to this view, some of our behaviour is shaped by evolution or by learning to be adapted to what has worked in the past, just like that of other animals. However, this theory includes the idea that we humans also have a *new* mind, the reflective mind, which gives us a higher form of reasoning, rationality, and purpose. In *The Robot's Rebellion*,[2] Keith Stanovich illustrates this idea with an analogy.[3] He invites us to imagine a future world in which a man decides to have himself frozen until a cure for death can be found. The problem is what to do with his body in the meantime. He first thinks to have it stored in secure facility. Realizing that he may need to be frozen for hundreds of years, however, he starts to worry about nuclear warfare, or perhaps unscrupulous planners exploiting future political regimes to gain permission to demolish the facility.

On reflection, it seems that his body would be much safer it was installed inside a robot provided with artificial intelligence, which would enable it to carry him around and keep him safe. The robot might be programmed to avoid all possible hazards. However, there is a new problem. The man cannot foresee all the possible hazards that might arise in hundreds of years of cold storage. He therefore decides to program the robot with a general form of intelligence and problem-solving ability, so that it can solve any novel problems that it comes across. At this point, Stanovich poses a key question. What if the robot, with its general intelligence, decides to *rebel*? For example, it may be programmed by its maker to destroy itself and transfer the frozen body to a new robot of superior design when such becomes available. But the robot with its higher form of intelligence might decide to act in *its* interests, rather than those of the designer.

In this very clever thought experiment, the robot actually plays the part of *us*, human beings, and the robot's designer that of our genes. What Stanovich is saying is that because we evolved our unique reflective minds, we are the one species on earth that is *not* the total slave of our genes. Like animals, we may in part be programmed to serve the interests of our genes, which is simply to survive long enough to reproduce and raise our offspring. But unlike other animals, we can pursue our own goals, such as a long life, well beyond the years of rearing offspring. We are robots that can rebel. For example, the genes gave us sexual pleasure to serve their interests, not ours. But we can have sex with contraception, serving our own goals while frustrating theirs. While our higher form of intelligence may have evolved originally by Darwinian processes, enabling us to outperform other hominids, it also created us as sentient beings with our own sense of self and purpose. This is a powerful idea that I will return to many times in this book.

The Darwinian algorithm

In any rational assessment of the greatest ever Briton, there could surely only be three serious contenders: Charles Darwin, William Shakespeare, and Isaac Newton. Inexplicably, in a popular poll conducted by the BBC in 2002, they finished up 4th, 5th, and 6th, respectively (behind Churchill, Brunel, and Princess Diana!). There is little doubt that for the creation of single idea—natural selection—that could change the social world forever, Darwin may be one of the most significant people of any nationality to have walked the Earth.[4] However, his idea is *still* changing the world and has a long way to go before it finishes the job. As Keith Stanovich recently observed, 'I refer to the present time as "The Age of Darwin" because, despite the fact that the *Origin of Species* was written over 140 years ago, we are in an era in which the implications of Darwin's insight are still being worked out.'[5] The implications of Darwinian evolution for the nature of the human mind, in particular, have particularly been the focus of much attention in the recent years.[6] To understand how the mind may have evolved, it is worth dwelling a little on the mechanisms for evolution in general.

In 1976, Richard Dawkins, published *The Selfish Gene*,[7] which brilliantly conveyed the key ideas of Darwinism for the general public. Darwin of course did not know about genes, but their later discovery provided the missing mechanism for the process of evolution he described. Dawkins invites us to be anthropomorphic in our view of genes, just as we were in the story of the 'man' who designed the rebellious robot. Of course, genes, unlike the reflective minds which they unwittingly created, have no beliefs, desires, or intentions. Dawkins calls them 'selfish' because this helps us understand the mechanisms by which they work. It is a common mistake to think of evolution in terms of the survival of individual organisms and a worse one to think in terms of the survival of species. The mechanism operates at the level of genes. Although genes are not sentient, they behave as though they were selfish. This is because they are *replicators*; they can reproduce themselves on a potentially indefinite basis. However, to survive they need *vehicles* (organisms) in which they can safely live. Genes determine the precise characteristics of these organisms, and these characteristics in turn have a degree of fit to the environmental demands with which their vehicles need to cope. Genes that build fit-for-purpose vehicles are more likely to survive and replicate. It is hence in the interest of the genes that the organisms in which they reside are able to survive long enough to reproduce (thus allowing the gene to replicate itself in a new vehicle) and raise the offspring so that they too will be fit to reproduce.

The 'strategies' that different genes have programmed into their vehicles for survival and reproduction are endlessly varied. Some animals are too big and strong to be attacked by predators (elephants and whales, for example), some develop sharp spines (porcupines), or hard shells (turtles); still others may use camouflage (stick insects). Some species (for example, mice and some kinds of fish) simply have the strategy of reproducing in very large numbers. The young will mostly be eaten by predators but some will survive. The selfish genes care not at all that suffering and early death is the fate of most of their vehicles, so long as enough copies of themselves survive to be passed on again. This endless variety shows the haphazard and semi-random nature of evolutionary processes. Natural selection has produced the daisy but also the giant redwood; the ant but also the rhinoceros. Evolution has but a single problem to solve, the successful replication of genes, but has come up with a billion different solutions to it.

Evolution is sometimes viewed as a design process: nature is breeding designs fit for particular purposes. Indeed, there is a branch of engineering which uses 'genetic algorithms' to solve complex design problems. Originally devised by

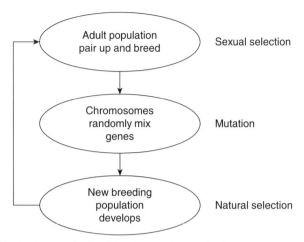

Fig. 2.1 The basic genetic algorithm in sexual reproduction.

John Holland to demonstrate the power of the Darwinian mechanism, these computer programs proved to have great practical application in engineering design.[8] Their methods are closely based upon the genetic algorithm, which works in nature via sexual reproduction, summarized in Figure 2.1. Assume that we have an adult breeding population available. As dictated by genes and circumstances, these will pair up and mate. At this point, the mechanism Darwin described as *sexual selection* can operate. Individuals that are more attractive to potential partners are more likely to find a mate, and thus have a greater chance to pass on their genes. We now know that there are many genes laid out along a series of chromosomes. The chromosomes from each parent line up and exchange genes randomly to form the chromosomes of the off-spring. This means that any two parents can produce a potentially vast number of genetically different children.

Once the offspring are born, they have to survive until adulthood in order to form the next breeding generation. In the process, those who are least well adapted to their environment will be more likely to die young and thus less likely successfully to breed and pass on their genes. This is how Darwin's mechanism of *natural selection* works and why sexual reproduction is such a powerful evolutionary mechanism. There is vast variation in the individuals that a population can generate, with selective retention in the next breeding population of those that are best fitted for survival. However, nature provides one more trick, which ensures the success of the system: *mutation*. A potential weakness in the algorithm is that when the parents have identical copies of a particular gene, the random mixing will have no effect and this gene will be passed on to the next generation. Without mutation, this would be a severe limitation. A gene may be fixed to certain state, which is initially adaptive, but no longer so when the environment changes. Due to small copying errors in the genes mixing, however, a gene is occasionally altered by accident in the offspring. Most such mutations have no benefit and quickly disappear from the population. However, if this new gene proves to be adaptive, then individuals with the mutation will flourish and eventually dominate the breeding population.

Sexual selection can speed up the evolutionary processes, once people inherit adaptive preferences for mates. Evolutionary psychologists have tested the theory that the mating preferences of humans are genetically programmed. The theory predicts some clear asymmetries between males and females when it comes to attractiveness of potential mates. From the male (selfish gene) point of view, he needs to find a mate who will reproduce his genes. This means that she should (a) be young, healthy, and capable of bearing children and (b) exclusively available to him. Clearly a woman who gets pregnant by another man is of no use to his genes. On this basis, men should be attracted to women by their youth and physical looks. Physical attractiveness, in turn, should have evolved to provide cues to potential successful child-bearing and raising of offspring. It is also to be expected that men will be possessive and sexually jealous. From the female (selfish gene) point of view, the issues are somewhat different. Physical attractiveness is less important, although men should still appear young and strong enough to support child-rearing. More important is the ability of the man to provide resources and a long-term relationship. Women should be less sexually jealous, but more emotionally jealous as they should fear losing their partner and with them their support system for child-rearing. Numerous studies of human mating preferences have been conducted, which broadly support these predictions.[9]

Computer programs based on genetic algorithms simulate in a highly simplified way what happens in evolution by natural selection of real organisms. The fact that engineers have found such programs to be enormously powerful for solving complex design problems is testament to the power of the Darwinian algorithm in nature. However, it is important to realize that the algorithm does not *optimize* its design solutions. There is a considerable element of randomness in the way that the genes mix in reproduction, as well as in the generation of mutations. Evolution produces something more like what engineers call 'kludges', approximate solutions that are good enough to solve the problem at hand. This creates a real difficulty in the logic of *retrospective* evolutionary arguments, made with the hindsight knowledge of what actually evolved.

Imagine we could put time back a 100 million years or so and observe the organisms then present on the earth. Armed with our time machine, the latest evolutionary theory and the most powerful computers, what could we predict about the future evolution of these species? We could, perhaps, predict the evolution of complex organisms that would be adapted to a range of environments on the earth including deserts, polar ice caps, and deep ocean trenches. But could we predict the evolution of the horse, the giraffe, or the killer whale? Absolutely not. If we could turn time back and let evolution proceed again, it would not produce these species, but something else. That is the nature of the process.

We can nevertheless assume that many of our characteristics are adaptations in the Darwinian sense because we have survived and because they have evident adaptive value.[10] Eyes, for example, are very useful as they enable organisms to extract information from light patterns and more than one kind of eye has in fact evolved independently in nature. We can easily imagine evolutionary pressures that would have produced seeing creatures and we can also trace stages in the evolution—say of the mammalian eye—by examination of lower creatures (whose evolution arrested at a much earlier date) and fossil records and so on.[11] However, not all useful features of organisms are adaptations. Some, known as 'spandrels', evolved accidentally as by-products of other evolutionary features with which they were coupled.[12] There is a major debate, for example, in cognitive science about whether human language is an adaptation (as argued by many evolutionary psychologists) or a spandrel (as argued by the world's most famous linguist, Noam Chomsky).[13] However, there is rather little dispute these days that there must be some innate basis for the human language facility.

While evolutionary biology is traditionally focussed on the adaptive nature of organs such as the eye, evolutionary psychology is concerned with the genetic basis of *behaviour*. In contrast with the 'blank slate' approach of behaviourism, this movement supposes that much animal and human behaviour has an innate basis, shaped by natural selection. For example, predator species need efficient strategies for locating and hunting their prey, while prey species need to be able to sense danger and be adept at hiding, fleeing, or otherwise protecting themselves. I have already given a possible human example of innate behaviour in the case of mating preferences. Such behaviours may be regarded as Darwinian adaptations within the brains of the animals, which evolve in the same way as physical characteristics. In essence, genes that program more effective survival strategies will be more likely to be replicated. With this in mind, we now start to consider how the modern human mind, or minds, may have evolved.

The evolution of the modern human mind

Of living species, humans are most closely related to African apes and especially the chimpanzee. However, we did not evolve from any surviving species. Rather, both we and modern apes descended from a common ancestor around 6 million years ago.[14] The ancestral ape is a theoretical inference, with no surviving remains, and so is often described as the 'missing link'.[15] There are, however, fossil remains allowing anthropologists and archaeologists to trace a number of hominids in the evolutionary story that runs from this period to the present day. They evolved originally in Africa but by around 2 million years ago, there were early humans in Europe and Asia who were making and using tools. It is matter of academic debate as to whether early humans such as Neanderthals had language and if so in what form. By around 100,000 years ago, our own species, *Homo sapiens sapiens* had emerged—a mere eye-blink in timescale of the evolution of life on earth. If we think of the time in which life has been evolving on earth as a 24-hour day, then our species did not appear until one-fifth of a second before midnight. (The time for which we have been the *only* hominid species on earth is even shorter. Neanderthals, for example, died out around 35,000 years ago.) These modern humans with their possession of language and higher mental abilities moved out from Africa and Asia to colonize the globe, reaching Australia around 50,000 years ago and migrating into the Americas via Siberia, colonizing from north to south. By around 12,000 years ago, there were modern humans living almost everywhere on Earth and adapting themselves to the widest possible variety of climates and terrain. Why this mass migration of a species, then relatively small in number, occurred at all remains a scientific mystery.

The modern environment in which we now operate is so recent as to have played almost no role in the evolution of our species. For most of the period in which early and modern humans were evolving, we were hunter-gatherers operating in often hostile conditions. Shortage of food and the presence of many dangerous predators may explain the nomadic nature of human tribes, although that can hardly account for a mass migration that required crossing seas, deserts, mountains, and glaciers to achieve. Perhaps our early ancestors, who were much more like us than we may realize, were just curious explorers who wanted to know their planet. What we do know is that our adaptation to a modern world of cars, airplanes, office towers, and computers was not a Darwinian process. This environment exists because we designed and built it, using our superior reflective minds. The human hand did not evolve to fit a glove; rather the glove was designed to fit the hand. In fact, much of human progress over the past 10,000 years or so can be described as a process of cultural rather than biological evolution.

Not only do modern humans have superior problem-solving abilities, but we transmit knowledge via written documents and organized education. Each new generation starts from where the previous one finished, so that knowledge and technology continue to progress. Human design, however, is in some ways analogous to nature's design. Just as some species (e.g. the horse, which has been around for 5 million years or so in its modern form) reach an evolutionary stasis, remaining stable for long periods, so do many human designs. Tables and chairs have remained unchanged in essential features for example, for thousands of years. Other designs evolve and change rapidly, such as the hardware and software associated with computer systems over the past 50 years or so. Some designs are so successful that life without them is almost unimaginable. Few of us now could imagine life without the Internet or mobile telephones, but these are very recent inventions indeed. Most of my life has been lived without either of these being available or perhaps even imagined. The analogy with evolution is a good one, because evolution is in fact a design process. However, it is not an *intentional* design process, in the special sense that applies only to the reflective mind. It is the blind progress of the Darwinian algorithm. Not a random process by any means, but one much influenced by chance, nonetheless.

Modern human intelligence, in the reflective mind, is only possible because of two other faculties that seem to have developed uniquely in our species. One is language and the other what we might term 'social intelligence'. Both are related to the size and shape of the human brain, whose evolution can be inferred from the examination of fossil skulls. Some scholars have concluded that the both the brain and the vocal tract development required for speech were present in early humans at least 250,000 years ago.[16] However, there is a great deal more to language than vocalization and vocal communication. Language provides the means by which we can represent complex concepts, ideas, and suppositions in our minds, as well as communicate them to others. Indeed, it is impossible to imagine how the reflective mind could operate without it.

Humans are a highly socialized species and one whose survival has depended upon our ability to co-operate in groups. Whether co-operating with your peers (for example, in an organized hunt of large and dangerous animals) or competing with other humans (for example in battle) the ability to perceive other people's desires, intentions, and goals would be greatly advantageous. This is often referred to as 'mindreading' although not in the paranormal sense. We are not talking about telepathy, but rather an ability to predict other people's future actions by in some way reading their state of mind from their behaviour. Researchers refer to this faculty as a *theory of mind*, meaning that we have a theory of other people's minds. It is also what is meant by 'folk psychology' in the technical way that many philosophers use that term. The generally accepted view is that people have a folk psychological theory of mind, which allows them to attribute to other people mental states such as belief, desires, goals, and intentions. It is a strong tenet of evolutionary psychology that this is a faculty like language, which evolved very distinctively in modern humans.

Scientific theories of psychology are those developed by academic researchers and hence known to a limited number of people. Folk psychology, by contrast, is used by everyone, including professional psychologists, and it is difficult to see how we could manage in a social world without it. We constantly and compulsively attribute mental states to others as we try to interpret, understand, and predict their behaviour. We face our next meeting with a colleague with apprehension, believing that the rash email we sent her yesterday may have made her *angry*. We offer a friend a drink after a round of golf believing that he is *thirsty* and that a drink will make him *happy* and more *favourably disposed* to us when we ask for a lift home. We avoid criticizing Paul in front of Mary because we believe that Mary *loves* Paul and will not *believe* our story about his bad behaviour at a party last night. Or if she does, it will make her *jealous*.

As these brief examples show, we are compulsive mindreaders and moreover, we, the folk, are mentalists, not behaviourists. Of course, that does not mean that mentalism is a better *scientific* theory than behaviourism. The philosopher Gilbert Ryle, writing in the behaviourist period, argued that such mentalistic terms really refer to no more than dispositions to behave in different ways.[17] An angry colleague is one who will tend to act aggressively and unpleasantly and is therefore to be avoided. A happy friend will give us a lift and a jealous Mary may act in a hostile manner towards us. Nor is it the case that we are unerringly accurate in our attributions.[18] Social psychologists have exposed evidence for a 'fundamental attribution error'.[19] In explaining the causes of other people's behaviour we tend to give too much weight to the individual personality. We assume people's actions are caused by their own personal dispositions (e.g. ambition, jealousy, anxiety) when they often simply a consequence of the situation in which they find themselves. Hence, our mentalistic folk psychology is applied rather too enthusiastically, perhaps because it is indeed hardwired by evolution.

During the period in which both language and social intelligence were evolving, the brain size of our ancestors was also increasing, especially in the frontal region.[20] Robin Dunbar[21] has suggested that this development was directly linked to our need for social communication. In support of this, he has shown that brain size of different species of ape is closely related to the group size in which they normally operate. He has also shown that larger group sizes are expensive to maintain, because of the large amount of time spent in the grooming behaviour required to maintain social relationships. This leads naturally to the possibility that language developed initially for social reasons: fast-track grooming at a distance. It is certainly the case that a large use of the language faculty in modern humans is devoted to inconsequential gossip, which can be regarded as a form of grooming! On this view, the ability to represent complex concepts through language might be a spandrel, an extremely handy by-product, which was not the initial evolutionary driver of language development.

Meta-representation

Both language and theory of mind are faculties, which are, in essence, uniquely human. The two in combination help to explain why humans were able to develop what I am calling the reflective mind, as they support higher forms of thought. Specifically, they allow us to represent other people's mental representations, known technically as *meta-representation*. Let us first be clear on what is meant by 'mental representation', a key concept in the computational theory of mind, defined in Chapter 1. All cognitive acts involve such representations. If I see an animal in my garden, I might recognize it as a dog, using a combination of perceptual features detected by my visual system and my stored knowledge of what a dog looks like. Together with other stored information, such as whether I like or dislike dogs, this may determine my subsequent actions: to approach the dog and stroke it perhaps, or to beat a hurried retreat into the house. In either case, there is no actual dog in my head! Instead there is *mental representation* of a dog in my mind, together with everything I know and believe about dogs in general and any individual dog that I might happen to know. Without such representations, my computational mind would have no means to compute an appropriate course of action.

Mental representations are not exclusive to human beings. Suppose a cat walks into the garden and sees the dog, who has not yet noticed the cat. The cat may arch its back or make a hurried exit. The dog has not yet behaved aggressively to the cat or even noticed it, but the cat too has a mental representation of the dog, and one which is enhanced by knowledge of its prototypical properties, such as the tendency to bark at and chase cats. If the dog in question has grown up with the cat, they may be on friendly terms, and so this default behaviour will be cancelled. A behaviourist might argue that all we need to explain the cat's behaviour is some conditioned fear response, but this can be viewed as a mental representation as well, albeit one lacking in complex conceptual organization.

All information processing systems must be able to represent objects and concepts and this applies equally to animal, human, and machine cognition. What is regarded as very distinctively human is the ability to represent mental representations themselves, as folk psychology requires. This is what is known as meta-representation. If the cat walks straight up to the dog, then we think that it is not afraid (a meta-representation) and may speculate that they are from the same household. Technically, a mental representation is described as having 'first-order intentionality', while a meta-representation must have at least second-order intentionality, such as 'I think that Sue is jealous'. To understand the sentence 'George *thinks* that Mary *believes* that Paul is *angry* because Linda *intends* to leave him' requires fifth order intentionality! This requires a lot of brain power and is around the limit of what most people can handle. Studies of animals suggest that their social intelligence is much more limited in this respect than that of humans. There is some evidence that chimpanzees have a rudimentary theory of mind[22] but certainly not beyond the level of second order intentionality. It is not sufficient for animals to behave *as if* they understood the intentions of their fellow creatures: they may simply be following fixed rules of instinctive programming.

Meta-representation is not limited to theory of mind. It is also linked to other uniquely human faculties, such as self-consciousness and hypothetical thinking. If my cat gets shut out of the house on a rainy day, I may come home to find a pathetic figure on the doorstep. He is (as we would be) cold, wet, and miserable. However, he is not capable of formulating the *thought* that he is cold, wet, and miserable or even the thought that he is a cat. Only mental representation is needed for the consciousness of immediate experience: *self*-consciousness requires meta-representation. Hypothetical thinking is another case in point. I only need representation to believe something, but I need meta-representation to *suppose* something. For example, most people know that George W. Bush won (at least legally) the U.S. presidential election in 2000. This requires only a representation, or first-order intentionality. But during his period of government, there was much debate and discussion about what would have happened had the narrowly defeated Al Gore won instead. Would the United States have invaded Iraq? Probably not, argue many. Would they have signed the Kyoto accord on global warming? Probably so, they claim. Our ability to engage in such debate is only possible because of our ability to meta-represent. In exploring these counterfactual[23] possibilities, we represent the proposition that Gore won not as an actual belief (which would be a delusion) but as a supposition. To know the difference between a belief and supposition requires second-order intentionality.

While animals have communication systems that are often based on vocalization, none remotely approach the human faculty of speech and language. Language is universally acquired by infants developing with speech around them, with no need for parents to teach it to their children. It is thought to have a complex underlying structure that is innately present, together with the ability to learn the surface form of any particular natural language to which the developing child is exposed.[24] While there is much academic debate about how and why language evolved, it clearly played a key role in the development of the reflective mind. Language permits concepts to be formulated explicitly and supports meta-representational thought. It should also be evident that language without meta-representation would be nothing like the faculty that humans actually enjoy. Language with only representation is basically nothing more than a code and in this sense many other species have forms of gestured or vocalized language. Young animals may communicate their fear or hunger to parents by the cries they make. Some animals are innately programmed with very specific forms of communication. For example, bees do a special dance to tell their fellow creatures the direction and distance of food sources.[25] Human language is immensely richer than this.

It is impossible to know whether language or mindreading evolved first, but this has not prevented scholars from speculating on the subject! It can be argued both ways. One story is that language evolved first, perhaps as a social communication device, allowing grooming at a distance. The representational power of language, however, gave it spandrel-like properties that were exploited for meta-representation, initially used for mindreading but later generalized to hypothetical thinking. Another story, favoured by leading anthropologist and cognitive scientist Dan Sperber, is that meta-representation, in the form of a theory of mind, preceded the evolution of language and as a result caused human language to develop in a much richer and more complex form than the simple communication systems of other animals.[26] Evidence for this view includes the fact that complex social organization of early humans preceded the development of the vocal apparatus required for speech. However, it is also possible that a sophisticated form of sign language preceded the development of spoken language which, being more efficient, eventually replaced it.

Mithen's account of the 'prehistory' of the mind

Whichever way we may choose to speculate about our ancestors, there seems little doubt that the evolution of language, social intelligence, meta-representation, and a large neo-cortex (also known as the forebrain, or frontal lobes) are all closely linked in the human story. All of these in turn are prerequisites for what is called the new or reflective mind in the two minds theory. One plausible account of how all this was put together has been presented by Steve Mithen in his excellent book, *The Prehistory of the Mind*. Mithen belongs to a rare breed of academics: he is a cognitive archaeologist. At a remarkably early stage in his career, he read widely in cognitive science and combined this with his detailed knowledge of archaeology and anthropology to put together his theory of how the human mind evolved.

Mithen proposes three broad stages of development from ancient to early to modern humans (see Figure 2.2). The earliest stage he calls 'general intelligence'. I put the quotes in because, while I understand his reasons for choosing the term, it is most unfortunate from the viewpoint of a psychologist. In psychology, the term 'general intelligence' refers to the kind that is measured by IQ tests: general reasoning and problem-solving ability. This cannot be what Mithen has in mind, since this is the kind of thinking that characterizes the new, reflective mind. What he is really getting at is that most animals (and very young children) depend upon a general purpose form of intelligence, mostly comprised of an ancient general learning system that we share with alligators, let alone chimpanzees. Being general-purpose is a strength, in that it can be applied to any problem, but also a weakness in that it cannot be designed for maximum effectiveness in any particular context. He comments that 'this general intelligence would have been constituted by a suite of general-purpose learning and decision-making rules … that can be used to modify behaviour in the light of experience in any behavioural domain. But they can only produce relatively simple behaviour …'.[27]

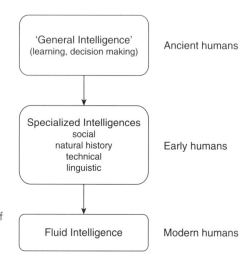

Fig. 2.2 Summary of Mithen's (1996) theory of the evolution of the human mind.

It is a basic tenet of the two minds hypothesis that older forms of intelligence, in the main, have been added to, rather than replaced by what followed.[28] Mithen claims that the human mind next evolved next by the addition, in early humans, of specialized intelligences in four domains: social, technical, natural history, and linguistic. The first and last have already been discussed. Technical intelligence includes the ability to build artefacts such as stone tools, which were very precisely engineered. Natural history intelligence includes such facilities as the classification of plants and animals and the ability to construct mental maps of geographical terrain. Mithen discusses evidence that (a) early humans had advanced knowledge and skills in each of these domains and that (b) these knowledge systems were relatively isolated from one another. For example, Neanderthals were unable to adapt the design of their hunting tools according to the available prey. Hence, they might continue to use close range weapons against animals whose size and strength made this very risky.

Something changed dramatically in the minds of early *modern* humans, however. By contrast with Neanderthals, they were able very rapidly to amend the design of their artefacts to changes in environmental demands. This may be the reason that we are the only surviving hominid species on the planet. Mithen believes that only modern humans reached his third stage, which he calls 'fluid intelligence'. At this stage, people were able to connect their specialized intelligences and reason across the domains, probably using meta-representation. Certainly, he regards the development of language and linguistic intelligence as key to this development. Fluid intelligence was highly adaptive. For example, unlike the Neanderthals, we could modify the design of tools, weapons, and artefacts to changing circumstances in the environment, demonstrating linkage between technical and natural history intelligence. It is also likely that our ancestors could use their fluid intelligence to apply their theory of human minds (social intelligence) to animals, allowing them better to anticipate the behaviour of their prey animals and thus achieve more hunting success.

Anthropomorphic thinking was not restricted to animals, as the primitive folk psychology became applied also to inanimate objects such as the sun, moon, and the rain, giving rise to early pagan religions in which the behaviour of these natural forces is attributed to gods. This also shows that the early modern human mind demanded causal explanations of the world. If abnormal weather devastated life, it was not due to chance but because the sun or rain god was angry. Paradoxically (to some) the cognitive foundations of religion and science are essentially the same, a need that humans have to explain, understand, and predict the world around them. In fact religious imagery, as well as more general art, is a distinguishing feature of what Mithen calls the 'big bang' of human cultural development, which started at least 60,000 years ago. There is no evidence to suppose that art or religion motivated the design of artefacts in earlier humans.

On the face of it, Mithen's theory does not fit too neatly into the two minds hypothesis, as it sounds more like a *three* minds theory. However, it is widely agreed that the modern human mind does combine general learning, as well as modular or specialized cognition with flexible and abstract forms of thinking and reasoning. Advocates of the two minds hypothesis initially tended to regard specialized intelligence as well as general learning as belonging to the old mind, while regarding flexible thinking and reasoning as the hallmark of the new or reflective mind. However, as I have recently argued,[29] there is a case for regarding social and linguistic intelligence as part of the new mind on the grounds that these faculties are very distinctively human and that reflective thinking would be impossible without them.

Is the human mind modular?

The term 'cognitive module' refers to the idea that there are self-contained areas of the mind dedicated to serving a particular function. Interest in modules in cognitive science dates from a landmark book by Jerry Fodor, *The Modularity of Mind*, published in 1983.[30] Fodor argued that the mind is comprised of a number of special purpose 'input' and 'output' modules together with a central and general purpose cognitive system. Input modules create mental representations for more general processing. The visual system, for example, extracts information from the patterns of light arriving at the retina. There are low-level receptors specialized for detecting points, edges, contours, brightness differences, colours, and so on. Higher level functions put these together to produce inferences or constructed representations of what is actually out there in the world. Thus a series of point detectors might feed a line detector one level up. If an edge is moving in the outside world, then a series of such line detectors will fire in turn in adjacent spatial locations. This in turn can feed higher level functions, which trigger perception of movement and so on. The highest level of this system will produce complex perceptual representations that become inputs to more general central cognition. Thus what we see may be combined with what we know or believe as well as our current goals and intentions in deciding what we actually do.

Fodor-modules are dedicated systems with their own isolated information processes. A line detector in the visual system, for example, is designed for that purpose and no other. It has built-in programming that enables it do this and these processes cannot be accessed by any other part of the mind. We might think of this as something like a microprocessor; say, one that is designed to implement the different programmes in your washing machine. There is a chip, which takes inputs (from the dial settings) and generates outputs (controlling water temperature, washing time, spin cycles etc). Its programming is fixed and impenetrable to any other part of the system. If the washing machine has a digital clock for example, then neither this nor the washing programme chip has any need to know about each other's internal workings nor any ability to control them. However, the output from the clock may be an input for the chip that is controlling the time of the wash.

Of course, a washing machine has no central cognitive system equivalent to that of a general purpose programmable computer, as we discussed in Chapter 1. But the brain apparently does, as we are able to apply our cognitive resources to a huge variety of different tasks. Hence, Fodor's account can be seen as a version of the two minds theory in which the intuitive mind is modular and the reflective mind is a general-purpose reasoning system. Fodor famously produced some very clear and strong definitions of what should count as a module. For example, modules should be innate, special-purpose, encapsulated (containing their own programming), inaccessible (not available to any other part of the mind), neurologically localized in the brain, and giving rise to specific patterns of development and disorder. Hence we might regard a particular form of memory as modular if it can be shown to be located in a particular region of the brain, and for it to be possible for its function to be impaired by brain damage, while leaving other forms of memory intact.

Modularity became very controversial when evolutionary theorists, led by John Tooby and Leda Cosmides, began to explore the idea that even apparently central and general-purpose cognition was really modular in nature. This has become known as the *massive modularity* theory. It goes well beyond the idea of input modules (such as language, vision, and perhaps a theory of mind module), which merely create mental representations for further processing. Here, we have to entertain the idea that cognitive modules may take direct control of human behaviour, or at least of the reasoning processes that are closely linked to our decision making. Before discussing what might constitute evidence for this claim, we first consider animal cognition where a case for massive modularity is easier to make.

Take the hunting behaviour of a cat. Cats are extraordinarily skilled and successful hunters. Moreover, all cats carry out essentially the same set of behaviours when hunting. It is quite noticeable that the stalking movements of even large cats such as lions and tigers are essentially similar to those of the domestic pet. This behaviour meets the criteria for a true instinct. That is, the behaviour is innate, fixed, and universal. It also appears to be an adaptation in the Darwinian sense, something which evolved in order to improve the survival prospects of cats (or more accurately, their genes). It ensures the food supply for the cat and has co-evolved with other relevant but physical features, such as a digestive system suited to a meat based diet.

Observing a domestic cat, it is hard to think other than that it has a mind, which is to some large extent modular. Once the hunting module has been engaged, a set pattern of behaviours will continue unless the cat is interrupted and severely distracted from its task. The hunting module is very powerful and flexible and it seems that modules like this are specialized learning systems, which can adapt to the environment in which the animal operates.[31] For example, cats can hunt in a variety of domains (including built environments that did not exist when the module was evolving) and hunt a variety of prey animals that behave in different ways and in some cases present potential hazards to the hunter. The behaviour also can be overgeneralized as when kittens (and often mature cats) will react to sudden movements, chasing, and attacking inanimate objects such as a piece of string that is manipulated for its benefit by a human being. Of course, the hunting module is not the only one possessed by the cat's mind. All cats wash, for example. Not only that, but they all do it in much the same way including some quite intricate manoeuvres like licking their paws and then rubbing behind their ears to reach an area to which their tongues have no direct access. Hence, this behaviour too must be controlled by a module.

The particular school of evolutionary psychology led by Cosmides and Tooby has proposed what is known as the Swiss Army knife model of the human mind, or the massive modularity hypothesis. The Swiss Army knife has many specialist blades designed for particular tasks. (Critics have pointed out that it also has a general purpose blade that tends to be used much more often than the others!) If the mind is massively modular then it is comprised wholly or mostly of cognitive 'organs' that evolved to deliver specific aspects of behaviour in adaptive ways. When this hypothesis first emerged in the early 1990s, it appeared to suggest that the human mind was comprised entirely of Fodor-type modules. That is cognitive modules that were innate, special purpose, isolated, and so on. Indeed, it was strongly argued at that time that not only was the idea of some central and general-purpose cognitive system unnecessary but that it was also evolutionarily implausible. In a paper published in 1992, Tooby and Cosmides confidently stated that '... there is a host of ... reasons why content-free, general-purpose systems could not evolve, could not manage their own reproduction, and would be grossly inefficient and easily outcompeted if they did'.[32]

This is a fairly extreme position, which has attracted much criticism (not least from Fodor) and from which its authors have since done a fair amount of back-tracking.[33] This proposal of what the mind *would be* like seems to defy both scientific observation and common-sense with regard to what it *is* like. First, both people and animals can seem to engage in a large amount of general learning. For example, it does appear that the domestic cat has an innate hunting module and can use this to survive as a feral cat in the absence of owners. Our own cat, Freddie, went missing for three months and was eventually found sheltering in a farmer's barn, having evidently been living off his innate hunting skills. On returning home, however, he gave no sign of his adventure and one of his first acts was to run to into the kitchen and look for his food bowl. As this shows, even a cat's mind is not fully modular: it can *learn* all kinds of things from experience like how to use a cat flap, where to find a safe warm place to sleep, and how to tell its owners that is hungry.

Consider now how we human beings go about gathering the food necessary for our survival. We evolved from hunter-gatherers and evolutionary psychologists might point to the fact that hunting (say with hounds, or with guns or with fishing rod) is still a popular human activity. That may be so, but I personally and many like me have never hunted anything in my life nor felt any inclination to do so. I have occasionally picked wild blackberries, but I am not much of a gatherer either. Not unless you count my shopping in supermarkets from time to time. As modern humans in the contemporary culture we largely gather our food by shopping, eating in restaurants, phoning for home delivery pizzas and so on. Nothing here looks very modular to me. Whilst they serve an innate drive (hunger) most of the behaviours associated with it are clearly shaped by learning and culture Also, none of these behaviours could have been selected for in the 'environment of evolutionary adaptation' (EEA) as the environmental psychologists like to call it.[34] Most of our evolution was stabilized during a period when we lived as hunter-gatherers in natural environments.

The claims of Cosmides and Tooby also fly in the face of 100 years of research on general intelligence or IQ. It has been known for many years that people vary considerably in their ability to reason and solve problems. Intelligence tests measure a 'general factor' that underlies performance on many different problems, also known just as 'g'. This is known to be *heritable* characteristic, meaning that the IQ of children is closely related to that of their parents, having been passed on genetically. Evolutionary psychologists have tried to downplay the importance of general intelligence, as well they might. If all human thought derives from special purpose modules, honed, and optimized by evolution for particular tasks, then why do individuals have a *general* ability to solve problems, which some are better at than others? Heritable general intelligence does not fit at all well with the old mind account of massive modularity theorists like Cosmides and Tooby. Indeed, I will show later in the book that it is closely related to the function of the new mind, predicting our efficiency in reasoning and hypothetical thinking.

The structured program view of the mind

In his recent book, *The Architecture of the Mind*, Peter Carruthers argues, like others before him, for a massively modular theory of the mind.[35] However, his proposals differ quite radically from those of earlier evolutionary psychologists. His modules are not Fodor-modules. He rejects the idea that modules are necessarily self-contained and isolated from each other and argues on evolutionary grounds that it is implausible that they would be. The problem is that a large brain is very expensive to maintain, consuming large amounts of oxygen and calories to run. Hence such brains could only have evolved (in humans) because they bring some great adaptive advantage to offset their cost. Even so, it is essential that brains develop to be *no larger than they need to be*. They must be frugal in their use of resources. Hence, evolution would avoid duplication of functions and to encourage co-operation and resource sharing where possible. The modules should interact with each other in the most efficient manner possible.

Carruthers draws an analogy with the modular design of modern computer programs, an idea I would like to explore in a bit more detail here. Programs written from the 1960s to the 1980s, before the advent of personal computers, tended to have a linear structure. Such a program carries out a series of functions in a fixed order. For example, a program to perform statistical analysis might read a set of data, transform, and arrange it, and then compute a series of statistics, before printing out the results for the user to read. Even for programs of this design, however, a modular construction was soon preferred, with languages like Pascal developed to encourage 'structured programming'. Such programs have a hierarchical organization, with a series of high-level procedures (or functions) that are executed in turn, each of which may call a lower-level procedure and so on. Programmers were also strongly encouraged to use local variables, so that data could only be accessed within a given procedure which 'owned' them. This is very similar to the idea of encapsulated information in cognitive modules.

The design of modern interactive computer programs provides a better analogy to a modular mind (see Figure 2.3). Such programs are designed to interact with users, for example, a word-processor or a web browser. They are no longer linear, because what the program does depends on the demands that the user makes. A user of a word processor might press a key for example, an

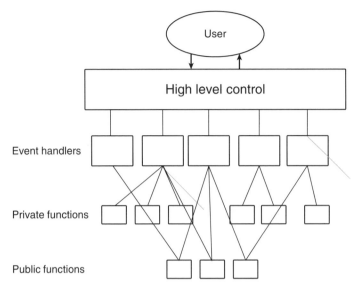

Fig. 2.3 Architecture of modern interactive computer programs.
Note: Private functions are available only to the event handlers that call them, but public functions are of more general utility and may be accessed by more than one event handler. In the analogy to the human mind, handlers with private functions are like Fodor-modules with encapsulated and isolated information processes.

event which requires insertion of text at the cursor. But they might also click the mouse on a menu item, which requires some quite different action. Hence, at the highest level of control (which is typically implicit in modern programming languages) the software detects events and assigns them to relevant event handlers. If the event is a click on the icon for italicized text, for example, then the program must respond by converting any highlighted text to italics. A relevant event-handler must be assigned to do this: a specialized procedure for responding to this particular input.

To envisage Figure 2.3 as a model of the mind (human or animal) we need to substitute 'environment' for 'user'. Organisms are constantly gathering perceptual inputs from their environment and responding with appropriate behaviours. The incoming information needs to be filtered and organized and assigned to 'event handlers' in the mind. Consider the following situation: you are travelling alone in a large city when you suddenly see a familiar face in the crowd who is an old friend. You go up to your friend and greet him before continuing with your planned business. The recognition of the face triggered an event handler for dealing with this social situation. But before this happened, other event handlers must have been activated. At a much lower level in the visual system, light patterns must have activated handlers for identifying contours and patterns that could lead to the recognition of faces as perceptual objects, prior to the recognition of a particular familiar face. So modules in the mind must be capable of generating their own events to which other modules can respond.

Much of the mind must work in this way, with different mechanisms being activated by features of the environment that are conveyed to us by our senses. However, this kind of 'stimulus control' is what features in the *old*, intuitive mind. There is also a form of high level control in our minds, which corresponds to conscious, volitional thought in the *new*, reflective mind. The reflective mind may come into play when dealing with novel problems, for example. The familiar but unrecognized face in the crowd might nag away at us so that we engage in conscious *reasoning* and *hypothesis-testing* to try to decide who it was. Perhaps it is someone we knew years ago when we lived in the city. We may try to decide how long ago that was, what age they would be now, and how much they might have changed. Unlike the massively parallel intuitive mind, such conscious reflection is a *singular* process: it must give up other tasks to focus on this one. It cannot at the same time do something else, like planning the business meeting which brought us into the city in the first place. Anyone wishing to argue for a massively modular human mind must provide some explanation for this apparently quite different mode of thought: singular, slow, conscious, deliberative, and capable of reasoning about novel problems with no immediately given solution.

Evolution and the brain: new mind = new brain?

What evidence might persuade us that our one brain has two minds within it? First, we might expect that different faculties assigned to either mind, for example, implicit and explicit systems of knowledge, will have distinct neurological locations. Second, we might expect that those functions attributed to the new mind will lie in regions of the brain known to have evolved more recently and more distinctively in human beings. Since the most recently evolved area is known to be the forebrain or frontal lobes, these should be especially associated with the new mind. While I examine this claim specifically here, I will actually discuss many studies of the brain throughout this book. Hence, I will first give a brief outline of the anatomy of the brain and methods that can be used to study its role in our behaviour.

The human brain is a very complex structure, estimated to contain up to 100 billion neurones or nerve cells. Although the chemical transmission process used by neurones is very much slower than information transmission speeds in modern computers, this very large number of cells with a potentially vast number of interconnections gives the brain quite enormous computational power. Anatomically, the human brain is dominated by two large cerebral hemispheres whose highly convoluted outer surface of grey matter is the cerebral cortex. The cortex is responsible, among other things, for perception, speech, memory formation, reasoning, planning, and decision making: in other words, all of the higher cognitive functions of the mind with which this book is concerned.

Evidence of the evolution of the modern human brain strongly suggests that any 'new mind' would have much to do with the frontal lobes of the brain. Brain size has increased from around 440 grams in early hominids 3–4 million years ago, to around 1400 grams in modern humans, an increase out of all proportion to the growth in our body size. As mentioned earlier, skull fossils suggest that the brain areas responsible for speech and language were developed prior to the emergence of the modern human species *Homo sapiens sapiens*. The most dramatic increase in brain size in modern humans, however, has been in the frontal and pre-frontal regions. Hence, it seems that the two minds hypothesis must predict a close relationship between the frontal lobes and the reflective mind.

There are two main methods for studying the relationship between brain and mind, which are called cognitive neuroscience and cognitive neuropsychology. Cognitive neuroscience is relatively new, but *cognitive neuropsychology* has been going strong since the 1970s. There is an important difference between the two. Cognitive neuropsychology, put simply, involves running cognitive tests on people with various kinds of brain damage. I will discuss some work of this type in Chapter 3, where studies of amnesic patients have been used to show that there are separate kinds of memory systems. That actually is its purpose: to understand better how the mind normally works by studying those whose brain damage has rendered them abnormal. As a leading exponent, Max Coltheart, recently put it: 'Cognitive neuropsychologists are not studying the brain.'[36] Neuroscience, on the other hand, most definitely *is* studying the brain, using methods developed quite recently and originally for medical purposes.

One of the biggest recent developments in medical science is a range of scanning technologies, which allow doctors (as well as researchers) to see what is going on in the human body, without actually having to do surgery. Some of these scanning methods, such as positron emission tomography (PET) can be used to track brain activity. By far the most popular in current neuroscience studies is functional magnetic resonance imaging or fMRI for short. MRI machines can take pictures in slices of any part of the body using very strong magnetic fields to take advantage of weakly magnetic protons in water molecules. Functional MRI involves taking successive pictures of the brain in order to track changes over time using powerful software.

Cognitive neuroscience attempts to study what happens in the brain by tracking pictures of its activity (neural imaging) while people perform some cognitive task. To simplify things, what happens essentially is that when a particular region of the brain is working hard, extra blood flows to it. PET tracks the blood flow directly, while fMRI tracks the oxygen it contains. Cognitive neuroscientists are thus able to look at which parts of the brain 'light up' when people perform particular tasks. Unlike cognitive neuropsychology, neural imaging can be applied to normal, intact brains. Of course, we might expect evidence from the two methods to converge. For example, if a particular region lights up when a person is perceiving speech, then we would expect damage to that area to be associated with a loss of speech perception. I will discuss studies using both methods at various times in this book.

The frontal cortex is sometimes described as the 'executive brain', implying that it is the source of controlled and volitional cognition. In fact, following a classic paper by the psychologists Don Norman and Tim Shallice[37] the forebrain has been the focus of intensive research on what are known as 'executive functions'. Recall that one popular way of framing dual-process theories of the mind is to contrast automatic with *controlled* processing. 'Executive function' is an essentially similar notion to that of controlled processing, and includes such high-level cognitive processes as planning and decision making. It also involves the ability to detect danger and difficulty and, when necessary, to override habitual responding in favour of novel reasoning. There is now a considerable body of neuropsychological and neurophysiological evidence linking these new mind functions with the frontal lobes.[38] However, reviewers have also noted the complexity of the studies and the inconsistencies between their findings, suggesting that executive functions are not limited to the frontal lobes but also involve multiple connections with other brain regions.[39]

A popular task used in the study of executive function is the Tower of London problem in which, typically, beads of different colours have to be moved between at least three 'towers' (wooden stakes on which the beads can be threaded) with the rule that only the topmost bead from any tower can be moved at one time.[40] Participants are shown a starting position as well as a desired goal state, an arrangement of beads on another tower to which they must move the beads, ending up with the correct colour sequence. In order to achieve the goal in the minimum number of moves, it is necessary to conduct a mental simulation in which you first imagine moving beads, and by (mental) trial and error discover the optimal method. This is very much the kind of ability that I have been attributing to the new or reflective mind. It has been known for some time that patients with certain patterns of damage to the frontal lobes perform poorly on this task, taking a large number of moves, presumably because they are unable to plan them in advance. Of course, this does not mean that *only* the prefrontal cortex is involved, but does indicate that it plays an important role. In fact, a more recent study using fMRI has concluded that regions of the parietal[41] as well as frontal lobes are involved in solving this task.[42]

As mentioned earlier, the two minds hypothesis clearly links general intelligence with the new, reflective mind. Correspondingly, researchers have investigated the role of the frontal lobes in individual differences in IQ. Performance on IQ tests is generally found to be impaired in neurological patients with frontal lobe damage, as expected. As with studies of planning, however, more recent and sophisticated study of this issue, combining data obtained from use of a wide range of methodologies, indicates that differences in IQ reflect a broader and more complex network of brain regions. While the frontal lobes play a major role, other brain areas, including the parietal lobes, are also involved.[43]

The research on frontal lobe function generally provides evidence that is supportive of the two minds hypothesis. The hypothesis attributes certain kinds of thinking to a mind which is evolutionarily new and distinctively human. The region of the brain, which is particularly recent and human in its development, is the forebrain. Research indicates that the frontal lobes are at least heavily involved in the kind of reflective thinking that we have been attributing to the new mind, as well as suggesting a major role for this brain region in performance on IQ tests. At the same time, functions normally attributed to the old mind such as emotion and associative learning are to be found in separate brain regions, which are much older in evolutionary terms and more similar to those of other animals.

Conclusions

How could it come about that we humans have two minds in the one brain? In this chapter, I have looked to evolutionary arguments and evidence for an explanation. The argument is that the new mind—reflective, distinctive human—has been added by evolution to an older mind—parallel, fast, and automatic. If the intuitive mind is indeed older then it makes sense that it should have more in common with animal cognition. However, I think it is probably a mistake to claim that the reflective mind is uniquely human, at least in origin. We may well be unique in our possession of language, meta-representation, and reflective consciousness, but the origins of these things may still be present in some limited form in apes and other animals. The biologist Fred Toates, for example, has reviewed much evidence for a distinction between what he calls stimulus-controlled and higher-order-controlled cognition in many higher animals, including rats.[44] Stimulus-control means that behaviour is directly triggered by cues in the environment. This can come about through instincts as well as through conditioning and learning. However, animals also have a mechanism in their brains (similar to one in ours) that will recruit their attention to deal with novel or hazardous situations where habitual learning will not cope. Such controlled cognition is known to take place in the frontal lobes of the brain, a region enormously more developed in human beings than any other species.

Why this mechanism developed into the reflective mind in modern humans is rather like asking how the elephant got its trunk. Evolution occasionally takes a unique pathway with a particular species and this seems to have happened with us. It somehow came about that we, modern humans, developed language, social cognition, reflective consciousness, and large forebrains, all in some way connected. The flexibility and creative power of our thinking sets us aside not just from apes but from all other hominid species. We are the only species that in any significant way has designed the environment to suit us, rather than simply evolving to adapt to the environment in which we happen to find ourselves. So developed is the reflective mind that for a long time philosophers and psychologists thought it was the *whole* mind, and that introspection was the only methodology needed to study it (see Chapter 1). Even today, the folk psychology that we all carry with us persuades us that we have much more conscious control over our behaviour than is really the case (see Chapter 7).

If we leave aside the restrictive definition of Fodor-modules then it may be reasonable to argue, in the way that Carruthers does, that the *old* mind is massively modular. However, as we shall see in this book, the new, reflective mind has a quite different character. It is singular, sequential, slow, and capacity limited—the opposite in all respects of the intuitive mind. Put this way, it sounds like a pretty limited device, which is true of its precursor mechanism in animals. However, the reflective mind is precisely what defines the uniqueness of our species and gives us every cognitive advantage that we hold over other animals. We have taken the ability to think about novel problems to a level completely without precedent in the rest of the animal kingdom. But the old, fast, parallel intuitive mind remains. This means that we have two ways of knowing, two ways of deciding, and two ways of acting upon the world. The rest of this book is concerned with exploring these dualities and their consequences for understanding the psychology of people.

Notes and references

1 I discuss the evolution of the brain later in the chapter. Some parts of the human brain evolved much earlier than others and have more in common with other animals. Conditioning and associative learning takes places in one of these older regions, called the basal ganglia.

2 Stanovich (2004).

3 Developed from the thought experiment originally proposed by Dennett (1995).

4 See Dennett (1995).

5 Stanovich (2004, pp. 3–4).

6 Particularly influential have been the chapters by John Tooby and Leda Cosmides in the edited collection of Barkow, Cosmides, and Tooby (1992) and the popularization of these ideas by Pinker (1997).

7 Dawkins (1976). See also Stanovich (2004) for detailed application of the selfish gene hypothesis to human behaviour.

8 For a detailed technical account of how they work, see Gen and Cheng (1997).

9 See, for example, Buss (2004).

10 Due to the hindsight problem, however, evolutionary biologists lay down strict criteria that have to be met before an adaptation can be claimed (Andrews, Gangestad, and Mattews, 2002).

11 Understanding how such a complex organ could evolve *gradually* is more difficult, but we let that pass.

12 Spandrel is an architectural term that refers to spaces left by other features. Its application in evolutionary psychology appears to have been coined by Gould (see, for example, Gould, 1991) who also uses the term 'exaption' to refer to features that were originally adapted to one purpose and then co-opted to another. For example, birds' feathers may have originally evolved to keep them warm and have later been adapted for the purpose of flying.

13 See Pinker and Bloom (1990).

14 For readable accounts of the story of human evolution, see Mithen (1996) and Dunbar (2004).

15 This is the modern use of the term. After Darwin, it was believed for a long time that people had indeed descended from apes, and there was much search for the remains of some intermediate creature that was then known as 'the missing link'.
See Mithen (1996) and Dunbar (2004).

16 See Aiello and Dunbar (1993).

17 Ryle (1949).

18 There is a vigorous debate amongst philosophers of mind as to whether folk psychology is a good theory of the human mind, having both advocates and stern critics (e.g. Haselager, 1997). My views are strongly with the sceptics. For a philosophical treatment of folk psychology within a two minds approach, see Frankish (2004).

19 The term was first coined by Ross (1977) since when much evidence has been accumulated to support it.

20 These are the frontal and pre-frontal lobes of the brain which account for the high foreheads in modern humans. Due to its recent evolution, this region is also known sometimes as the neo-cortex.

21 See Dunbar (2004).

22 See Mithen (1996) and Whiten (2000).

23 The term 'counterfactual' has a technical meaning which is not quite the same as 'contrary to fact'. Counterfactual conditional statements are often used in the past tense to refer to things which were once, but are no longer, possible, such as 'if I had taken that job offer, I would be a rich man now.' Present tense counterfactual statements are also possible, such as 'if I were President, I would withdraw the troops from Afghanistan.' Counterfactual statements are common in everyday language and evidence of our ability for meta-representation and hypothetical thinking.

24 The belief that language is innate became widespread following a series of seminal publications by the linguist Noam Chomsky (e.g. 1986). He argued that the structure of language could not be learnt, as behaviourists had tried previously to argue, and that there must be an innate language acquisition device to enable infants to learn languages. Curiously, Chomsky does not believe that language evolved by natural selection, although many other authors argue that it did (e.g. Pinker, 1994).

25 Real (1991).

26 Sperber (2000).

27 Mithen (1996), p. 68.

28 This is something of a simplification. For example, when flexible modern human intelligence developed and was widely applied, some specialized innate technical abilities may have dropped out of our store of innate knowledge.

29 Evans (2009).

30 Fodor (1983).

31 A recent advocate of a massively modular mind is Carruthers (2006) who proposes that most cognitive modules are designed for specialised learning. Carruthers also relaxes a number of Fodor's original criteria for modules, which makes the hypothesis more plausible.

32 Tooby and Cosmides (1992, p.112).

33 Cosmides and Tooby (2000) acknowledge a very important and distinctly human ability for meta-representation and hypothetical thinking that does not seem to be consistent with the idea of a domain-specific module. It certainly cannot be a Fodor- module. The same applies to the proposal of Sperber (2000) that we may have a mental-logic 'module' for general reasoning.

34 This is the environment in which most of the characteristics of modern humans evolved and stabilized. It is generally considered to be the Pleistocene period, which ended 12,000 years ago.

35 Carruthers (2006).

36 Coltheart (2004).

37 Norman and Shallice (1986).

38 Ward (2006).

39 Andres (2003) ; Baddeley (2007).

40 Not to be confused with the Tower of Hanoi problem, which involves moving discs of different sizes, with the additional constraint that a larger disc cannot be placed on a smaller one. This more complex problem can also be used to study executive function, with similar results.

41 The cortex has four principal lobes on each side. From front to back these are termed frontal, temporal, parietal, and occipital.

42 Newman et al. (2003).

43 Jung and Haier (2007).

44 Toates (2006).

Chapter 3

Two ways of knowing

Here are some of the things that I know:

1. I know how to play the piano.
2. I know that my father's name is John.
3. I know that Paris is the capital of France.
4. I know that biology is the study of living things.
5. I know how to walk.
6. I know how to play chess.
7. I know how to design psychological experiments.
8. I know that it poured with rain last year on my birthday and I had to cancel the planned barbeque.
9. I know how to speak English.

Like everybody else, I know a lot of things, but not all these kinds of knowledge seem to be of the same kind. Looking at this brief list, one obvious distinction is between 'knowing that' and 'knowing how', technically referred to as declarative and procedural knowledge. If we look at the 'knowing that' items, we can see that some of these things I know, most other people will know too (3,4) but some are personal to me (2,8). There is nothing surprising about that and not necessarily an indication that any different kind of memory system is involved. If we learn lots of facts, many but not all will be shared with others due to our common exposure to education, news media, and so on. There is a more significant difference between items like 3 and 8, however. I know as a fact that Paris is the capital of France, but I have no idea when and where I learnt this. On other hand, my recollection of my washed-out birthday barbecue is very personal: I know exactly when and where it happened and how I felt about it at the time.

Psychologists describe knowledge like 3 as belonging to *semantic* memory whereas knowledge like 8 is from *episodic* memory. We know that these are, in fact, two different memory systems. For example, patients suffering from amnesia caused by traumatic brain injures lose access to personal and episodic memories but do not lose their general knowledge about the world. In extreme cases, they may lose knowledge of their names and identities and fail to recognize their spouses, but they still know what names and spouses *are* and what the capital of France is. Although distinct, both kinds of memory are *explicit*, so that they may be called to mind and consciously reflected upon. For example, if plan a barbeque for my (mid-summer) birthday this year, I will likely recall what happened last year and perhaps develop a contingency plan for a wet day. Or if someone asks me in a quiz which is the largest capital city in Europe, I may call to mind Paris and try to figure out whether it bigger than London, Madrid, or Berlin. Explicit memories provide fuel for the reflective mind.

Consider now the 'knowing how' items. The personal/impersonal distinction is here to some extent as well: most people know how to walk, but only minority how to play the piano or chess, and still fewer how to design experiments. Knowing how to do a physical thinking like walking or playing golf also seems rather different from a mental thing like knowing how to play chess or design psychological experiments. And some kinds of procedural learning are related to general intelligence whereas others are not. With the exception of savants (individuals with special isolated abilities), it is difficult to become master chess player or a successful scientist without a minimum level of IQ, whereas everyone without a specific disorder can learn to walk and to speak at least one natural language. So there are probably a number of different systems involved in procedural learning as well.

What is interesting about 'knowing how' or procedural knowledge for our purposes, however, is that it seems largely to be *implicit* and hence not directly accessible to the reflective mind. As the linguistic Noam Chomsky famously pointed out, possession of a natural language, like English, enables us potentially to generate and understand an infinite number of sentences.[1] So we, or our brains, must in some way 'know' a complex set of rules that allow this to happen. But we clearly do not know them in the sense that we can call these rules to mind and write them down. Even the world's greatest linguists cannot agree what these rules are. The same is true for other kinds of procedural knowledge. I don't actually have a clue what is required physically for a person to stand up without falling over, let alone walk around. Even with an intellectual game like chess, much of the knowledge that distinguishes strong from weak players is implicit. Early designers of artificially intelligent computer programs were disappointed when chess masters, like other experts, could not describe the rules that they used to select chess moves. In fact, it turns out that much chess expertise is perceptual: players look at a board and just 'see' that some moves are worth considering, and strong players see better moves than weak ones.[2] So although reflective thinking is involved in chess as players try to project and analyse the consequences of potential moves, much of the process is preconscious and intuitive.

To take another example, compare an expert snooker (or pool) player with a physicist who has a strong grasp of the theory of mechanics. The snooker player knows how hard to hit the cue ball and with what degree of spin, not only to pot the object ball but to bring the cue ball into the correct position for the next shot. In doing this, he takes into account the speed of the cloth, the elasticity of the cushions, and so on. The physicist understands the process theoretically and could provide a set of equations for computing the motion and finally resting place of the balls. Very few snooker players, however, have explicit knowledge of these equations, even though in some sense their intuitive minds must represent them. Needless to say, equally few physicists are expert snooker players. And if they are, it is because they have acquired the implicit procedural knowledge required by an *entirely separate* learning process.

Does this mean that the reflective mind has no role to play in the acquisition of procedural knowledge? Far from it, it has a crucial role. It is pretty obvious that if you want to be an expert piano player (or an expert anything else) you need to practice for many years. In fact, the psychological evidence suggests that the idea of natural talent is something of a myth, and that the acquisition of any physical skill to international standards is mostly a function of the number of hours and years of practice that is put in.[3] So if you spent 10 years studying the theory of playing the piano, without ever touching the instrument, you could not expect to walk up to it knowing how to play it. But how do piano teachers teach their pupils to play? The answer is partly by example, but mostly by *verbal instruction*. But does not verbal instruction simply communicate explicit knowledge to the reflective mind?

We will see many examples in this book of the interaction between the intuitive and reflective minds, but skill learning provides a good example. What piano teachers, driving instructors, and other teachers of skills do is to provide instruction on *how to practise*. The rules that they impart to their pupils are internalized so that they can then practise correctly in the absence of the teacher. For example, a child may be taught the finger movements to play a scale of C major and then told to practise this repeatedly until they can make the intervals between the notes and the sound level of each note as even as possible. The repetition of these movements and the response to feedback (noticing how accurate and even the notes are and attempting to correct errors) creates the implicit knowledge of how to play. But the allocation of time and effort to practise in the correct way is under the control of the reflective mind. The pupil will also instruct herself by recalling the explicit rules for practise given by the teacher. Some theorists think that rehearsal of action through inner speech is one of most important ways in which the reflective mind operates.[4]

It has been understood for many years that the acquisition of skills requires what is known as *controlled attention* in the early stages, but that such skills become progressively 'automatic' with practise. In fact, the distinction between automatic and controlled processing was applied in this field before it became popular in dual-process accounts of thinking and social cognition.[5] 'Controlled attention' is one of the terms that psychologists use to refer to what I am calling the reflective mind. Even when the knowledge to be acquired will be implicit and procedural, attention is generally required to learn it. For example, when learning to drive a car with a gear shift, much conscious effort is required in the early stages to synchronize the clutch pedal with the gear lever and to co-ordinate the movements, whilst also steering the vehicle correctly and looking out for hazards. At first, this activity takes all our attention and conscious effort, but with much practice, we can do all this while listening to the radio, talking to a passenger, or planning our day's work ahead. This automation is just as well because the reflective mind has a limited capacity: it is very difficult for it to be applied to more than one task at a time.

Experts generally acquire a mixture of implicit and explicit knowledge, but the balance depends on the field of endeavour. Where physical skills are particularly important, as in professional sports, the balance is heavily implicit. But explicit knowledge and the reflective mind are important too. In a team sport, the player will endeavour to follow tactical instructions that the coach may have imparted prior to the start of the game. And a player may use self-instruction through inner speech at times, for example in telling themselves to stay calm and take their time when a chance arises to shoot at goal. At the other end of the continuum, an academic researcher might rely heavily on explicit knowledge and reasoning in order to give a lecture or write a book. But experience inevitably generates implicit knowledge and intuitions in researchers as well, particularly for disciplines involving empirical research methods. Even in academia, the traditional apprenticeship model works well. It is hugely advantageous for young researchers to work with established researchers or strong research groups who *know what they are doing*, rather than trying to learn research in a purely theoretical manner.[6]

There are multiple learning and memory systems in the human mind, of which I have already mentioned several in this book (conditioning, episodic memory, semantic memory, skill learning, modular learning systems). However, it is central to the two minds hypothesis that these can be classed as either implicit or explicit according to whether they support the intuitive or the reflective mind. In the next chapter, for example, we will see that the claim that we make decisions in two different ways is based on access to these two forms of knowledge. Implicit knowledge systems may either control behaviour directly by some kind of 'automatic' processing, or deliver at best *intuitions* which are conscious, but only in the sense of having a feeling of an answer or a course of action with some degree of confidence. Explicit knowledge, however, may be called consciously to mind and reflected upon by deliberative reasoning. In the rest of this chapter, we will look more closely at some of the evidence that the brain does indeed acquire and use knowledge in two distinct ways, starting with a discussion of visual perception.

Two ways of seeing

Everything we learn comes to us initially through the senses, of which perhaps the most important is vision. One form of knowing is the immediate apprehension that accompanies a perceptual experience. For example, I see someone in a crowd and recognize their face, knowing immediately who they are, whether I like them and how to talk to them. In cognitive terms, a lot of things happen here in a short space of time. The visual system processes the incoming light patterns to extract features, which are mapped on to the face recognition system that registers a hit. This in turn leads to recall of knowledge about the individual and the social context triggers knowledge in my social cognition systems about appropriate courses of action. Of all this processing, a small amount becomes conscious. For example, I may think 'That is Jim. I had better be polite to him because he is my boss'.

Common sense and the Chief Executive model of consciousness (Chapter 1) explains this interaction something like this. Automatic slave processes provide 'us' (the conscious person) with the knowledge that we have by chance encountered Jim, our boss, while out walking around town. We then consciously decide to be ingratiating in the hope that this will please our boss and gain us advantage in the work place. Having decided what to say we leave it to the appropriate slave system (in this case, speech production) to carry out our wishes. Hence, consciousness is a place where everything comes together and mediates between perception and action, something like this:

Sensory stimuli → perceptual experience → conscious knowledge → conscious decision making → action

The philosopher Daniel Dennett[7] has described this place where consciousness apparently mediates between perception and action as the *Cartesian Theatre*. He then goes on to show that this is a myth; there is no such place. Dennett's analysis is similar to the Chief Executive model. The Chief Executive receives information from some underlings and transmits orders to others. His office is in effect a Cartesian Theatre. To understand why this is a problem, let us look at the belief that action is mediated by conscious perception.

An accumulation of evidence in recent years, both experimental and neurological, has shown that perception does not have to be conscious at all. One method, which was a specialism of one of my old tutors at University College London, Norman Dixon, is that of subliminal perception. Participants can be shown brief exposures of stimuli which they are unable to identify, or even to see, but which still influence their behaviour in some way. For example, if presented with either letters or digits at random, they can 'guess' the category at well above chance rates, even though they are unable consciously to identify the stimulus. It is interesting to note that at the time that Dixon was working on this in the 1960s and 1970s the topic was extremely controversial, to the point where some psychologists regarded the claim that we could respond to stimuli we could not see as akin to parapsychology.[8] Nevertheless, some governments including that of the UK were sufficiently concerned by the evidence to ban subliminal advertising methods, on the basis that people might be persuaded involuntarily to buy products by brief exposures to advertisements that were not consciously seen.

A related method is that of *visual masking*. If you present a stimulus for a short but sufficient duration such that people would normally see it, this perception can be obliterated by a visual mask: an interfering pattern that appears in the same location. In a famous paper, Marcel showed that such masked words, though not perceived, would 'prime' the recognition of subsequently presented words of related or associated meaning.[9] For example, a word like 'chair' would be recognized more quickly if preceded by the masked presentation of a related word like 'table' than an unrelated one like 'diary'. This method and related ones are still somewhat controversial, however, due to the difficulty of determining that the perception of the prime word was entirely unconscious.[10] Perhaps the word is consciously perceived and it is the *memory* of this experience that is deleted by the mask, which is why people are unable to report it.

Another classic study that suggested the possibility of unconscious perception was the discovery of 'blindsight' in neurological patients, originally described by Weiskrantz and colleagues.[11] Information carried by the optic nerve into the brain is channelled through several routes, one of the most important of which is through the primary visual cortex, or striate cortex, located in the occipital lobes (at the back of the brain). Animal experiments have shown that when this area is surgically removed, the animals still retain some residual visual abilities to discriminate objects. When the striate cortex is (accidentally!) damaged in human neurological patients, it affects *conscious* visual perception such that there are blind areas in the visual field. If stimuli are presented in these blind regions and the patients are instructed to guess their properties, however, they can do so remarkably well. Although the visual acuity is less than with normal vision, blindsighted patients can often 'guess' features such as colour, movement, position, and even simple shapes that are to them, as conscious persons, invisible.

Perhaps most interesting of all for the two minds hypothesis is the now widely accepted view that there are two visual systems, one which leads to conscious perception and one which leads to *direct control of action*.[12] The second system is heavily involved, for example, in tracking the movement of a ball in flight and preparing the correct movements required to catch it. These are known as the ventral (conscious) and dorsal (unconscious) systems, terms that refer to their location within the brain. The ventral system can only be accessed through the striate cortex, which is where its conscious nature presumably arises. One way of demonstrating their different functions is by studying patients who have neurological damage to one system or the other. But the difference can be shown in normal participants as well. For example, it has been shown that a number of visual illusions affect only the ventral and not the dorsal system.

As an example, look at the Ebbinghaus illusion (Figure 3.1). When a circle is surrounded by other large circles, it appears smaller than when surrounded by small circles. It is possible to use this illusion in a slightly different way. The size of the circle on the left can be increased so that it appears subjectively equal in size to that on the right even though it is not. Suppose we do this with actual disks, lying on a table. Participants can then be instructed to pick up the central disc. While their hand is in motion towards the coin, the aperture between thumb and finger—anticipating the grasp on the coin—can be measured using attached light emitting diodes. This aperture is *not* equal in the two cases, but wider when the coin to be grasped is, in fact, bigger. So the ventral visual system, which gives rise to phenomenally experienced size of the discs, is subject to the Ebbinghaus illusion, but the dorsal system which controls the grasping movement is not. The two minds see different things.

These examples show that what we, conscious persons, see reflects only one means by which sensory information can reach the brain. There must also be a part of our brain that monitors input from the senses, most of which never becomes conscious. For example, when having a conversation in a crowded room, we (normally) listen to the person with whom we are immediately conversing. But if someone across the room mentions our name, our attention will immediately switch. Then we hear what that voice is saying instead.

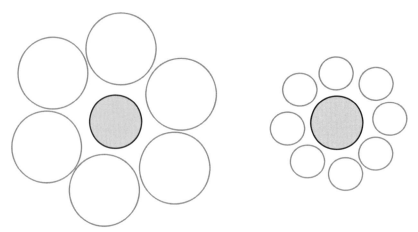

Fig. 3.1 The Ebbinghaus illusion. The grey circle to the left looks smaller than that on the right but is actually the same size.

We (conscious persons) were not hearing that conversation before, but clearly something in our brains was, for how else could its relevance ever be noticed and come to our attention? This is clear illustration of the fact that what 'we' see, hear (and I will argue later in the book, *think*) is largely determined by *pre*conscious control systems in our brains.

Multiple memory systems: evolutionary arguments

As discussed in Chapter 2, evolutionary psychologists tend to argue that the mind contains a number of 'modules', i.e. specialized components for performing given tasks, each with their own evolutionary story. Sometimes an analogy is drawn between physical and mental organs. Parts of the body such as the eye or the knee or the heart can each be given an evolutionary account, which reflects distinctive Darwinian forces. There is an adaptive advantage in being able to perceive patterns of light, bend one's legs, and pump blood around the body, but the exact development of each of these body parts reflects the interaction of our forebears with differing aspects of the environment. In the same way, it is argued, there are distinctive mental 'organs' responsible for such diverse cognitive acts as mind-reading, face recognition, or speech production. We need a specific account in each case of how this facility evolved in response to the relevant evolutionary forces.

It is not at all surprising, then, that there should be evolutionary arguments for multiple memory systems in the brain. If we consider the different kinds of learning that we need to accomplish, it is difficult to see how a single mechanism could realistically be responsible. Here are a few examples of things that we can learn:

+ How to perceive the world around us, identifying and locating objects in a three-dimensional space.
+ How to perform wide variety of actions and physical skills.
+ How to speak and understand a natural language and any number of further languages.
+ How to develop a spatial mental map of geographical areas that we have explored.
+ How to behave appropriately in social situations.

A contemporary view of innate cognitive modules is that they are primarily specialized *learning* devices.[13] One of the first such proposals in modern cognitive science was by the leading linguist Noam Chomsky, who suggested that we are born with a *language acquisition device.*[14] Chomsky has long argued that the structure of human language could not be learnt by experience and so its basis must be innate. There are several arguments to support this claim. First, the development of natural language in humans is universal and almost impossible to suppress except in the most severely deprived linguistic environments (as when a child is locked, isolated in a room during the critical years). Second, the linguistic environment provides quite impoverished stimulation. If children simply imitated what they heard, then they would learn all the hesitations, grammatical errors, and incomplete sentences, and also be limited to the particular sentence forms experienced. But in fact, we all acquire the abstract conceptual basis of the language around us, and the competence (in principle) to generate and understand a potentially infinite number of sentences. Finally, there is evidence of linguistic universals, i.e. structures that are common to all natural languages to be found around the world.

If the basis of language is (or must be, as Chomsky argues) innate, then what exactly is built in to the DNA? Clearly not English, Mandarin, or Swahili. The particular language (or languages) that children acquire depends upon those that are spoken around them (or signed, in the case of deaf children of deaf parents). So what must be built-in at birth is a set of algorithms for *learning* one or more languages, with a predefined structure and underlying set of rules. But if we accept this argument for one modular learning system, why not others? For example, we have to learn to see. Perceiving a three-dimensional world from the 2D image on the retina is hugely ambiguous. There are infinitely many ways that the brain might construct the picture we see. For example, some visual illusions seem to be related to the ways in which we see corners and angles in a built environment and such illusions are less strong in nomadic tribes who lack the same learning experiences. Even as adults we (our brains) can quite rapidly adapt to changes in visual input. If this were not the case, then spectacles with varifocal lenses would not be the great success they have become. Such glasses provide clear in-focus vision at long, mid and near distances, but to do so must create distortions due to their curiously shaped lenses. As anyone who wears these will know, these distortions are initially quite disturbing, but after a few days they just 'disappear'. The brain (with practice) creates the illusion of perfect sight at all distances, simply because it has been provided with the information that enables it to do so.

It does seem pretty obvious that the mechanisms for language and visual learning must be specialized and cannot be the same as those involved, say, in remembering a telephone number or replaying a piece of music in your head. However, evolutionary arguments for multiple memory systems are not restricted to such specialized modular systems. It can also be argued that we have more than one kind of general purpose memory, that is, systems that allow us to learn about the world across a wide variety of domains and contexts. In a classic paper, Sherry and Schacter[15] argued that we do have distinct forms of explicit memory (episodic, declarative, knowing that) and implicit memory (procedural, habits, knowing how) because they evolved in response to different Darwinian drivers. These systems are distinct, they argue, because their functional requirements are fundamentally incompatible. One system learns *invariances* in our environment while the other responds to *variances*. Both are adaptive, but for different reasons.

I noted above that when children learn language, they disregard variations in how sentences are actually uttered and abstract their underlying form. The same is true of habit and procedural learning generally. When we learn to play a scale of C major on the piano under initial and clumsy conscious control, our fingers will make many mistakes, missing a note or hitting two together. However, these errors will be random, not consistent. When the skill is automated these variances are not retained; what is learnt is the average position and movement of the fingers, abstracting the underlying and correct form of the skill. Even if we look at a much higher form of automated thinking involved in social cognition (Chapter 6), we find the same encoding of *invariances*. When we judge a person by his or her social category, we use a *stereotype*, which is by definition insensitive to variations among the individuals who make up that category. When you learn to play chess, the skill does not depend on the size of the chessboard, the shape of pieces or even whether they are on an actual board or just a picture in a newspaper or on a computer screen. All these kinds of learning and memory involve extracting the invariant features of our environment.

By contrast, consider the nature of personal, episodic memories. These encode what is distinctive or different about particular experiences. In fact, our ability to recall such memories depends critically upon variance. Like many people, I commute to work, driving the same route at the same time of day, with little variation. Most days, when I arrive at work, I can recall very little about this 30 minutes of my life. I kept my car on the road, stopped at traffic lights, obeyed speed limits, and so on, so I must have been attending reasonably well to the environment. If you rang a buzzer at a random interval on the drive, I would be able to describe in detail what I was seeing and what I had recently seen. But the detail will be quickly forgotten unless something *unusual* happens. My drive takes me across the Tamar Bridge from Cornwall into Devon and occasionally the bridge is blocked by an accident further up the road leading to long delays. I remember *those* journeys very well. So where the first learning system retains the invariant and discards the variant, the second does the precise opposite.

As Sherry and Schacter point out, episodic memory, like procedural memory, is adaptive. For example, when an animal remembers where it has stored food or where a dangerous predator was seen, these are specifics that will enhance its survival value. But as they also point out, it is most unlikely that a single mechanism could evolve to abstract variances without invariances and vice versa. In any case, the distinction between these two memory systems is strongly supported by neuropsychological evidence, as we shall see later in the chapter. For the moment, however, note how relevant this discussion of variances is to the two minds hypothesis. The intuitive or autonomous mind deals with invariances because it is the mind of routine and habitual behaviour. When we don't reflect, then we do what is habitual, what has worked (on average) in the past. When the reflective mind is engaged, however, we can deal with individual circumstances on their merits. So the two ways of thinking with which this book is primarily concerned have a lot in common with the two kinds of memory upon which each principally draws.

Rule learning with and without awareness

When we learn, as when we think or decide, the two minds may be simultaneously active. Attending to events in our environment provides an opportunity for both kinds of learning to occur, so that some of the experiences that lead to implicit, procedural learning also result in explicit, episodic memories. For example, if we think back to the time when we were learning how to drive a car, we may recall particular episodes: a conversation with the driving instructor perhaps, or a near accident they helped us avoid, or a car whose gears were very hard to locate. These episodic memories have nothing to do with the process of learning to drive, however, they were merely formed in parallel. As discussed above, our driving skill depends upon its indifference to the particulars of the learning experiences.

An interesting method used in psychology is that of rule or concept learning. In the real world, we learn somehow to classify objects into categories. Some of these categories seem natural, with some fairly obvious shared properties, like birds or trees. Others are clearly cultural creations and may include a number of objects with quite diverse features, for example, furniture. Many concepts and categories are learnt by children, but we retain the ability for concept learning all our lives. Some of the concepts I now use frequently, such as computer virus, web links or satellite communications, did not exist when I was growing up. But how do we acquire such concepts in cognitive terms? Do we do it by some form of explicit hypothesis testing and reasoning (reflective mind) or by some automatic learning process (intuitive mind) or some combination of the two?

Laboratory studies can be a little misleading in addressing this kind of question due to the artificial nature of the tasks. In other words, what happens in the lab may not be representative of everyday life. A good example is an influential study run in the 1950s[16] by Jerome Bruner and colleagues, which strongly gives the impression that concept learning is a task for the reflective mind involving explicit hypothesis testing. Their methods generally involved giving people positive and negative examples of concepts, that is cases which are included or excluded by some rule, and asking people to figure out what the rule is. Suppose we have cards displaying coloured shapes and I tell you that the following cards are positive and negative examples of the rule:

Positive	Negative
3 blue triangles	1 red square
1 red triangle	3 green triangles
2 green squares	2 blue circles

If you are puzzled by the above, do not be concerned. I have chosen here a rule of a kind that is the most difficult to learn, technically known as an exclusive disjunction. The actual rule used to classify the above cases is 'A card which has triangles or green figures *but not both*'. Such rules are really difficult because common features may be shared by positive and negative cases. You probably assumed (incorrectly) that triangles were not part of the definition of the rule, for example, because they appear in both the positive and negative lists. To solve such problems requires difficult explicit reasoning. Most examples of the concepts we use at least in everyday life have some common features. For example, computer viruses, worms, trojans, adware, and spyware are all technically distinct concepts, but for the average user (as opposed to the professional programmer), they are all bad things that come from the Internet and that we want a single program to remove for us. So we devise a term like 'malware' to cover them all.

Bruner and colleagues did also study much simpler concepts that do have common features but still reported that people used explicit hypothesis testing strategies to solve them. A key criterion here was that when they solved the problem, they could not only correctly classify new cases but they could also *state the rule*. For example, they might say, 'the rule is any card that has red triangles'. If this were always the case, then we might think that such rule learning was an explicit process of the reflective mind. Rule learning would also be a quick and simple process. However, there is plenty of evidence that concept learning may also be a slow process that can be effectively achieved by implicit learning processes belonging to the intuitive mind.

A very early demonstration of this kind of learning was by the famous behaviourist Clark Hull, published in 1920.[17] Hull asked people to classify ideograms resembling Chinese characters into two categories, A and B. These were quite complex visual patterns. However, the A characters had a common element called a 'radical' although it was hard to pick it out. On a task like this, people are trained by 'outcome feedback'. That is, they guess the category first and then are told what it was afterwards, thus finding out if they were right or wrong. Eventually people learnt to classify the characters correctly. Moreover, they were able to do this for a new set of characters not previously seen. But the interesting finding in this study was that they could not state the 'rule'. In fact, people had no idea how they knew the As from the Bs. Hence, in this case the learning seemed to be implicit.

Findings of this kind have been replicated in many more recent studies using a variety of different tasks.[18] Such tasks also involve rule learning, but where the rules are far from obvious. A popular method is artificial grammar learning. An example of an artificial grammar is shown in Figure 3.2. The 'sentences' in this grammar are actually strings of letters. The system has five states including an entry (S1) and exit (S5) state. In between you can move to any state where there is an arrow, and S3 can also move to itself. Each such movement generates a letter as shown. This grammar can be used to generate legal or grammatical strings as follows:

Positive	*Negative*
PW	PTV
PRXXTV	PRXXVW

VXXTV	VRWW
PRTWRXTV	VTXXW
VXXXTWW	PWXXXV
VTV	PWW

All the strings listed as positive cases can be generated by moving through the grammar according to the arrows. The negative list, although containing similar letters and some subgroups of letters, cannot. The question is, can people learn such grammars merely by studying examples? The answer is yes and no!

It has been known for many years that complex rules are more easily learnt by studying just positive examples, omitting the negative cases. In this case, people also perform better if they are *not* told that there are rules underlying the strings and do not attempt to reason out what they are. It seems sufficient simply to make sure that the examples are attended. A typical method involves giving people sets of four positive examples at a time and instructing them to memorize them. Only following such training, are participants told that there are rules that link the examples they have seen together. They are shown new sets of strings, only some of which conform to the rules, and asked to classify them as grammatical or ungrammatical. People can do this with well above chance accuracy, but they are quite unable to state the rules they are using. So they have learnt the rules in the sense that they can use them, but not in the sense that they can state them. Findings like these have been replicated many times both using artificial grammars and other methods.

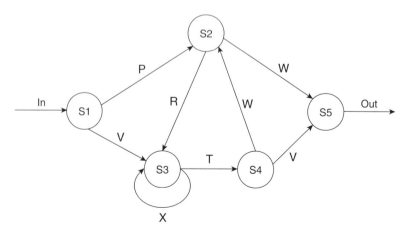

Fig. 3.2 An artificial grammar.

From the evidence reviewed here, it seems that simple rules can be learnt by explicit reasoning and hypothesis testing, but complex rules and patterns are instead acquired by automatic, implicit learning processes. Correct classification of Chinese radicals and artificial grammar strings seems to be a function of the intuitive, not the reflective mind. Experiential learning in such cases leads to intuitive feelings that some cases are right and others wrong but with no explicit knowledge in the reflective mind of the rules involved. In fact, instructing people to reflect can lead to *worse* performance on such tasks. Surely it is this kind of implicit learning that must underlie many forms of intuitive expertise in the real world: the experienced police detective who feels that the witness is lying, the nurse who suspects the imminent onset of a heart attack, and the salesman who believes his customer will eventually sign the contract. There is nothing mystical about such intuitions; they are based on the perception of cues that have been learnt by experience to be predictive.

Gary Klein[19] conducted a study of naturalistic decision making among U.S. Fireground commanders. In one case, they were called to what appeared to be simple fire in a one storey building. They entered the building and sprayed water on the fire, but with little effect. The commander was puzzled because the fire was not responding as it should. Feeling that something was wrong, he ordered his men to retreat. Shortly after, the floor of the building collapsed. It turned out, contrary to their knowledge, that the building had a basement where the fire was actually raging. The decision to withdraw saved the lives of him and his men. The commander attributed this decision to his 'extra-sensory perception', at least until he met Klein. Of course, it was no such thing. What happened here was that an apparently familiar situation set up expectations that failed to materialize. This led to an intuitive feeling that something was wrong and fortunately to an intervention by the commander's reflective mind with an executive decision to withdraw while figuring out what was going on.

Implicit rule learning, like all forms of learning, requires that people attend to the relevant information. Unlike explicit learning, however, it does not need any conscious intention or effort to learn or any explicit reasoning in the reflective mind. Attention is required, but that is ensured by asking people to memorize the examples they are given. The fact that a conscious effort to learn can result in poorer performance indicates that the task is not amenable to the explicit learning system; it also suggests that applying the reflective mind to a task interferes with ability to process it intuitively. We will see in later chapters how the two minds can often come into conflict. But there is a good example of a rule learning task where we can see the two minds at work also. This is a problem that was invented by Peter Wason called the 2 4 6 problem.[20] Participants are told that the experimenter has as rule in mind, which classifies triples of three whole numbers. An example that conforms with the rule is 2 4 6. They are then told to try to discover the rule by generating number triples. In each case, the experimenter tells them with the triple belongs to his rule (yes) or not (no). They are instructed to announce what the rule is only when they are very confident they have it correct.

While this is clearly an explicit rule learning task, the experimenter has played a rather nasty trick. The rule he actually has in mind is any ascending sequence. But of course, the sequence 2 4 6 suggests something much more specific, like ascending with equal intervals. Now here is the difficulty. Any sequence that belongs to such a more specific rule *also* belongs to the more general one. So if the participant gives triads like 10 20 30, or 1 4 7 or 21 22 23, the experimenter will always say yes. So most people on this task become very convinced that they know the rule, when they do not. In fact, the only way they can disprove their hypothesis is to do something which few think of: to test a negative case of it, like 1 2 6. In this case, the experimenter would still say yes, even though the intervals are uneven.

The 2 4 6 problem is very difficult, but what interests us here is the way people respond to being told that their rules are wrong. Consider this protocol, reported by Wason:

No.4. Female, aged 19, 1st year undergraduate
8 10 12: two added each time; 14 16 18: even numbers in order of magnitude; 20 22 24: same reason; 1 3 5: two added to preceding number.
The rule is that by starting with any number two is added each time to form the next number.
2 6 10: middle number is the arithmetic mean of the other two; 1 50 99: same reason.
The rule is that the middle number is the arithmetic mean of the other two.
3 10 17: same number, seven, added each time; 0 3 6: three added each time.
The rule is that the difference between two numbers next to each other is the same.
12 8 4: the same number subtracted each time to form the next number.
The rule is adding a number, always the same one to form the next number.
1 4 9: any three numbers in order of magnitude.
The rule is any three numbers in order of magnitude.
(17 minutes)

This participant first thinks the rule is ascending in intervals of two, but then switches to a rule based on ascending in equal numbers. Now what is really interesting about this protocol (and others like it) is the last three rules announced before the problem is solved:

The rule is that the middle number is the arithmetic mean of the other two.
The rule is that the difference between two numbers next to each other is the same.
The rule is adding a number, always the same one to form the next number.

These are, in fact, three statements of *almost exactly the same* rule, although the first two attempts are not explicit about the ascending order. What can be going on here? This looks to me like an example of a conflict between the intuitive and reflective minds. The constant reinforcement, 'yes' to generated triples, is cementing the equal interval rule in the intuitive mind. So compelling is the intuition that the reflective mind invents alternative wordings to express it. Eventually, however, the reflective mind asserts its authority and superior reasoning ability. This individual finally escapes the intuition and finds the correct solution. Many others, however, do not.

Multiple memory systems in the brain

Both the evolutionary arguments and experimental evidence strongly support the case for two kinds of learning. In addition, the evidence from neuropsychology is very strong. There are different methods for studying the neurological basis for cognitive functions (see Chapter 1), one of which is focussed on the effects of various kinds of brain damage in human patients. There are also animal studies in which brain damage is intentionally inflicted, usually by surgical means and the behavioural effects investigated. The animal studies can be informative, whatever you may think of the ethics of such experimentation. However, they can also be quite limited sometimes, because of the significant differences in cognitive function that humans have, compared with even our closest, monkey relatives.

The most famous neurological patient in the scientific literature is known only as HM.[21] As a child, HM was knocked off his bicycle and suffered a head injury. He later suffered from epileptic seizures, which became more and more frequent so that his life as an adult was intolerable. Finally, at age 27, he was given a drastic cure when a neurosurgeon removed both temporal lobes of his brain, including the organs known as the hippocampi. As we now know from many other neuropsychological studies in humans and animals, the hippocampus plays a very significant role in learning and memory. The effect on HM was immediate and drastic; he lost all ability to form new long-term memories as well as losing access to such memories for several years prior to the operation. In many other respects, however, HM was remarkably normal. For example, his perceptual and motor abilities were unaffected, as was his linguistic ability, although his conversational skill was obviously limited by his inability to remember what had been said to him a few minutes previously. He could retain information briefly so that he still had what psychologists call short-term or working memory (see next section). His IQ actually *increased* somewhat after the operation.

HM and other amnesic patients provide clear evidence for a distinctive hippocampal learning system that is responsible for the laying down the kind of memories that I have been referring to as episodic and personal. It is the explicit learning system. But if the conclusions from earlier sections are right, this is not the only kind of learning system in the brain. What about learning new skills or acquiring habits, the kind of knowledge that I have attributed to a separate, implicit learning system? As it turns out these kinds of learning are generally *spared* in amnesic patients with localized damage to the hippocampus. This includes cognitive skills of the kind discussed in the previous section. For example, amnesics can perform equally as well as normal control participants when learning artificial grammars, the task discussed earlier. That is, they are just as able, after training, to classify new letter strings correctly. This is in spite of the fact that their ability to recognize the exemplars they studied in training is greatly impaired.[22] Again, it seems that attending to the relevant information gives both implicit and explicit learning systems a chance to operate. If one of these systems is impaired by neurological damage, then the other can still function.

If this conclusion is right, then we should be able to find the opposite pattern: patients whose explicit learning is normal but whose implicit learning is impaired. Once again, this is proved by neuropsychology. Procedural, skill, and habit learning appear to be located in the striatum or amygdala, organs associated with motor control and emotion respectively. Damage to these regions can indeed result in impaired implicit learning but leave intact explicit learning. This is what neuropsychologists call a *double dissociation*. Assume that brain area A is responsible for cognitive function X and region B is responsible for function Y. Then a patient with damage to A should be able to do Y but not X, while a patient with damage to B should be able to do X and not Y. This is considered the strongest form of evidence for localized cognitive functions in the brain. On this basis, the neuropsychological evidence strongly confirms that there are indeed distinct explicit and implicit learning systems in the brain, as required by the two minds hypothesis.

Working memory, general intelligence, and the reflective mind

Some of the key properties of the reflective mind, as defined in Chapter 1, are that it is slow, sequential and singular. It has a very limited capacity for processing information, compared with the intuitive mind, and can essentially perform only one task at a time. It is also, in some sense, conscious. In spite of its limitations, use of the reflective mind seems essential for solving novel problems where past experience is not directly applicable. Reflective thinking is also associated with measures of general intelligence or IQ. Strangely enough, all of these properties can be explained by reference to a field of work that originated in the psychology of memory a little over 30 years ago. This is the topic that psychologist call 'working memory', a kind of memory that perhaps has more to do with attention and thought than it does with the storage of information.

In the behaviourist period of psychology, human learning was regarded as an extension of animal conditioning, leading to a disproportionate emphasis on habit learning. With the cognitive revolution came a switch to studying what we can now see to be mostly explicit learning processes associated with episodic memory and the hippocampal learning system. Research methods also changed. Instead of studying slow learning processes that took many repeated trials for habits to be acquired, psychologists started, for example, giving people lists of words (just once) and asking them to recall them. Suppose I read you a list of 10–20 unrelated words and then ask you to write down as many as you can (in any order). Of course, you will forget some of them, but those that you recall best and will write down first will be the *later* words in the list: those most recently presented. Suppose now, I give you another list and ask you to recall them in the order in which they were presented. Now the advantage for recently presented words will disappear, because you have to recall them last. Why should this be?

The apparent answer to this question, offered by a number of psychologists in the 1960s was that people must have two different kinds of memory 'store': short-term and long-term.[23] In the word recall tasks, the last few words are still in short-term memory and can be recalled better than earlier ones, which rely on having been transferred into long-term storage. However, if you are forced to recall the words in order, this short-term storage is lost and with it the advantage for later items. Note that this technical use of the term 'short-term memory' does not correspond to its everyday use. It is not recall of what you did yesterday, this morning or even a few minutes ago. All of those require long-term memory. Short-term memory refers to the ability to hold a few items in mind on a temporary basis like remembering a phone number long enough to dial it. In fact, to retain such a number for more than a few seconds requires us to rehearse it using inner speech: we say the number to ourselves in our minds. Such rehearsal also increases the chances that the number will be transferred into long-term memory.

Of course, saying that something is stored in long-term memory is not the same as saying that it is permanent. Most memories are quickly forgotten.[24] For example, if I am watching a film on television with my wife, who leaves the room for a few minutes, I can give her a summary of the action she missed. If I was tested even the next day on what happened in that period, however, little would remain. In fact, it is *adaptive* to forget most of the minutiae of our lives. Consider, for example, the case of parking in a large car park every day with no reserved space. At the end of each day, you need to remember where exactly you parked to find your car. If the memories of all the other locations you have parked in on previous days at work were equally strong, this would be a near impossible task.

If there is a short-term memory store, what is its purpose? One early idea that seemed very reasonable was that it was a kind of temporary store in which information could be held or refreshed by rehearsal to give it time to be transferred to more permanent storage in long-term memory. Although widely accepted for a few years, this view was undermined by the report in 1970 of a neurological patient who had a severe impairment of short-term memory without any apparent deficit in his ability to form long-term memories.[25] This was an extremely important study, not just for the theory of human memory, but also because it was one of the first to establish the research method known as cognitive neuropsychology. That is, the use of psychological testing of brain-damaged patients in order better to understand the cognitive systems in the mind.

In the 1970s, the idea emerged that short-term memory was more than just a temporary storage system but should instead be regarded as a *working memory*, a term which is now much more often used. One of the pioneers of this approach (as well as its most prolific researcher up to the current time) is the British psychologist Alan Baddeley. He recently defined working memory as 'a temporary storage system under attentional control that underpins our capacity for complex thought'.[26] This definition more than strongly suggests that working memory is central to what I am calling the reflective mind in this book. Although working memory appears to have specialized devices for the rehearsal of sounds and images, it also has several attributes, which link it directly to reflective thinking. It is of limited capacity, associated with consciousness and 'controlled attention' and appears to be highly general in its application. Information, which flows though our conscious minds from moment to moment, is thought to be held in this working memory system.

Working memory is needed by any system that does calculations or computations. Suppose you type into your pocket calculator: 5 times 4 divided by 2 equals? Of course, it will return the answer: 10. Until you press the equals key, however, the computation cannot be done. So the calculator must be able to hold the rest in some temporary memory system: the numbers 5, 4, and 2, the instruction to first multiply and then divide. Once the calculation is done, however, this working memory store can be wiped and re-used for something else. If you want a human example, consider that problem of understanding a sentence that is spoken to you. Even understanding a simple statement like 'your dinner is on the table' requires that by the time you reach 'table' both the subject of the sentence 'dinner' and the relation 'is on' have been retained so that they can all be put together to extract the grammatical relations and the actual meaning of the sentence. In this sense, the brain must have multiple specialized working memory systems, for example those that are able to relate together multiple inputs from the visual system in order to construct a mental picture of the world. But like most psychologists, when I use the term 'working memory' in this book, it will refer to a single general-purpose system that reflects our current focus of conscious attention. This is what gives the reflective mind its distinctive properties of being slow, sequential, limited in capacity and associated with conscious experiences.[27] It is also the basis for differences between people in the kind of ability measured by tests of general intelligence or IQ, which we now consider.

First, let us consider briefly the history of intelligence testing. I mentioned in the previous chapter that IQ tests measure a heritable factor of general intelligence. The idea that intellectual ability could be inherited and passed down through families was proposed by the 19th century psychologist, Sir Francis Galton. The IQ or 'intelligence quotient' was, however, invented by the French psychologist Alfred Binet, early in the 20th century. The notion of an intelligence *quotient* was originally devised from the idea that children have a 'mental age', which is more or less advanced than their actual age and computing their ratio. It was originally calculated by dividing the mental age by the chronological age and multiplying by 100; hence the term 'quotient' and the convention of setting the population average to 100. However, it is impossible to extend this method of measurement to adults, as performance on IQ-type tests peaks at around 16 years of age. So nowadays 'IQ' scores are generated by arbitrarily fixing the mean population performance to 100 and producing a range of scores on either side. What is important is that such scores provide a reliable measure of individual differences in some kind of general intellectual ability. That is to say, some people consistently score higher on such tests than others. These scores, in turn, are related to general measures of intellectual achievement, especially getting good marks at school or university.

The study of intelligence has had more than its share of controversies. For example, there have been arguments throughout the 20th century about whether intelligence is a singular ability, whether and to what extent it is inherited and most notoriously whether there could be differences in average intelligence between races. To cut a long story short, the evidence strongly indicates that there is a general factor of ability measured by IQ tests, which are primarily tests of abstract reasoning and problem-solving. This general factor is often known simply as *g* (so named by the English psychologist, Charles Spearman) and it has a high degree of heritability.[28] This means that the IQ of a child is strongly related to that of its parents and other close relatives. The best evidence of this comes from numerous studies of the IQs of twins both fraternal and identical, raised both together and apart. Identical twins have identical genes and even when raised separately (as has happened in enough cases for such studies to be viable) their IQ scores are highly correlated. However, IQ scores are subject to large environmental influences as well,[29] which is why it is difficult to find 'culture-fair' methods of comparing different ethnic or socioeconomic groups. There have been recent advances in understanding both the genetic basis of IQ, and its neurological location in brain.[30]

IQ has also been controversial with regard to such questions as what does it measure and how important is it in life to have a high score? As we shall see later in the book, recent studies of thinking and reasoning shed some light on these questions. In post-war Britain, the psychologist Sir Cyril Burt was highly influential in promoting the idea that intelligence was fixed, general, and innate and one of those responsible for implementing the eleven plus test, in which children were selected for two kinds of school, basically as the result of an IQ test. Although many education authorities in the UK now have only comprehensive secondary education, selection by eleven plus examination remains in some areas and has made something of a comeback in recent years. Selection at age 11 has not been a feature of U.S. education, but intelligence testing, in a disguised form, comes in at university level in the form of the Scholastic Aptitude Test (SAT) and Graduate Record Examination (GRE) tests that are widely used in the selection of undergraduate and postgraduate students respectively. The GRE includes abstract reasoning problems, not unlike those used in IQ tests. Although the SAT is apparently composed of tests of scholastic attainment in preuniversity education, it is in fact so highly correlated with IQ scores, that it can reliably be used to estimate them. SAT scores are also routinely used as measures of general intelligence in contemporary psychological studies of reasoning and decision making.[31]

The link between general intelligence and working memory has been discovered comparatively recently. There is now a large body of work that looks at individual differences between people in their *working memory capacity*. This is generally measured by asking someone to hold some items in memory while also performing a cognitive task of some kind. For example, you may be given a list of digits to remember and then asked to read a sentence and judge whether it is true or false. The number of digits you can recall after doing this is a measure of your working memory capacity. As with intelligence tests, some people consistently have higher scores on such tasks than others. These scores, in turn, can be used to predict their performance on a variety of other tasks. When such correlations are found, it is inferred that working memory must be important for the task in question. On this basis, it seems that very many tasks require working memory. Working memory capacity is correlated with, among other things, reasoning, problem-solving, reading, language comprehension, planning, and most kinds of learning. In addition, all of the above tasks can also be disrupted by requirement to perform them while simultaneously doing another task that also involves working memory.[32]

Although the study of intelligence and memory have entirely different histories, they are now firmly connected by the finding that when individual differences in working memory capacity are compared with those of general intelligence, the two are very highly correlated indeed.[33] So the mysterious 'g', discovered early in the 20th century now seems to have a clear location within the (reflective) mind. It turns out that the same people who are good at the kind of abstract reasoning and problem-solving tasks used to measure IQ, are also the ones who are also good at holding items in memory while performing another task. And these people do have some general advantage in learning, reasoning and problem-solving: all activities that heavily involve the reflective mind.

It is important, however, not to attach too much importance to intelligence scores, for several reasons. First much of our 'intelligence' is unrelated to scores on IQ tests, or tests of working memory. Unless people have some specific genetic or neurological disorder, many aspects of brain function seem quite independent of such scores: the mechanisms of visual perception and language acquisition, for example. Where people can solve problems by relying on previous experience though the intuitive mind, their ability to do so is little affected by their intelligence score.[34] Second, having a high IQ is no guarantee that people will behave *rationally* or make good decisions. I will return to this problem in Chapter 8.

So what it boils down to is this. Not all brains are born equal: some are *potentially* faster and more efficient in their computational power than others. Some people are luckier with their genes than others. But this innate advantage is (a) subject to much environmental influence and (b) limited to the functions of the reflective mind. Most of the many automatic calculations that the human brain performs are not related to the performance of the singular working memory device. But, of course, some very important ones are. As we shall see, the reflective mind does enable us to achieve a flexibility of thought and a capacity for rational decision making well beyond that of experience-based intuitions.

Conclusions

The two minds hypothesis, which I have primarily defined as a distinction between intuition and reflection in thinking, reasoning and decision making (Chapter 1) is in fact supported strongly by research on learning and memory. The hypothesis rests critically on the idea that there are two main forms of knowledge. Implicit knowledge is reflected in our behaviour—what we can do—and in the intuitions that come to mind without any conscious knowledge of their basis. Explicit knowledge, which we can call to mind and reflect upon, is quite separate. This distinction is critical to the claim that we have two minds: two different ways of thinking, deciding, and acting, which can come into conflict with one another. In this chapter, we have seen strong experimental and neuropsychological evidence for this claim. There are, indeed, two ways of knowing.

Research on memory and attention also supports the two minds hypothesis in a different way. The study of what was originally thought to be a short-term memory store has developed into a major programme of research on 'working memory' over the past 30 years. This is much more than a memory system. In fact, according to some authors, it has much more to do with attention.[35] There are very strong reasons to suppose that working memory is a key element of the reflective mind. First, if reflection requires working memory, we can see why it can only do one thing at a time, has a limited capacity, is slow, sequential, and associated with conscious experiences. Second, measures of individual differences in working memory capacity are very closely correlated with measures of general intelligence. The best measures of general intelligence are, in fact, abstract reasoning tasks. And there is much evidence that the ability of the reflective mind (but *not* the intuitive mind) to solve problems is closely related to measures of intelligence.

Notes and references

1 Chomsky had an enormous influence on psychology and cognitive science. He came to fame originally in the 1950s and 1960s by his critique of Skinner's behaviouristic theory of language acquisition and his now widely accepted argument that language must have an innate basis in the human mind (see, for example, Chomsky, 1986).

2 Chase and Simon (1973).

3 See Ericsson et al. (1993).

4 See Carruthers (2002, 2006).

5 Schneider and Shiffrin (1977); Shiffrin and Schneider (1977).

6 I have written a book on this: Evans (2005).

7 Dennett (1991).

8 Dixon (1971).

9   Marcel (1983).

10 See, for example, Merikle and Reingold (1998).

11 Weiskrantz (1986).

12 Goodale (2007; Goodale and Milner, 2004).

13 See Carruthers (2006).

14 Chomsky (1986).

15 Sherry and Schacter (1987).

16 Bruner, Goodnow, and Austin (1956).

17 Hull (1920).

18 For review see Reber (1993), Berry and Dienes (1993), and Sun (2001).

19 Klein (1999); see Chapter 4.

20 Wason (1960, 1968).

21 HM has been the subject of many published papers from 1957 onwards. For an overview of these, see Eichenbaum and Cohen (2001).

22 Knowlton, Ramus, and Squire (1992).

23 See Baddeley (2007) for a more detailed history of research on memory.

24 There is debate about whether forgetting is due to loss of the memories or an inability to access them for recall. However, this is of no importance for the purpose of the current book.

25 Shallice and Warrington (1970).

26 Baddeley (2007), p.1.

27 In my recent scholarly writings on dual-process theory, I have proposed that the key distinction is between processes that require this central working-memory system and those which can operate independently of it. See Evans (2008).

28 For a brief introduction to IQ testing and its history, see Deary (2001). For a more thorough and detailed treatment, see Mackintosh (2009).

29 Dickens and Flynn (2001).

30 See Jung & Haier (2007); Plomn and Spinath (2004).

31 See Frey (2004); Stanovich (1999).

32 For a detailed recent review of individual differences studies (Mackintosh, 2009), see Barrett, Tugade, and Engle (2004) and for detailed discussion of dual-task studies, see Baddeley (2007).

33 See Colom et al. (2004).

34 A massive research programme on this topic has been conducted by Keith Stanovich and Rich West (Stanovich, 1999, 2009c; Stanovich and West, 2000, 2008b). This work shows the conditions under which reasoning performance will and will not be related to cognitive ability.

35 See Engle (2002).

Chapter 4

Two ways of deciding

How many decisions did you make today? One? Two? Hundreds? Thousands? The answer depends on what I mean by a decision and on what I mean by 'you'. 'You' the conscious person, or 'you' your brain? For example, suppose you went to work today, stopped at a red traffic light on your drive in, and checked your email when you arrived in the office. Were these decisions? Yes and no. They don't feel like decisions because such behaviours are *habitual*. On working days, you go to work. When a red light shows, you just automatically stop without thinking about it. And checking email is always the first thing you do on arrival at the office. But in a sense these are decisions because you could have acted otherwise. You could have phoned in sick even if you were not and taken the day off. You could have driven to within a mile of your work place and then just turned off and headed for the beach instead. You may even choose to drive through a red traffic light. Nothing physically prevents you from doing so. The habitual behaviours will assert themselves unless the reflective mind intervenes. And only if it does will you be conscious of making a decision.

In this chapter, I will only consider situations where we know we are making a decision. However, that only means that the reflective mind is involved, and not necessarily *in charge*. Decisions can be made intuitively or emotionally and not necessarily as the result of reflective thinking. Decision making is hence a key topic for the two minds hypothesis. The intuitive mind and the reflective mind may both be involved and they may be in conflict. This is popularly expressed by the saying that the head tells us one thing and the heart another. When the reflective mind is engaged the decision making will be slow and effortful. But even so, it may not have the final word.

Consider two cases where we would know we were making a decision: A: You drop in to see a friend and they offer you a hot drink: 'Would you like tea or coffee?' B: A head-hunting agency contacts you and out of the blue you are offered a new job. It is much better paid than your current one, but involves a rapid relocation to a city 500 miles away with obvious disruption for your family. In both cases, A and B, we know there is a decision to be made, but B is evidently much more important. Not only that but it is a novel decision, one you have never had to make before, at least not in a precisely similar form. By contrast, you probably have a long-established habitual response to the offer of tea or coffee. You might reflect briefly before answering, but little time and effort will be expended and your immediate, intuitive feeling will most times provide the answer.

Closely related to decision making are judgements of various kinds that I will also discuss in this chapter. For example, decisions involve the imagination of future events, which makes the judgements involved in *forecasting* particularly relevant. Even choosing between tea or coffee involves forecasting: anticipating which you will enjoy more, assuming there are no special factors like trying to please your host. Maybe you normally prefer (real) coffee, but dislike the instant kind, which appears to be on offer and opt for tea. But the forecasting here is really no more than extrapolation from past experience. Such habitual decision making often serves us well but has its limits. For example, some people who have routinely refused a particular food for many years on the grounds that they don't like it may discover by accident that they do, after all! Unlearning habitual behaviours takes conscious effort, as we shall see in Chapter 8.

On the other hand, being offered a job in another town involves a much more complex form of forecasting which is technically known as a *mental simulation*. To make such a decision reflectively involves imagining how your life will be if you take the offer and comparing it with the life you have. Which of these two future worlds would you rather live in? This is really a very complex business and one that we are not necessarily very good at. The new job will be better paid and have more status, but there is much to set against taking it as well. The effort and disruption of moving for a start, the need for children to start in a new school and for you to make new friends, and to find a new golf club, or whatever you need to continue your way of life. There is more risk and uncertainty in this prospect than that of staying where you are. There are many unknowns that make it difficult to perform a good simulation: for example, will you get on with your new work colleagues? When making this kind of decision, it is easy to forget that the nonaction, staying where you are, is a choice too and that *also* should be simulated. Suppose you get a promotion in a few months if you stay where you are: would it then be worth the effort and expense of moving?

Some decisions seem obvious and easy but others can be very evenly balanced. Decisions made intuitively are usually based on a 'feeling of rightness' or preference that requires little or no deliberation.[1] If I always or nearly always drink tea (or coffee) then the choice is automatic. If I am indifferent, then the choice is theoretically hard, but I don't want to be left dithering and lost in thought while my host patiently waits for an answer! So we must have the capacity to make an apparently random choice in such circumstances. When the decision is important and the reflective mind is fully engaged, however, it is quite a different matter. Suppose you are offered the new job, but your initial analysis results in the belief that you are almost indifferent between going and staying. Few people would be happy to make such a choice on the spin of a coin! In fact, as anyone who has been in this situation can attest, such choices become very stressful. One reason is that we generally go through life 'remembering' the future as well as the past. That is, we see ourselves in a temporal context, which includes an anticipation of what we will be doing next week, next month, and next year (at least). When suddenly there is a fork in front of us, leading to two very different futures, we can feel very anxious and insecure. This might occur with decision B, in spite of the fact that you were quite happy and content with your projected future until you answered the call from the head-hunter. How could adding a choice, without subtracting anything, make you unhappy?

In fact, too much choice makes us both unhappy and confused as much recent research has shown.[2] In the UK, a recent large advertising campaign by a leading bank exploited this fact. They ran a series of TV adverts to tell people that while other lenders offered a bewildering array of different kinds of mortgage loans for private home purchases, they offered just two! A truly remarkable campaign when you consider that their competitors offered the same deals plus others as well. Less is truly more, it seems.

Playing the markets

My main purpose in this chapter is to discuss the interplay of the intuitive and reflective minds in our decision making. To illustrate this, I will consider first the buying and selling of shares and other commodities in the 'free markets' so beloved of Western economies. Markets can behave in ways that seem very rational, so that the price of items reflects very accurately information about them. As an example, I can recall my own experience in the UK housing market. A few years ago, my wife and I decided to move house but as I was not changing my job, there was no great hurry. In the event we looked at many houses over a period of months before choosing one. The houses varied on many dimensions such as size, condition, location, quality of garden, access to amenities, and so on. I became very impressed by something that an economist could have told me in the first place: absolutely everything factors into the price. If you receive details on a new house, which (with your market experience) looks 10% too cheap, you don't suspect but *know* there is something wrong with it. It will turn out to have no garden, or to back on to the railway or have some other drawback. If it were otherwise, someone would have bought it before the details even reached you. Of course, the odd house is too expensive for what it is, because the owner thinks they can beat the market. Such houses simply do not sell, until eventually the price is lowered.

In the same way, stock market values largely reflect expert evaluation of a company's strengths and weakness by professional fund managers and other investors. If the price falls below its true worth, investors will quickly snap it up, raising the price to the right level. However, stock markets do not always behave rationally and reflectively. There are herd effects, like panic selling, which can cause a major crash as one investor after another tries to sell and drives the price down. And sometimes the opposite occurs, when the herd agree on optimistic buying, as in the apparently crazy 'gold-rush' for dot-com companies in the late 1990s. Massive amounts of money were invested and lost in Internet companies that mostly went bust, often without having developed any products at all. Which mind should we blame that on? While it is true that social influence—the herd effect—is deep-rooted in the intuitive mind, so that we all tend to feel safety in numbers, the dot-com boom and bust cannot simply be attributed to that.[3] It appears that people also based their decisions on explicit reasoning with their reflective minds but to poor effect. If our assumptions are wrong, then good reasoning will still lead to bad decisions. In this case, false assumptions included the belief that companies involved in transforming technology will necessarily be very profitable and that companies that enter the market earliest will dominate those who join later. History supports neither proposition.[4]

Of course, people can also use their reflective minds to avoid intuitive errors, but they must first have the correct training, or what Stanovich[5] calls the 'mindware' for the job. To illustrate this again with stock markets, there was a sharp and largely sustained increase in world share prices between 1980 and 2000, which allowed sales people to produce a very impressive looking graph to persuade customers to invest in the stock market, or market-related products. This was a blatant appeal to the intuitive mind; it has worked in the past, so it will work in the future. And of course, many were persuaded, only to see their investments halve in value over the next few years. Tim Harford, a trained economist, explains how the same graph rang alarm bells for him.[6] Essentially, the 'true' value of shares is based on the profitability of the companies and should only exceed a given ratio to current profits if future ones can be expected to increase sharply. Between 1980 and 2000, share values rose much faster than company profits leading to a ratio between the two that was historically unsustainable. No realistic level of economic growth could fill the gap. So to an economist, these same figures indicated that stock markets were highly overinflated and would likely fall. This is a case where the (trained) reflective mind would draw precisely the opposite conclusion to the intuitive mind.

Another big factor in stock market values is uncertainty. This was most dramatically illustrated in recent times by the large and sustained fall in world stock markets that occurred after the 9/11 terrorist attack on New York. This cannot simply be written off as an irrational herd effect. The problem here is that while stock market values are mostly determined by the reflective reasoning of expert investors, much of this reasoning concerns attempts to *forecast the future*. This is most dramatically illustrated in the 'futures' markets, in which investors will buy quantities of oil, grain, sugar, and so on that have not yet been produced. Such investors have no storage tanks and warehouses, for they will never take a delivery. The commodity they buy is later sold again, eventually to someone who can actually make use of it. The art of futures trading is to compute what the value will be when the commodity is actually produced.

In fact, all stock market trading involves forecasting, because the value of shares in the future will depend upon whether a company's profits rise or fall. This is why stock markets hate uncertainty, of which the 9/11 attack created an extreme case. All simulations of future events, whether carried out by computers or purely mentally, rest on assumptions. After 9/11 no one knew what the power of terrorists' actions would be to disrupt the Western way of life and business. Standard assumptions were suddenly questionable. And while people will quite happily cope with risk when they can calculate it, they absolutely hate unknown levels of risk. Unable to simulate the future with any confidence, a lot of investors simply decided to take their money out of the stock markets, forcing the price down.

The theory of rational decision making

There is a close relationship between the psychology of decision making and the discipline of economics. In fact, psychologists sometimes win the Nobel Prize for Economics, as in the case of Herb Simon (1978) and most recently, Daniel Kahneman (2002). And psychology owes the theory of 'rational' decision making to economics from the time when the psychologist Ward Edwards reviewed the economic literature and presented it to academic psychology in the 1960s. The theory had been familiar to economists much earlier, following the classic work *Theory of games and economic behaviour* (1944) by von Neuman and Moregenstern.[7] In game theory, the idealized player is traditionally described as 'rational man', although in these politically correct days, she should be probably known as rational person.

According to the theory, rationality embodies total selfishness. A rational choice is one that maximizes benefit, or minimizes cost to the decision maker. For example, if I am shopping for a new jacket, it is rational to choose the cheaper one when comparing it with another of equal quality and suitability. Or if two jackets are the same price, it is rational to choose one of high quality and so on. The principle is more complex to apply, however, when risk and uncertainty is involved. For example, I may be tempted to buy a new wristwatch when travelling on another continent because it is cheaper than the equivalent quality product back home. But it is also more risky, because if the watch goes wrong I cannot take it back to the shop for a free repair or replacement. In such cases, the theory tells us to choose the option which has the higher *expected* benefit for us. This involves trading off risks and benefits as I will explain shortly.

The theory works well for free market choices, like the house price example I discussed earlier. But surely, total selfishness cannot be the basis of all our decisions? What about altruistic acts, like donating money to charity? Well according to the theory, what the decision maker is trying to maximize is *utility* or subjective value. People only give money to charities, for example, because it has some personal utility for them: for example, they want to impress their friends with their generosity, or they like to see themselves as a compassionate and caring person. Of course, this may seem like a circular argument and this is indeed something of a problem for the theory.

It is actually quite hard to get away from the idea that a rational act is one which maximizes expected benefits for the actor. Evolutionary psychology (Chapter 2), for example, is based on Darwinian principles and the selfish gene hypothesis. Genes are 'selfish' because they confer attributes to the organism that promote its success and survival. Given the way that evolution works, they cannot be anything but selfish. Natural selection does indeed maximize the expect benefits for the genes, in terms of their goal to reproduce and survive. The Skinnerian learning principle works in the same way: animals and people tend to repeat behaviours that have been rewarded in the past. Thus it might seem that the intuitive mind, driven by genetic influences and experiential learning, might be rational in the sense of economic theory. It is certainly true that animals can behave in ways that seem consistent with game theory: for example, bees seem to trade off risk and benefit in very efficient ways when searching for food.[8] However, closer examination of the theory makes it apparent that a rational person must have a very well-functioning reflective mind. This is because rational person is expected to calculate the future rather than simply rely on the past.

The theory can be applied to various decision situations, but I will focus for the moment on decisions made under risk. This is still a game to a game theorist. When we make decisions under risk, there is another 'player' but it is not a person, but rather Nature or God or chance or whatever you think is responsible for uncertainty in life. We still try to win by computing what the other 'player' will do, although in this case it involves calculating the probabilities of various uncertain events. Let us start with the fairly obvious case of gambling. When, according to the theory, is it rational to place a bet and when should you walk away? Most commonly applied in this situation is the *expected value* rule. What this means is that you should play if, *on average*, you would win more than you would lose.

On this basis, no one should ever play roulette in a casino, because of the zero on the wheel (or the even greedier, two zeros used on wheels in some casinos). For example, you get an even money bet on black versus red, or odds versus evens, which would be fair, if it were not for the fact that you lose if the ball rolls onto a zero. The same applies on all other bets. If you bet on any of the numbers 1–36, you get odds of 35 to 1 against. Again, this would be fair, except that you lose if you hit zero as well as the wrong numbers. So the odds are really 36 or 37 to one against, depending on whether the wheel has one or two zeroes. Despite belief in various 'systems' (see Chapter 8), punters can never escape the mathematics. In the long run, they lose and the casino wins.

The question of why people gamble is fascinating and I will return to it later in the book. But here it looks like a problem for decision theory. Many millions of people bet on national lotteries, for example, which are taxed heavily with governments pocketing large profits. Of course, they all have an expected loss, so is this not something of an embarrassment for the theory? Is the great bulk of humanity to be deemed irrational? With the slippery notion of 'utility', however, decision theory can wriggle. For example, people may have a 'utility for gambling', a pleasure in taking part, that outweighs the expected loss. Or perhaps their utility for money is not directly related to its value, so they overvalue the prize relative to the stake. Or perhaps their decision might be rational if we take into account their *subjective* probability for the events. For example, if people overestimate their chances of winning the lottery then their subjective expectation is of a gain, rather than a loss. So they are 'rational' after all except for getting the probabilities wrong, of course!

Given social attitudes towards gambling, we might simply be able to write it off as an irrational activity, in spite of mass participation. However, the case of insurance is even more embarrassing for the theory. Insuring your house, your life, your holiday, or your car is generally considered a 'good thing' by society and not just by the insurance companies that stand to profit from the policies. But profit they do, of course. Actuaries are people employed by insurance companies to calculate risks. For example, if you buy motor insurance, the premiums will be set for certain categories of people based on age, gender, history of accidents, and so on. These premiums will be calculated on the basis of how often people in such categories make claims, and what these claims cost the company. But of course, the companies put their own zeroes on the roulette wheel. On average, they will take more in premiums than they pay out in claims. The expected value rule works for them, so it works against you. So why buy insurance?

The problem is that if buying insurance is rational, then game theory is not a good theory of rational decision making. I have long understood both game theory and the fact that insurance companies make profits, and it has not stopped me, or many like me, from buying insurance. Expected value is a good rule for an insurance company because they are underwriting large numbers of cases and can calculate with some precision what their gains and losses will be. It is not a good rule for an individual, however, because they are dealing with one-off cases. If the main bread winner dies without life insurance it is a disaster for their family. If the house is burnt down or the new car is stolen, it will be a massive financial blow. Some risks just cannot be tolerated. In fact, individuals seem to be focusing not on expected values but on the worst case scenario. So we could regard insurance selling and buying as mutually rational, because the sellers and buyers are (appropriately) applying different rules.[9]

Consider this simple scenario. Suppose I suggest the following wager (A). I will toss a coin and if it comes down heads, I will give you $200. If it comes down tails you give me $100. Now consider this slightly different one (B). The game is the same, except that we repeat the process for 100 spins of the coin. At the end, we total up the wins and losses. Now would you take the wager? Most people say they would refuse A but accept B and this has been described by decision theorists as being irrational, a violation of decision theory.[10] It certainly violates the expected value rule, because on average you will win $50 for each play and so should accept the gamble, according to decision theory, whether it is offered once or many times. But why should people apply the rule to a single case? If you cannot afford to lose $100 then refuse the bet. Of course, if it is averaged over 100 trials then something changes: the chances of coming out ahead. On a single spin, you have a 50% chance of losing money. Over 100 spins, the chances of losing are very small. To lose on B, the coin would have to come down tails at least 67 times, and the chances of that happening are around 3 in 10,000. It seems to me that in the one-off case the participant thinks like an insurance buyer. In the long-run case, she thinks like an insurance *seller*, because the fluctuations are smoothed out by averaging.

I never cease to be amazed by how adamant some academics are that the expected value rule is *the* rational way to make decisions under risk, even in one off cases. I once saw a mathematician playing *Who Wants To Be A Millionaire?* on TV. It was evident to me from the start that he had decided to play the expected value rule. Fortunately for him, he was paired with a normal person and so had to moderate his strategy. Otherwise he might have got himself into this situation.[11] Suppose you have correctly answered the £500,000 question and are now going for a million. When the question comes up, you have no idea, but have one life-line left: 50-50. Should you take the money or guess between the two remaining options? 'Rational man' as he obviously thought himself to be, would presumably have guessed among the two remaining answers. This would have given him an equal chance of either gaining £500,000 or losing £468,000 (because he would take home a minimum of £32,000 under the rules). So the guessing prospect has a higher expected value than taking the money (see Figure 4.1). I doubt that anyone has made such a decision in the history of the game. In general, when given a choice between a sure thing and a risky prospect of higher expected value, people have a strong preference for the former.[12]

We can, of course, make people's economic decision making look 'rational' by assuming they have idiosyncratic and subjective ways of valuing different amounts of money, and determining subjective probabilities for different events. This gets pretty messy, though, and it was left to two psychologists, Danny Kahneman and Amos Tversky, to come up with prospect theory, a good

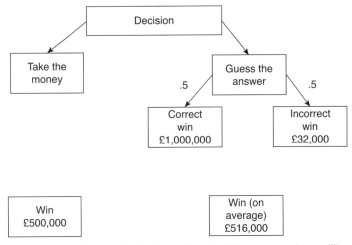

Fig. 4.1 Decision tree for a choice facing a player in Who wants to be a millionaire? (See text for details). According to the expect value rule, the contestant should guess.

descriptive account of how these decisions are made by ordinary people.[13] In general, people tend to avoid risks when considering prospective gains, but seek them when considering prospective losses. If this were the only factor, however, people would not bet on lotteries or buy insurance. However, the authors also showed that people attach considerably too much weight to very small probabilities. Suppose I offer you $500 for sure or the chance to win $1000 on the spin of a coin? Most people will take the $500, the kind of behaviour that contestants regularly show on *Who Wants To Be A Millionaire?* Now suppose that I offer you a 2 in 10,000 chance to win $500 or a 1 in 10,000 chance to win $1000? Most people will now switch and go for the large prize at the lower probability. Again, this accords with everyday observation. When people are offered raffle tickets in the pub, they often enquire about the attractiveness of the prize. However, I have yet to hear anyone ask how many other people have bought tickets. Below a certain value, a long-shot is a long-shot—the number (apparently) does not matter much.

Prospect theory was very important in economics and one of the main foundations for Kahneman's Nobel Prize (Tversky was deceased by the time of the award, and therefore ineligible). But it does not help us much with our quest to understand the underlying mental processes. Are these processes intuitive or reflective? The same applies to much psychological work on decision making inspired by economics. Fortunately, there are a number of other kinds of study on judgement and decision making much more helpful to our enterprise. I turn to these now.

Intuition and reflection in cognitive biases

There is something of a current fashion for authors to praise humans' ability to make decisions intuitively, without conscious reflection. I will discuss these approaches later in the chapter. Historically, however, intuitive judgement has had pretty bad press in psychology, as it has been blamed for a large number of cognitive biases observed in our experiments. A defining characteristic of intuition is that we have no conscious access to the processes which underlie it: only a feeling of what the right answer should be. To make matters worse, the reflective mind is prone to *confabulate* rational sounding explanations for our intuitions that may be quite misleading. So people can easily be biased without being aware of the fact.

Terms like 'bias' and 'prejudice' are in everyday use, and we all suspect biases in expert opinion when the expert has a commitment to a particular position. We would not expect, for example, that an analysis of the current state of the economy would be independent of left or right wing political affiliations of the commentator. Similarly, if we hear a debate on global warming between a spokesperson for the oil industry and a member of environmental interest group, we know what we are going to hear. The same data would be given different interpretations. A key research study for one side would be dismissed as 'junk science' by the other and so on. This kind of bias is real and is of interest to psychologists, of course. However, the term *cognitive bias* refers to many phenomena that would not be at all obvious but for the relevant experimental studies. Although less apparent to the public, such biases are equally important. Let us consider a few examples.

Reasons for and against

Imagine you are the judge in a child custody case. Parent A has average income, average health, average working hours, reasonable rapport with the child, and a relatively stable social life. Parent B has above-average income, a very close relationship with the child, an extremely active social life, does a lot of work-related travel and has minor health problems. In one study, when participants were asked to whom they would award custody, 64% chose B and only 36% A. However, when a separate group were asked to whom they would *deny* custody, 55% chose B and 45% A.[14] Does something strike you as rather odd about these figures? If B is the better parent, then not only should he/she be awarded custody, but obviously A should be denied it! B cannot be both the better and the worse parent.

This simple but clever experiment shows just how easily our intuitions can be biased by context. A, you will have noticed, is average on everything, while B has good points and weak points. It appears that when you are asked to award custody, you look for positive reasons to do so and these are to be found on B's list. You can point to the higher income and closer bond with the child. When asked to deny custody you look for negative reasons to do so, and these are to be found on B's list as well: B's social life and business commitments seem to take him/her away from home a lot, for example. So the framing of the questions sensitizes you to different aspects of the information available, resulting in a significant number of changes in which a different decision is made.

The child custody problem is a good example of how intuition and reflection can interact in decision making. People are using their reflective minds and would be quite capable of giving you reasoned arguments for their choices, whichever form of the problem they happen to be given. The problem is that the information, which appears to them to be relevant, has been predetermined by intuitive and unconscious processes. Because attention has been focussed (unconsciously) on positive attributes in one case and negative attributes in the other, the reasoning they apply is inevitably biased towards different decisions. The same applies to experts whose judgements are biased by their political beliefs or other prior interests. The cogent and detailed reasons they provide for their judgements can only be the product of reflective thinking and reasoning. But the process is biased nonetheless, because their beliefs affect both the selection and interpretation of the evidence on which these arguments are based. This is what I meant earlier when I said that just because the reflective mind is involved in a decision, it does not mean that it is in charge. It also shows that errors and biases of judgement are not just down to the failings of the intuitive mind. The reflective mind seems to have a fundamental bias towards trying to justify the action under consideration, rather than considering alternatives.[15]

Outcome bias

Now consider this problem.

> A surgeon is contemplating whether to operate on a 55-year-old man with a heart condition. His chest pain is preventing him from working and also from enjoying travel and recreation. Successful heart bypass surgery would relieve the pain and also increase his life expectancy from 65 to 70 years. However, 8% of patients have died from the surgery in similar operations in the past. The surgeon decides to go ahead with the operation and the patient survives. How good was the decision to operate?

In the relevant psychological experiments, one group receive the version above while another is given exactly the same scenario with one critical difference: the patient dies. The second group rate the surgeon's decision as somewhat less good than the first group, even though the only difference is the outcome, which follows the decision. If the general intelligence of the participants is measured, we find that the effect is reduced (but still present) for those of high intelligence.[16] This phenomenon is known as *outcome bias*. Unless the surgeon is a clairvoyant, she cannot know in advance whether the patient will live or die, but can only take into account this probability and weigh it against the benefits of a successful operation. The decision may be good or bad, but it depends only upon the information available at the time and cannot be affected by the actual outcome.

Research on outcome bias shows that as judges of the situation, with the outcome known, we cannot help but be influenced by it. Outcome bias is rampant in society, the press, and everyday life. In the precarious professional life of a football manager in the English leagues for example, a ball striking the goal posts and deflecting either into or out of the goal, might determine whether or not his team avoids relegation to a lower division, and with it whether he keeps his job for the following season. Public decision makers may be, and often are, pilloried for good decisions (based on the information available at the time), which turned out badly, or praised for lucky guesses that turned out well. Moreover, something akin to outcome bias is enshrined into the criminal justice system of many countries like the UK and United States.[17] Consider the case of a man who gets into a fight in a bar, and knocks another man down. If he is unlucky, he might get arrested and charged with assault and could spend a short time in prison. Suppose, however, that his victim hits his head on a hard object when falling and dies of a brain haemorrhage. Now he will certainly be charged with manslaughter, which carries much more severe penalties. The action and the intent are exactly the same, but the outcome determines how harshly it will be judged and what punishment will be handed down.

Hindsight bias

Closely related to outcome bias is 'hindsight bias'. I can illustrate this with UK media reporting of football games. In the 2007/8 season, Arsenal led the premiership league table for most of the season, but then slumped to third place following a series of poor results late in the season. The most obvious causal factor in this decline was injuries to three of their best attacking players who were all unavailable during the period of poor results. The same sporting press, who had predicted a poor season for Arsenal in the previous summer, now proceeded to castigate the team manager, Arsène Wenger, for not having bought new forwards in the January transfer window, which preceded the injuries and loss of form. Their rivals Manchester United, who also had bought no forwards at this time, but experienced no serious injuries to the ones they had, were the main beneficiaries. Their manager, Sir Alex Ferguson, of course, was heaped with praise. This kind of hindsight bias is a serious matter for the individual concerned. A manager less secure in his job than Wenger, for example, might well be sacked as a result.

It has been argued that hindsight bias is so prevalent in human thinking that it effectively prevents us from learning from history.[18] In prospect, life is full of uncertain events that we were unable to predict with any accuracy. This, of course, includes the results of sporting events, upon which a large gambling industry is based. This industry could not exist if the outcome of these games was determined and predictable in advance. In hindsight, it is easy for everyone from sports fans to professional historians to give seemingly inevitable causal accounts of why things had to happen the way they did. One manifestation of hindsight bias is that people assign much higher probabilities to outcomes of an uncertain process when they know (or are told that) these outcomes actually occurred, than when they are asked to predict them in advance. Another is that our memories for what we predicted in the past are biased. Experimental studies have shown that people consistently overestimate the confidence they had in answering a question or forecasting a future event when later questioned after the answer is known to be correct.[19]

Again, we can see that outcome and hindsight biases are not simply the result of intuitive thinking. The reflective mind is very much involved, even in the most prejudiced of soccer fans. In the case of outcome bias, two things are seen to co-vary, a decision (say to operate on the patients) and the outcome (say the patient dies). One is assumed to cause the other and the features of this particular case dominate our thinking, to the exclusion of the other possibilities and probabilities that needed to be considered at the time the decision was made. It is poor reasoning that leads us immediately to conclude that the surgeon got it wrong. But it is reasoning, nonetheless. The same applies to hindsight bias. Injuries to key players gave a plausible causal account of Arsenal's decline in form in 2008, but the inference that their manager should have anticipated this and bought extra players was highly questionable. Although injuries are to be expected, the scale of these can vary greatly from season to season. Also, the real problem for football managers happens when several players get injured from the same section of the team (defence, midfield, or attack) as happened in this particular case. To cope with this by purchasing a larger squad of players is quite unrealistic for most clubs, because you have to have several top (and highly paid) players for every position on the pitch. So again, people are engaging in reflective reasoning, but doing so rather poorly.

In another work,[20] I have described what I believe to be a fundamental bias in the reflective mind, namely, that we tend to focus on only on single possibilities and ignore alternatives. This applies in both thinking about the future and thinking about the past. If I am right, then the way in which our reflective minds work is far from the 'rational' ideal described in the theory of decision making. We rarely analyze all the alternative actions and deliberate between them, an observation that has been confirmed in studies of real world expert decision making. Instead, our intuitive minds focus attention on particular options or information, which our reflective minds then analyse, often to the exclusion of alternatives. Outcome and hindsight biases occur because we fix actual outcomes into our assessment of events and fail to consider alternative ways that things might have happened. Focusing on single scenarios can be effective, however, provided we have enough relevant expertise. The psychologist Gary Klein[21] has studied expert groups such as fire service commanders or nurses working in intensive care units who have to make rapid decisions where people's lives depend on the outcome. In most cases, these experts simply recognize a situation and retrieve the appropriate actions from memory. Reflective reasoning may contribute little more than minor accommodation of the recalled procedures to the details of the individual cases.

Disjunction effect

Just as we prefer to think about only one scenario when analysing the past, so we like to work with a single mental simulation of what may happen in future. A good illustration of this is the phenomenon known to psychologists as the 'disjunction effect'.[22] Suppose that a student is taking an important examination and has the chance to book a holiday in a tropical resort the following week. In a relevant experiment, people were asked if they would book the holiday if the exam was passed and most said yes. In another group, they were asked if they would book it if the exam were failed, and also said yes. However, a third group, who were told that the result of the exam was unknown, opted to pay a fee in order to defer a decision on the holiday until after the result was known. Why waste the money? If you prefer to take the holiday when you pass and when you fail, why do you need to know the result first? Why not just book it now?

The disjunction effect is often described as irrational or as an error of reasoning, but in a sense this a bit harsh. The problem is that the participants are tested in separate groups and only get one version of the task. The group who don't know the outcome of the test have no way to know how they would have responded in one of the other groups and hence to perceived the inconsistency. We feel good about the holiday when we imagine that we have passed the exam—celebrating and relaxing. When we imagine failing an exam, we also feel a holiday would be a good idea, perhaps to cheer ourselves up. For some reason, we cannot easily combine two such mental simulations and consider that we would want the holiday either way. As I mentioned earlier in the chapter, we find close decisions that would take our lives in very different directions quite stressful. Even when the event that divides our future is beyond our control, as in the result of an exam, we still find it difficult to imagine and compare how we would feel in alternative future worlds.

The (apparent) power of intuition

It is important to understand the limitations of the reflective mind and its role in the operation of cognitive biases. Dual-process theorists in psychology have tended traditionally to attribute biases to intuition and correct reasoning to reflection.[23] Some even go so far as to describe reflective cognition as the 'rational' system.[24] However, I think it is a major mistake to think that the reflective mind is either logical or 'rational' in the decision theory sense. For one thing, *what* we think about is typically directed by the intuitive mind. Reflective thinking is much constrained by the preconscious process involved in attention and the retrieval of relevant knowledge. We reason and reflect constantly, but not always to very good effect, and sometimes simply confabulate (that is, invent) an explanation for an intuitive decision (see Chapter 7). So might we do better if we don't reflect at all and rely solely on our intuitive minds? Some authors have come very close to recommending precisely that, and I consider their views in this section.

There is a long history in philosophy of equating logical reasoning and reflection with rationality and of disparaging decisions made on the basis of emotions. This has been reflected in educational practice, as well as the value that society places on individuals with high general intelligence or IQ, which essentially measures reasoning ability. As already mentioned, intuition has also been widely blamed for the presence of cognitive biases in judgement, even though, as I have shown, reflective thought is often involved. However, the intuitive mind has been getting a much better press lately, with a number of recent books appearing on the subject ranging from journalistic to heavyweight academic.[25] These authors claim, or come very close to claiming, that intuition is king and that we are better off not trying to second guess its powers with conscious reasoning. We might call this the 'no-mind' position, as these fashionable views are in strong conflict with the two minds hypothesis that I am advocating this book. Why on earth would humans have evolved their unique reflective minds if we were better off not using them? I will describe this 'no-mind'[26] hypothesis as clearly as I can and later explain what I think is wrong with it.

Malcolm Gladwell's popular book, *Blink: The Power of Thinking without Thinking,* published in 2005,[27] has been particularly successful and has made some impact on popular culture with its coverage in the media. Gladwell describes a number of cases where experts can make very quick but surprisingly accurate judgements, such as the case of an art expert noticing that a statue (which is eventually proved to be a fake) did not look right, or a psychologist who can predict with high accuracy the long-term success rate of a marriage on the basis of observing a 15 minute video of the couple interacting. Gladwell claims that less can be more, meaning that when people have a lot of information, or engage in a lot of reasoning they may end up with a worse decision.

Gladwell is a journalist, but his arguments have much in common with that of a leading decision researcher Gerd Gigerenzer, who has recently published an accessible book on the topic called *Gut Feelings.*[28] Gigerenzer argues against logic and complex reasoning and in favour of intuition and short-cut decision making. In fact, he claims that when intuition and logic conflict, it is usually a good idea to trust your intuition: 'Often what looks like a reasoning error from a purely logical perspective turns out to be a highly intelligent social judgement in the real world' (p. 103). His research programme, which has been very influential in academic psychology, is based on an evolutionary perspective, related to the modular mind hypothesis discussed in Chapter 2. Evolution, he says, has created an adaptive toolbox, which provides 'fast and frugal' solutions to complex problems. These come in the form of 'rules of thumb' technically known as *heuristics*. These heuristics provide us with reliable and adaptive intuitions for our decision making, which generally outperform attempts at reflective reasoning.

Like Gladwell, Gigerenzer wishes to persuade us that less can be more, at least within certain limits. Total ignorance is bad, but partial ignorance can apparently be good. As an example, Gigerenzer describes a study where German students rated the relative size of cities in Germany and in the United States. Despite the fact that the students were much more familiar with the German cities, they actually were more accurate in their judgements about the American ones. He argues that this is achieved by use of the 'recognition heuristic'. When judging under partial ignorance (American cities) participants simply judged the city that sounded more familiar to be larger and this recognition cue proves to be remarkably accurate. When judging the size of German cities, by contrast, they knew too much, thought too much, and came up with poorer answers. Gigerenzer even claims in the book that ordinary people can match the performance of professional investors in constructing portfolios of stocks and shares.

There is an important ambiguity in Gladwell's and Gigerenzer's approach as to exactly what is *less*, in these 'less is more cases'. Is it less time taken, less information used, or less conscious thinking applied? I will return to this problem in the next section, but first let me describe another line of work in the 'intuition is better than reasoning' movement. How should we make decisions when there are multiple pieces of information available that bear on their outcome? For example, a doctor trying to diagnose a patient's illness might have a host of information available: demographic information such as age, gender, and occupation; medical history, family history of related conditions, symptoms, results of diagnostic tests, and so on. To take another example, a personnel manager selecting recruits for her company may have information about their previous employment experience, education and qualifications, interview performance, results of psychometric tests, and so on.

The traditional decision theory approach to this kind of problem is to try to take account of *all relevant information*. Each problem has a number of different 'cues', which have different predictive values. The first stage is to assign them appropriate weighting. It may be, for example, that previous experience and qualifications are good predictors of job performance, psychometric tests reasonable predictors and interview performance rather poor. In that case, the actual value of a given applicant on each cue must be weighted accordingly: good interview performance, for example, should not be allowed to compensate for poor qualifications and experience. Actually, this is a case where intuition might seem to let us down: numerous studies show that the subjective weighting given to interviews is far higher than it ought to be. However, even if we assume the decision maker is unbiased, the task of combining multiple pieces of information with different weightings is obviously a complex one.

Again, we find that Gladwell and Gigerenzer have a common agenda. Gladwell discusses the problem of doctors in a busy emergency room trying to decide whether a patient with chest pain is having a heart attack. According to Chapter 4 of *Blink*, clinicians are overburdened by the amount of information they have and do a lot better following a simple algorithm, which responds to only a small subset of cues. This has apparently been demonstrated by an experimental change of procedures in a U.S. hospital. While this may be a case of 'less is more' it is an odd example, surely, in a book extolling the virtues of intuitive thinking? Following an algorithm is anything but intuitive! Similarly, Gigerenzer's solution to making judgements under multiple cues is the 'take the best' heuristic, in which people focus on just a *single* cue, ignoring other relevant information. Suppose you are a personnel manager reviewing selection decisions against successful performance of appointed candidates. Statistical analysis might show that the three most important factors, in order, were (a) work experience, (b) qualifications, and (c) interview performance. In selecting new candidates, however, Gigerenzer claims that you will do better to ignore (b) and (c) and rely entirely on (a), the single best predictor (see Chapter 8 of *Gut Feelings*). Well, this is certainly fast and frugal but I am not sure I would want my doctor to diagnose an illness on a single symptom.

The claim that we may make better decisions with multiple cues when we do not think too much is supported by some published psychological experiments. One approach, taken by Tim Wilson and colleagues, is to argue that when good intuitive judgements are available, allowing people to reflect on them may lead them to inferior choices. [29] This was supported by experiments showing that students who analysed preferences in choices ranging from strawberry jam to college courses, made judgements *less* in line with experts than those who just made immediate, intuitive inferences, a case for the Blink school of decision making. More dramatically, a psychologist called Dijksterhuis[30] has recently been claiming that people can make better decisions by *unconscious* deliberation than by conscious reasoning. This idea is also odds with the two minds hypothesis. The concept of an unconscious mind that can reason deliberatively is more consistent with the Freudian than the cognitive unconscious, and plays no part in the definition of the intuitive mind that I gave in Chapter 1.

What evidence is there for this extraordinary claim? Basically, the method involves presenting three groups of participants with the same decision problems under three different conditions:

Immediate judgment:	A decision has to be made immediately
Conscious deliberation:	Participants are required to think for a couple of minutes before deciding
Unconscious thought:	The decision is deferred by the same amount of time as for the conscious deliberation group, but with a distraction task to prevent conscious thinking about the problem, e.g. solving anagrams.

On the basis of experiments like this, Dijksterhuis[31] claimed that 'unconscious thought improved the quality of decisions' because the unconscious thought groups outperformed those instructed to engage in conscious deliberation. Not only are people happier with decisions when they are processed unconsciously, but these decisions are objectively superior when the requirements of the task are assessed. This is attributed to superior reasoning processes in the unconscious mind.

What is wrong with the above claims?

I have summarized above a number of arguments to the effect that we do better when we do not think, or think less or think unconsciously—the no-mind hypothesis. If we accept these arguments, then it seems that the reflective mind evolved for little purpose and we are better off not using it. We should just trust our feelings and try not to think too much at all. There must be something wrong here. There is.

First of all, a decision does not belong to the intuitive mind simply because it is *quick*. I agree strongly with the views recently expressed by Tilmann Betsch[32] that psychologists working in decision making have confused two quite different kinds of rapid decision making which he calls (a) intuitive judgement and (b) heuristic judgement. Intuitive judgements belong to the intuitive mind as I have defined it in this book. They occur when we have a 'feeling of rightness' about a choice or action, whose character is not consciously accessible. Gladwell's case of the art expert who felt that something was wrong with the statue, but could not explain why, is a good case in point. This judgement was indeed intuitive and turned out to be correct. But we cannot take such cases in isolation as evidence for the superiority of intuition. Other intuitive judgements can let us down badly, as shown by much of the research on cognitive biases I discussed earlier. For example, we feel that a decision is better when it turns out well, leading to outcome bias. So just because intuition works well in one situation, there is no guarantee that it will do so in another.

As Bestch also argues, in effect, heuristic judgements are quick (and dirty) acts of the *reflective* mind. So when Gladwell talks about doctors following a simple rule for treating patients with chest pains, this is clearly reflective and not intuitive cognition. Their decisions reflect not feelings, but an explicit rule. The 'less is more' jingle is misleading too when talking about these different kinds of fast decision making. True intuitive judgements take account of *more* information than reflective ones—derived from past learning—which is why they can sometimes be superior. On the other hand, because our reflective minds are slow and can only consider a limited amount of information, they can only make quick decisions by following simple rules. Although in general, the reflective mind is slower than the intuitive mind, it still can work quickly if minimal reasoning and information processing is required. While Gigerenzer's *Gut Feelings* is purportedly about intuition, the heuristics he discusses based on recognition and 'take the best' are actually quick and dirty methods of the reflective mind. What is less here is the information considered and hence the time that the reflective mind needs to reach a decision. If these rules are intuitive, it is in a different sense of the word, perhaps meaning naïve, that is, something which occurs to someone without special training.

Before Gigerenzer started his work, there was an established and highly influential programme, dating from the early 1970s, led by Danny Kahneman and Amos Tversky, which associated heuristics with *biases* in 'intuitive' judgement.[33] The difference in Gigerenzer's work is the emphasis on the idea that heuristics can lead to good judgements rather than bad. For example, Kahneman and Tversky proposed an 'availability' heuristic for judging frequency. Suppose that an experienced doctor is trying to diagnose a patient with an unusual set of symptoms. She might search her memory for similar cases. If most cases that come to mind turned out to have diagnosis A, then she will probably assume that is the case here. The availability and recognition heuristics are obviously closely connected, but the 'spin' that the authors put on them is different. Kahneman and Tversky chose to emphasize the circumstances where relying on availability could lead you to error: for example, some items may come to mind because they are easier to recall rather than because they were more often experienced.

In fact, the recognition heuristic can lead to biases too. For example, people who assume that the best choice is the one with the highest recognition value are an advertiser's dream. It is well known that most people will prefer to buy products with high name recognition than a supermarket's own brand, even though the latter may be both cheaper and of equal quality. The whole point about heuristics is that they are simple rules that do not guarantee success. So different researchers can make them look good or bad according to how they set up the experiments. Despite the strong and somewhat acrimonious debate between Gigerenzer's research on heuristics and that of Kahneman and Tversky, the two programmes share rather imprecise labelling of the judgements as 'intuitive'. It is fairly easy to show that such judgements may be *naïve* but far less clear that they simply result from operations of the intuitive mind that take place without reflection.

If the recognition heuristic, for example, were simply some hardwired evolutionary tool that is applied automatically and without thought, then it would be seriously misapplied in some circumstances. Gigerenzer tries to avoid the problem by saying that the choice of heuristic (from our plentiful adaptive toolbox) will depend on the context. It will only be applied in a situation where it is useful. (Somehow the toolbox knows which tool to select, but I let that pass.) Thus we will not use recognition as a basis for judging someone's height, for example, to which it is irrelevant. So let us consider a context in which he says it *is* useful: judging the size of foreign cities. Suppose (as a Brit) I am asked to judge the relative size of German cities. Doubtless, I will use the recognition heuristic for most of these, and judge more familiar sounding cities to be larger. Suppose, however, the experimenter mentions a small city, which has high recognition value for me: perhaps I visited it on a recent holiday. I won't say it is a large city (because I recognize it) but will rather use my actual knowledge that it is *small* to make the opposite judgement.[34] This shows that the recognition heuristic is under full control of the reflective mind and not being applied *mindlessly*.

So when the term 'intuitive' is just used to refer to everyday, untrained naïve judgements, we should not assume that it reflects simply the operation of the intuitive mind. Nor should we assume that quick judgements are necessarily intuitive in this sense if they require only minimal processing of information. The tendency to rely on simple heuristics when exercising the reflective mind could reflect its limited capacity and the high effort that complex reasoning requires. And yes, in some cases, these simple heuristics serve us well. But they are not applied blindly, without the possibility of reflection, as the German city examples show.

What of the studies of Wilson and Dijksterhuis? Recall that these authors have run experiments suggesting that people do better when they do not engage in conscious thinking and reasoning. They make better decisions when given no time to think, or when distracted by another task they need to perform at the same time. Note first that all these studies involve a particular kind of task: one in which multiple pieces of information are relevant to the decision. Such tasks are bound to be difficult to solve by conscious reflection, because of the amount of information involved. Hence, where people have relevant experience they may be able to take account of more information when they exercise intuitive judgement (in the true sense) than when they exercise conscious reasoning. As discussed in Chapter 3, there are both implicit and explicit forms of knowledge with different cognitive and neural mechanisms for acquiring them. Implicit learning is slow and gradual and requires a lot of experience, which is why I also call this experiential learning. But we can learn more complex rules in this way than we can consciously, so that our judgements eventually take account of more of the relevant information in the environment. This means that multiple cue judgment is an ideal case for the intuitive mind, with relevant experiential learning, to outperform the reflective mind. This is why, say, an experienced police detective could develop strong and accurate intuitions about whether or not a witness is telling the truth, without knowing how he is able to do so.

When people consciously try to combine a lot of information using their reflective minds then they can get confused and make errors, the same reason, in fact, why heuristic rules need to be very simple. But Dijksterhuis, remember, went further than saying that we do better if we rely on intuition in these situations. He claimed that people solve problems by *unconscious deliberation*. But the version of the two minds hypothesis discussed in this book restricts deliberation to the conscious, reflective mind. I have no time for the idea of an unconscious mind that can think and reason in parallel with the conscious one. And in fact, I can see no way in which Dijksterhuis's experiments support his extraordinary claim. In any case, the reliability of this research programme has been called into question by a major recent study, which fails to replicate the unconscious thinking effect.[35] In the recent study, people if anything did better when they deliberated *consciously*.

When intuition may let us down badly: the case of probability

There is a great deal of evidence that we have poor intuitive understanding of probability. The mathematical theory of probability was not developed until the 17th and 18th centuries and before that everyone relied on faulty intuitions, such as that in the absence of other knowledge, all outcomes are equally likely. On this basis, for example, you would reckon that totalling 7 with a roll of two dice would be as likely as totalling 12 whereas it is actually six times more likely. Equipped with a time machine, you could travel back to 1600 and make a lot of money! Alternatively, of course, you might be burnt as a witch.

A fundamental problem is that what feels random to us is not and vice versa. When we view a series of events that are generated both randomly and independently, like say, odd and even numbers on a roulette wheel, we expect the two outcomes to alternate to a greater extent than they actually do.[36] One of the most important consequences of this is known as the *gambler's fallacy*. If a roulette wheel comes up black five times in a row, people will start betting on red. They know that it is 50–50 (discounting the zero) and so they expect that over a period, there will be about as many red as black spins. But they are wrong when they imagine that the roulette wheel has any obligation to balance out earlier outcomes. The wheel has no memory at all, so it is 50–50 each time, no matter what has gone before. However, belief in the fallacious 'law of averages' is at the heart of most of the false theories that support gambling behaviour.[37] Casinos actually encourage gamblers to use such systems, say by publishing the run of numbers that a particular wheel has generated. Gamblers using such (useless) systems, play with more confidence, hence losing more quickly.

The gambler's fallacy seems to be a case of a heuristic rule that we formulate and apply with the reflective mind, but on the basis of what feels right. Its origin is still in the intuitive mind and our intuitive feelings about randomness. This must be the case because even when a person is trained in probability theory, they may still experience a strong intuition that the colour of the wheel must change. They may experience a conflict between what they feel (intuitive mind) and what they know (reflective mind) and there is no guarantee that the latter will win the argument. However, it is certainly the case that a person with formal training in probability and statistics will make better judgements about probability in the everyday world.[38]

Sometimes when we are observing a process that is random, we think that it is not, and make false attributions of causality. A good example is the 'hot hand effect' in which basketball fans believe that players have streaks of good form, enabling them to shoot many baskets in succession. Statistical analysis shows that such runs are purely random: the reason that good players have longer runs of successful hits is simply because they have a higher probability of success each time they take a shot. What is particularly interesting about this faulty intuition is that it seems to be shared by a number of academic authors who have tried (erroneously) to argue that the hot hand effect is real![39] What this means, in general, is that the idea of sporting *form*, such as that of the soccer player who 'can't stop scoring' goals, may be mostly illusory.

One of the most compelling intuitive errors yet discovered also involves probability and is known as the Monty Hall problem. This is named after the host of a 1970s U.S. game show called *Let's Make A Deal*. The scenario is the following. The contestant can see three doors: A, B, and C (see Figure 4.2).

Behind one is a valuable prize—a new car—and behind the other two is an undesirable prize: in each case, a goat. The contestant chooses one door at random, say B. Monty then opens one of other two doors, in this case A, to reveal a goat. The contestant is now offered the choice of sticking with B or switching to C. Should she stick or switch?

Most people presented with this problem stick with their original choice. If asked what the probability of finding the car is behind B or C they say 50:50. This intuition is compelling but wrong. You should switch because there is a 2/3 chance that the car is behind C. It can be difficult to convince people of the right answer, but I will have a go. The initial choice is random, so there is a 1/3 chance that the car is behind door B. This probability does not change. Once A has been revealed as a goat, the only other place the car can be is behind C. Since the chance of it being behind B remains at 1/3, the chance of finding it behind C has gone up to 2/3. But how could the probability change?

The important thing to understand about probability is that it is not a fixed objective property of events, but rather a belief held by an observer, which is relative to their state of knowledge. Traditionally, when a coin is flipped we assign .5 as the probability of a head. If someone tosses the coin but covers it with their hand, we still assign a probability of .5, even though the coin has actually landed heads or tails. Relative to our state of knowledge, it is still 50:50. If we are now told that it is a trick coin with tails on both sides, we change the probability to zero and so on. So probabilities are always relative to knowledge. In the Monty Hall problem, once gate A is open, we know something we did not before. But it is tricky nonetheless. Had A been open from the

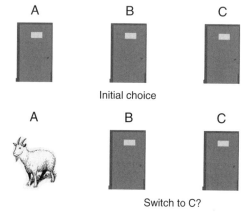

Fig. 4.2 The Monty Hall problem. The contestant chooses a door at random (B). Monty then opens door A to show a goat. Should the contestant now switch choice to C?

start, our choice between B and C would indeed have been 50:50 as people usually believe it to be. But when you choose between three possibilities your state of knowledge is different from that of choosing between two.

Here is a related problem. Assume that every human baby has a 50–50 chance of being a boy or a girl. A couple have two children. One is a boy. What is the chance that the other is a boy? Most people say 1/2 but the answer, surprisingly, is 1/3. With two children, there are four possibilities, all equally likely:

1. boy—boy
2. boy—girl
3. girl—boy
4. girl—girl

When I tell you that one child is a boy, this is new information, like Monty opening a door. It now eliminates possibility 4: they cannot have two girls. The other three possibilities are equally likely: they could have had a boy followed by a boy (1), a boy followed by a girl (2), or a girl followed by a boy (3). Only in case 1 is the *other* child a boy, so the probability is 1/3. Of course, if had told you that their *first* child was a boy, and asked what the probability was that the second was a boy also, then the answer would be 50%. That information would have eliminated case 3 as well as 4.

If you are still struggling with the Monty Hall problem, then you are in good company. When the switching response was first proposed by Marilyn vos Savant in the *New York Times* in 1990, it sparked a major debate. Most readers were unimpressed despite Savant's holding one of the highest known IQ's in the world. Many wrote in claiming that the answer was 50–50, including some with PhD's in mathematics. The argument raged in halls of the CIA and the mathematics department of the Massachusetts Institute of Technology and it took computer simulations to finally (almost) settle the argument. If you actually play the game repeatedly, the switching response will in fact win twice as often. When participants in a psychological experiment had this experience, they learnt to switch their choices but they did not change their belief that the probabilities were equal![40] The training modified their intuitive minds, while leaving their conscious opinions unchanged.

In the case of probability, then, everyday beliefs can be compelling but wrong. The gambler's fallacy, in which people deliberately bet on outcomes that have not appeared recently, seems to be an example of a heuristic rule. People may apply it deliberately, but because it is a bad rule, they lose money. Of course, it is possible to master an understanding of probability with our reflective minds, as many professional gamblers do. Card counters, for example, know how the odds have changed on successive deals, and when they are in their favour for a bet. Skilled poker players have remarkable knowledge of the probability of different hands, recalculating these as some cards are exposed. However, 'gut feelings' in Gigerenzer's sense are very unreliable indeed as applied to probabilities. As an example, the gambler's fallacy is a fast and frugal heuristic that makes us dumb rather than smart.

Conclusions

Both intuition and reflection play an important role in our decision making. We can make decisions on the basis of what feels right, and often do so. We can also try to make decisions, with our reflective minds, by simulating different actions and trying to calculate their outcomes. However, there is not too much evidence that we make decisions 'rationally' according to formal decision theory. We tend to explore particular scenarios that interest us rather than to give a full and equal consideration to all the options available. While we need to use our reflective mind to calculate consequences of decisions, this mind is sharply limited in the amount of information it can cope with. So we tend to focus on one option at a time. The intuitive mind will also have a strong influence on what we think about.

There is a view in the psychological literature that we need conscious reflection for good decision making and that reliance on intuition will lead us into errors and cognitive biases. There is a contrasting view (the 'no-mind' hypothesis) that we will do better by trusting our intuitive feelings and not trying to reason about our decisions at all. As one might expect, the truth lies in between. Relying on intuition sometimes leads to good decisions. This is true of much expert decision making, or that of an ordinary person who has a lot of relevant experience. Experience can lead us to have implicit knowledge of complex relationships where multiple pieces of information are relevant to the decision. Where we lack such experience we will need to apply reflective thinking and reasoning, often applying simple heuristics. Such heuristics may be well founded and lead to successful decisions. However, they may also originate from faulty intuitions and let us down badly. In general, we need some formal study and learning to acquire good explicit rules. A notable case involves probability. Without training, people develop and apply unreliable rules based on popular culture or intuitive feelings, such as the 'law of averages'.

Those who would persuade us that 'less is more' in decision making seem to confuse two very different things. Implicit knowledge is slow to acquire but quick to apply. So fast decision making, on the basis of intuition, may be superior to reflective reasoning, but only if we have had a lot of relevant experience. We may also make fast judgements with our reflective minds, but only by using heuristics—simple rules. There are situations where such heuristics can be very effective but others in which they can result in cognitive biases.

Some decisions can only be made well by slow and careful study of the evidence with the reflective mind. An example would be a judgement made by a high court judge, which may take weeks to prepare, after a long and complex case lasting many months. Another would be an assessment of the scientific evidence, very extensive and very complex, for the likely development of global warming in the atmosphere. I, for one, would not want such decisions to be made on the basis of gut feelings.

Notes and references

1 While we normally use the term 'feeling' to refer to emotions, psychologists also describe *cognitive* feelings, which involve intuition. For example, researchers studying human memory have examined the 'feeling of knowing' that people experience in recollection and recognition. The reasoning researcher Valerie Thompson recently coined the term 'feeling of rightness' to describe the subjective confidence that accompanies intuitive judgements (Thompson, 2009).

2 See Schwartz (2004).

3 For a discussion of what went wrong, see Howcroft (2001).

4 See Harford (2006).

5 Stanovich (2009a).

6 See n2.

7 See Edwards (1954, 1961); von Neumann and Morgenstern (1944).

8 Real (1991).

9 That is not to say that all insurance is a good deal for the consumer. Expensive warranties sold with now highly reliable electric goods, like television sets, are a case in point.

10 Samuelson (1963).

11 The text assumes the original structuring of the game where contestants winning £32,000 were guaranteed to keep that amount. Under recent rule revisions this holding point has been increased to £50,000. This makes no essential difference to the argument given. Contestants using the EV rule would still be obliged to guess the £1,000,000 question under the conditions stated.

12 Kahneman and Tversky (1979).

13 See n8.

14 Shafir (1993).

15 I discuss many examples of this in my recent book, *Hypothetical Thinking* (Evans, 2007a).

16 Stanovich and West (2008b).

17 It is not technically a bias if the legal system follows its own rules. However, the fact that we design laws to punish people variably according to the outcomes of identical actions, may be indicative of general outcomes bias in our evaluation of decisions.

18 Fischhoff (1982).

19 For a review of both forms of hindsight bias, see Roese (2004).

20 Evans (2007).

21 Klein (1999).

22 See Tversky and Shafir (1992).

23 This includes my own earlier writing on cognitive biases (Evans, 1989) as well as influential work by Keith Stanovich (Stanovich, 1999; Stanovich and West, 2000).

24 Epstein (1994).

25 The list includes Myers (2002), Gladwell (2005), Gigerenzer (2007), and Plesner, Betsch, and Betsch (2008).

26 My thanks to Shira Elqayam for suggesting this label.

27 Gladwell (2005).

28 Gigerenzer (2007).

29 Wilson and Schooler (1991).

30 For examples of his work, see Dijksterhuis (2004), Dijksterhuis, Bos, Nordgren, and von Baaren (2006).

31 See Dijksterhuis (2004, p. 596).

32 Betsch (2008).

33 For an early collection of papers from this programme see Kahneman, Slovic, and Tversky (1982) and for a more recent collection, see Gilovich, Griffin, and Kahneman (2002).

34 See Oppenheimer (2003).

35 Newell et al. (2008); see also Lassiter et al. (2009)

36 For a more detailed discussion of the psychological evidence, see Evans (2007).

37 See Wagenaar (1988), discussed further in Chapter 8.

38 See Fong, Krantz, and Nisbett (1986).

39 For the original demonstration of the hot hand effect see Gilovich, Vallone, and Tversky (1985) and for a discussion of the controversy it engendered, see Alter and Oppenheimer (2006).

40 Franco-Watkins, Derks, and Dougherty (2003).

Chapter 5

Reasoning and imagination

As I shall use the term here, 'reasoning' refers to making a conscious effort to draw conclusions from some given information. By definition, the reflective mind is involved and indeed many authors think that reasoning is one of its most important functions. As we saw with decision making in the previous chapter, however, involved does not necessarily mean 'in charge'. The intuitive mind always has an influence on our reasoning processes and sometimes hijacks the process altogether, substituting a conclusion of its own!

Reasoning is hard work, and we may sometimes be tempted to let our intuitions take over and make an easy choice. For example, a chess player thinking over a complex position might despair of calculating the consequences of an attacking move and just play it because it feels right. If his time is short, then he may have no choice but to play this way. Some players excel at speed chess, in which, say, they have a total of five or ten minutes to play all the moves of the game. In such games, very little time is allowed for the slow process of reflective reasoning and calculation. But even when time is available, intuition still plays a strong role in a chess game, as mentioned in Chapter 3. So even if the reflective mind is engaged to calculate the consequences of a move, the intuitive mind has already played a crucial role.

Good reasoning draws the correct conclusions from assumptions. Whether the conclusions are actually *true* depends on the accuracy of what is assumed. For example, in theoretical physics, the assumptions of the theory are laid out as a set of explicit postulates and the consequences of these are then inferred by mathematics. Mathematics is a form of logic, so if correctly applied, the predictions and theorems derived by the theorists will hold for sure, given these assumptions. Of course, there is no guarantee that these conclusions are *true*, because they depend on the initial postulates. The difference between Newton's mechanics and Einstein's theory of relativity, for example, depended upon changing fundamental assumptions, in particular that the measurement of time was relative and not absolute. Einstein's reasoning (that is, his mathematical proofs) was no better than Newton's. But this change of assumption allowed him to explain and predict things that the earlier theory could not cope with. Einstein's genius lay in his *imagination* of alternative possibilities. The mathematics (hard though it may have been) was just a matter of technique.

Logicians distinguish between deductive and inductive reasoning, where the former is logically valid and the latter is not. What 'valid' means is that if the premises are true, the conclusion is sure to be true as well. Inductive reasoning is invalid, because it does not carry this guarantee. A classic example is that deduction allows us to go from the general to the particular, but the reverse requires induction. For example, the universal gas laws allow us to state that a gas will increase in temperature if it is compressed. We can apply this to any particular gas, compressed by any method. This is deduction. However, observing the temperature of any number of gases under compression, in any large number of experiments, will not allow us to infer that all gases heat up when compressed. This is the so-called 'problem of induction' that has plagued philosophers of science for centuries. If you think that science should consist of universal laws, then no amount of evidence will allow us to infer these laws by a deductive process. But should science be built on illogical reasoning?[1]

In reality, the distinction between deduction and induction is fuzzy, because uncertainty enters into assumptions, if not the process of reasoning itself. As an example, consider some reasoning by the world's most famous fictional detective, Sherlock Holmes. In the extract from *The Sign of Four* shown in Box 5.1, Holmes amazes Watson by 'deducing' that he has been to Wigmore post office to dispatch a telegram. Let us consider his two conclusions separately, starting with his inference that Watson has been to this particular post office. What he observed was some reddish mould on Watson's shoe. He combines this with three other premises based on his knowledge that (a) such red clay is outside the post office, (b) that it is hard to avoid stepping in it, and (c) that there is no other earth with this particular tint in the district. Is this an induction or a deduction? If Holmes is right in his belief that this is the only way in which Watson could have acquired the red earth, then his conclusion is indeed a deduction. But it is still an uncertain conclusion, because he cannot be absolutely sure (for example) that there is nowhere else where Watson could have stepped in the earth.

Now consider the second conclusion: that Watson sent a telegram. This involves more speculation than the first. He had not seen Watson write a letter, knew that he already had stamps and postcards, and therefore assumed that he must have gone to the post office to send a telegram. This inference strikes me as quite insecure. Perhaps Watson went for a walk for another purpose, which

Box 5.1 Extract from Conan-Doyle's, *The Sign of Four* (1890)

(HOLMES TO WATSON) "Observation shows me that you have been to the Wigmore Street Post-Office this morning, but deduction lets me know that when there you dispatched a telegram."

"Right!" said I. "Right on both points! But I confess that I don't see how you arrived at it. It was a sudden impulse upon my part, and I have mentioned it to no one."

"It is simplicity itself," he remarked, chuckling at my surprise,— "so absurdly simple that an explanation is superfluous; and yet it may serve to define the limits of observation and of deduction. Observation tells me that you have a little reddish mould adhering to your instep. Just opposite the Wigmore Street Office they have taken up the pavement and thrown up some earth which lies in such a way that it is difficult to avoid treading in it in entering. The earth is of this peculiar reddish tint which is found, as far as I know, nowhere else in the neighborhood. So much is observation. The rest is deduction."

"How, then, did you deduce the telegram?"

"Why, of course I knew that you had not written a letter, since I sat opposite to you all morning. I see also in your open desk there that you have a sheet of stamps and a thick bundle of post-cards. What could you go into the post-office for, then, but to send a wire? Eliminate all other factors, and the one which remains must be the truth."

took him past the post office where he acquired the mud. Or perhaps he did visit the post office, but for another reason that Holmes has not thought of. Perhaps he was a friend of the postmaster and so on. Despite Arthur Conan Doyle's seductive story of observation and deduction, the truth is that all of Holmes's inferences (in all of the books) had varying degrees of uncertainty. The most remarkable thing about them was that his conclusions were never wrong!

Strict deductive reasoning does occur in the real world sometimes when arbitrary rules and regulations are involved. For example, most countries have a rather complex set of tax laws. From these laws and knowledge of your own circumstances, you may be able to deduce (literally) your liability to tax, and your entitlement to certain tax breaks. The premises here are certain because they are made-up and not natural laws. So with logical reasoning, the conclusions should be certain as well. In spite of this many of us are not confident to do the reasoning ourselves, preferring to leave it to accountants or professional tax advisers. We employ such professionals because they are experts, not so much in reasoning but in their detailed knowledge of the tax laws. But there must be something else going on here beyond knowledge and deduction. If they just reasoned from premises to conclusions, how would they know which of the many tax laws to apply to your particular circumstances? When they examine your details, ideas will occur to them as to how you might best organize your financial affairs to minimize your tax payments. So their initial reasoning is not deductive: it goes from the particular to the general and the intuitive mind almost certainly plays a role here. The tax adviser has learnt *from experience* that certain kinds of clients will benefit from certain kinds of arrangements. We pay them particularly for this kind of expertise.

Can ordinary people, untrained in logic, engage in deductive reasoning? The answer to this is yes, although as we shall see later, they may make many logical errors. However, at least some people *enjoy* reasoning as evidenced by the popularity of games and puzzles requiring logic. A good example is the now highly popular Sudoku game, which has a purely deductive nature. That is, Sudoku puzzles have a unique solution that can be found without any knowledge other than the rules of the game. An example of an easy puzzle is shown in Figure 5.1. The rule is:

> Every row, column and box of nine squares must contain exactly one of the digits 1–9.

Consider the square on the bottom left corner of the figure shown in Figure 5.1. It cannot be 4, 6, 7, or 5 because the bottom row already has those. It also cannot be 1,2, or 3 because the left hand column has those. So it must be 8 or 9. Now suppose that it is 8. We must then be able to place a 9 in the 3×3 square at the bottom left. But we can't place it in the middle row because there is a 9 further to the right. And we can't place it in the top row either, for the same reason. So a 9 can't fit at all! Hence, our supposition that the bottom left hand square had an 8 was wrong. That must be a 9. In this case, Sherlock Holmes's wisdom applies: when you have eliminated the impossible whatever remains must be the truth. And the inference that the square has a 9 is a true deduction, achieved by logical reasoning.

Obviously, people can solve Sudoku puzzles or they would not be endlessly published in newspapers and books. Recent research shows that people untrained in logic can solve hard Sudoku puzzles, developing some very sophisticated strategies in the process, which the authors claim to go beyond the ability of current theories of human reasoning to explain.[2]

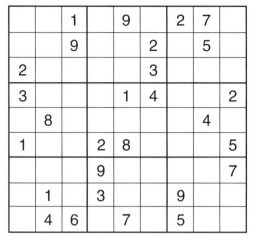

Fig. 5.1 Example of an (easy) Sudoku puzzle.

Logic, mental logic, and mental models

Consider the following argument:

> Paul is taller than John. 5.1
> George is shorter than John.
> Therefore, Paul is taller than George.

This is an argument that most university students[3] can see is valid, even when they have had no training in logic. Here is one that most people can see is invalid.

> Paul is taller than John. 5.2
> George is taller than John.
> Therefore, Paul is taller than George.

Height is a relationship that is *transitive*, that is, putting objects in sequence. 5.1 is a valid argument because, given the truth of the premises, the conclusion must follow. In 5.2, however, the conclusion is consistent with the premises but might be false. On the information given, Paul may or may not be taller than George: we simply cannot tell.

How can we describe the logic of transitivity? One was is to define rules. Let us say, that for a transitive relation, the sign '>' means higher on the dimension and the sign '<' lower. So for any set of objects A, B, C ... we can define rules like the following:

1. If A > B and B > C, then A > C.
2. If A < B, then B > A.

We cannot apply rule 1 to argument 5.1 as is stands but we can apply rule 2 to the second premise, transforming it to

Paul is taller than John.   5.3
John is taller than George.
Therefore, Paul is taller than George.

Now the argument fits rule 1, so it is valid. Assuming these are the only rules allowed, we cannot declare that 5.2 is valid, because it cannot be made to fit to rule 1. Some psychologists think that we reason by using built-in rules of logic, like these.[4] However, there is a lot of evidence to support an alternative view, called mental model theory. This theory draws an explicit link between reasoning and imagination. On this theory, the way we reason is by imagining 'mental models', which are states of affairs compatible with the premises. Given the premises of 5.1, for example, we order the boys (from tallest to shortest) as

Paul
John
George

In fact, this is the only mental model we can build. The conclusion we are offered—Paul is taller than George—is true in this model. Since it is the only model, it must be true if the premises are true, so it is valid.

Now consider 5.2. There are actually two mental models we can build of this one:

Paul   George
George   Paul
John   John

The conclusion 'Paul is taller than George' is true for one model, but not for the other. Hence, it cannot be a valid conclusion. On this theory of reasoning we don't need lots of rules to cover different situations, but just one general principle: *an argument is valid if there are no counterexamples to it.* Now consider this problem:

Paul is taller than John.   5.4
George is taller than John.
Therefore, John is the shortest.

This argument is valid, although it would need an extra rule to prove it so in the rule approach. For mental model theory, however, it is straightforward. 5.4 has the same two models as 5.2, shown above. But the conclusion is true in *both* models, so there is no counterexample to it. However, the author of the theory, Phil Johnson-Laird, argues that people will find problems like 5.4 harder than ones like 5.1. That is, the more mental models we need to consider to draw an inference, the more likely we are to make a mistake.[5]

Although this kind of reasoning might seem to be exclusive to the reflective mind, the intuitive mind is always present and likely to contribute ideas. Unfortunately, when strict logical reasoning is required, these tend to be unhelpful! For example, my choice of names in this example may have brought to mind images of the young men who played with the Beatles, with an impulse to compare the heights of the three I named. Surely, John (Lennon) was the tallest? No sooner than this thought comes, one realizes its irrelevance and tries to disregard the image. But one cannot prevent such associated knowledge form coming to mind the first place, and it does often influence the reasoning that people do, as I shall show below.

Let us revisit the reasoning of Sherlock Homes in the extract from *The Sign of Four* (Box 5.1). It is fairly easy to relate this to mental model theory. Model theory concerns reasoning about possibilities, which is exactly what Holmes does. In fact, his final comment 'Eliminate all other factors, and the one which remains must be the truth' expresses this quite directly. In deducing that Watson went to Wigmore Street post office Holmes reasons that (a) he could easily have picked up the red mud entering the post office and (b) it is most unlikely that he could have acquired it elsewhere, mentioning the distinctive colour and the absence of anything similar in the area. (a) states a provisional inference and (b) the elimination of counterexamples to it. The second inference involves a similar thought process. Holmes considers a number of possible reasons for Watson to visit the post office and then eliminates alternatives to sending a telegram—he had not written a letter to post, did not need to buy stamps etc.

Mental model theory provides a plausible story for how ordinary people can do logical reasoning. As mentioned above, the main alternative to it is that people have logical rules built in to their minds, hence the term 'mental logic'. A number of philosophers and psychologists have argued that logic is fundamental to rational thought and that there must be some kind of logic innately programmed into the human mind. One way this could happen is through language, in which words serve as logical devices. Consider, the words *not*, *and*, and *or*:

Not p—is true whenever some proposition p is false. For example, 'Al Gore is not President of the USA' is true.

p and q—is true, when both propositions p and q are individually true.

p or q—is true, when either proposition is true.

The ordinary meaning of these words in everyday language seems to capture basic logical relations and may support some simple deductive reasoning. For example, if I say that all the lecturers in my department are either men or under 40 years of age, and then I tell you that my new colleague is a woman, you will infer pretty easily that she is under 40. The logical relations involved are given by the meanings of 'or' and 'not', provided that you can interpret 'woman' to mean 'not man'. Of course, we can also tell a story here in terms of mental models rather than rules, if we assume that we reason by imagining and eliminating possibilities. For example, my first statement suggests that we may have men of all ages in the department but women only under 40. Once, the possibilities involving men are eliminated, the conclusion readily follows.

What happens when logic and language diverge? A serious case of this occurs when we use conditional statements, involving *if*. I will return to this later in the chapter.

Belief bias in reasoning

The reflective and intuitive minds can clash head-on if we ask people to reason about problems involving real-world beliefs. Consider this argument:

> No addictive things are inexpensive.
> Some cigarettes are inexpensive.
> Therefore, some addictive things are not cigarettes.   5.5

Do you think this argument is logically valid? Does the conclusion necessarily follow from the premises? Most university students think so—71% in one major study.[6] Now consider this argument:

> No millionaires are hard workers.
> Some rich people are hard workers.
> Therefore, some millionaires are not rich people.   5.6

Is this one valid? Most university students think not. Only 10% thought this conclusion to follow in the same study. Let us look a bit more closely at these. In the first argument, substitute A for addictive things, B for inexpensive, and C for cigarettes. Now we see that the logical form of the argument is

> No A are B.
> Some C are B.
> Therefore, some A are not C.

For the second argument, substitute A for millionaires, B for hard workers, and C for rich people. Now we see that the form of this argument is … exactly the same! To be valid, you can *never* have a situation where the premises are true and the conclusion false, no matter what you substitute for A, B, and C. In this case, the syllogism can have true premises and a false conclusion, as in

> No Democrats are Republicans.
> Some people are Republicans.
> Therefore, some Democrats are not people.

So, in fact, neither 5.5 nor 5.6 is a valid logical argument. So how come 71% of students think that one version is valid and only 10% the other, when logically they are exactly the same? What is going on here? The critical difference, as much research has confirmed, is that the conclusion of argument 1 is *believable* and that of argument 2 is not. Could the participants in this task somehow have confused what they were supposed to do? They were told that they would be asked if the conclusion followed and instructed, 'You should answer this question on the assumption that all the information given … is true. If you judge that the conclusion necessarily follows from the statements … you should answer "yes", otherwise "no"'.[7] Not much ambiguity there. So why can't university students (or most of them) follow these instructions?

Belief bias is a critical case for the two minds hypothesis. If we compare the valid and invalid problems (ignoring believability) we find that people accept many more of the former than the latter. So apparently, they are using their reflective minds to reason about the logic of the problems as instructed. But if we compare believable with unbelievable conclusions (ignoring validity), we find they accept many more believable ones, apparently ignoring the instructions! Particularly interesting are problems where belief and logic give different answers. This happens when the argument is valid, but the conclusion unbelievable or the argument is invalid but the conclusion is believable. On such problems, it seems that the intuitive and reflective minds go to war. Sometimes people go with belief and sometimes with logic. The same person may go with an intuitive mind on one problem and with reflective mind on the other.[8] The balance of power, however, varies across individuals. For example, those with higher general intelligence, and hence larger working memory capacity, are more likely to give the logical answer. Aging adults, in whom working memory is declining, are more likely to go with their beliefs.[9]

So what seems to happen here is as follows. Using their reflective minds people read the instructions and understand that they are required to reason logically from premises to conclusion. However, when they look at the conclusion, their intuitive minds deliver a strong tendency to say yes or no depending on whether it is believable.[10] This intuition clearly *competes* with any reasoning that is going on in the reflective mind. This competition in turn is affected by the ability of the individual as mentioned above. However, there are other means of shifting the balance of power that have emerged in recent research on this topic. For example, if people are required to respond very quickly or while carrying out a second mental task in competition with the reasoning, the intuitive, belief-based response is more likely to dominate.[11] What this shows is that our conscious attention and effort must be applied to the problem if we are to reason logically. But even under the most favourable conditions, and with the strongest instructions for logical reasoning, belief bias persists.

What should we make of findings like these? Does it mean that the intuitive mind is a source of irrational biases and prejudice? Consider the case of how we evaluate evidence from research studies. Research findings may accord or conflict with our existing beliefs. If these beliefs are strongly held, will we be objective and even-handed in assessing the methods of the study? The evidence suggests not. In one famous study,[12] students were asked to comment on the research methods of studies claiming to show that capital punishment either was or was not an effective deterrent to murder. Cleverly, the researchers presented several different versions to different participants. Some used method A and some B. Each method was equally often linked with an outcome that the participant agreed or disagreed with. Nevertheless, participants were much more critical of studies whose results opposed their own personal belief, whether this was for or against capital punishment.

Before we dismiss this sort of behaviour as irrational, consider that we all live our lives within belief systems. For example, I don't believe in the paranormal and supernatural and this disbelief is central to my identity as a scientist and an individual. So if I hear a report of a dramatic demonstration of telepathic communication, I will be strongly inclined to think that the methodology was suspect or the result a statistical fluke. And if Jehovah's Witnesses or other proselytizing Christians come to my door, I will not waste time listening to their arguments. Is this irrational? I have spent a lifetime building a belief system based on what I feel is good evidence and reasoning. Why should I not be sceptical and dismissive of arguments against these beliefs? Life is too short for us to be open to all arguments on all topics.

If you are less than convinced by the above paragraph, then consider what real scientists do when their *own* experiments come out against their theoretical predictions. A recent research study examined the behaviour of a number of research groups in molecular biology.[13] Of 417 original experiments, more than half (223) failed to conform with the predictions of the researchers, an amazing finding in itself. Did the scientists therefore conclude that their theory was wrong? No! In most cases (69%) they doubted the experiment itself, and repeated it with improved methodology. The majority of these repeat experiments confirmed the original finding, but even then the scientists revised their theories in only 58% of the cases studied. To a nonscientist, this may seem very surprising. But scientific theories, like personal life beliefs, take a lot of time, effort, and evidence to develop. When contrary evidence is found, it *is* rational to make very sure that this evidence is right before abandoning the theories.

What is most interesting about belief bias experiments is that they show the limited control that we, conscious persons, have over our own thinking and reasoning. 'We' really reside in our reflective minds and enjoy an illusion of being control of our behaviour. The beliefs involved in these experiments are not usually what social psychologists call 'core' beliefs, central to our identity. Moreover, we may be very motivated to reason logically, both to comply with the instructions given and to feel good about how smart we are. In spite of all this, our intuitive minds often exert control and hijack our reasoning. And surely we cannot be aware that this is happening. Certainly, no participant in a reasoning experiment reports that belief bias is the basis for their answer!

Support from neuroscience studies

Recent studies of belief bias using neural-imaging have provided strong support for the account of belief bias given here. The neuroscience of reasoning is a relatively neglected topic, with few brain imaging studies compared with those run on perception, memory, and executive functioning. There are by now, however, enough studies using deductive reasoning tasks to yield some insights. One early conclusion is that there is no singular system for reasoning in the human brain. This follows from surveys of relevant studies by one of the pioneers in this field, Vinod Goel.[14] First, there is considerable inconsistency in the brain areas, which 'light up' when people engage in reasoning tasks. No two studies show exactly the same pattern of activation, and no single brain area appears in every study. Some of these differences, however, can be traced to specific features of the tasks used. For example, there are consistent differences between reasoning with abstract statements, such as 'All X are Y', and realistic ones, such as 'All dogs are animals'.

Several studies have focussed on belief bias and on related problems where an intuitive and reflective response may come into conflict. Two brain areas have been of particular interest. One is the anterior cingulate cortex, or ACC for short, which is known to monitor conflict and hazardous situations. For example, in higher animals, the ACC will light up when habitual responding is failing to deal with a situation. When this happens, the ACC will in turn activate what is known as *controlled attention* to the problem, in animals and people, engaging resources in the prefrontal cortex. Essentially, the problem that was previously being monitored unconsciously becomes the focus of working memory. In other words, control is passed from the intuitive mind to the reflective mind. The other brain area, about which also quite a lot is known, is the right inferior frontal cortex (IFC), a region which becomes active when a habitual response is, in fact, inhibited. There are now several studies that show that these two brain areas deal with conflict in belief bias problems exactly as one might expect: the ACC becomes active when conflict is present (e.g. belief and logic lead to different answers), but the right IFC is activated *only* when the decision made is to override the belief bias.[15]

These studies provide important confirmation that the brain is indeed processing a conflict between logic and belief, just as was proposed on purely psychological grounds many years ago.[16] In order for intuition and reflection to battle for control as outlined earlier, it must first be necessary for conflict to be detected. What is fascinating in the findings of these recent neuroscience studies is that there are many occasions upon which conflict is indeed detected (activating the ACC) giving notice to the reflective mind that it has competition to deal with from the intuitive mind. But only on *some* of these occasions does the reflective mind in fact assert itself, overriding the belief based choice. This is signalled both by the choice itself (to go with logic) and the very highly correlated activation of the right IFC. The two minds do indeed battle over such problems, and the outcome is not determined: even when the reflective mind is engaged, the intuitive mind may still win the day.

If and the imagination

The word 'if' has fascinated me throughout my entire career. I first studied 'if' in my PhD work and since then have run dozens of experiments trying to understand how people understand and reason with this little word. Such is my obsession that I recently wrote a whole book about 'if', together with the philosopher David Over.[17] So what is the big deal?

A critical contention of the two minds hypothesis is that we human beings have one form of intelligence that is similar to that of other animals, but another form that is distinctively human. For example, I showed in Chapter 4 that we can make decisions intuitively, relying on our past learning and experience of what has worked previously in our lives. This is the way our old, intuitive, animal-like mind works. But we can also make decisions in a quite different way: by imagining the consequences of our actions. To do this, we have to run mental simulations. Just as scientists use computer simulations to try to forecast the future (how the economy will behave in the next 12 months, what the climate will be like in 2050) so ordinary people also simulate the future in their imagination. One reason we do this is to try to make the best decision by anticipating its consequences. However, we use our imagination of possibilities for a number of other reasons as well. And this distinctively human mental activity—which I call *hypothetical thinking*[18]—is often triggered by the word 'if'.

There are lots of uses of 'if' in ordinary language. One is to make predictions. For example:

5.7 If the President is a Democrat, then taxes will be high.

5.8 If interest rates are held low then the economy will recover.

5.9 If the use of private motor cars is not controlled, then global warming will accelerate.

5.10 If a plant is well watered, then it will thrive.

How can we decide whether to believe such statements? There are several possibilities. One is to trust the authority of the speaker. For example, on hearing or reading 5.8, we may not feel well enough versed in economic theory to make a judgement. But if we find the statement in a reputable source, like the *Financial Times*, we may be inclined to believe it is true. People are in fact influenced by the credibility of the source when they make inferences about conditional statements.[19] Another way might be to retrieve beliefs directly from memory. For example, a lifelong Republican may have a strongly held belief that Democrats always raise taxes, and hence agree with 5.7 without very much reflection at all. Another method, related to mental model theory, is to judge the statement true if you *cannot* retrieve counterexamples to it. Consider 5.10. Most plants thrive on watering but there are exceptions that may come to mind, like cacti and other desert plants. Or we may think that there are other reasons why a plant will fail to thrive, such as disease, which would not be prevented by watering.

With more novel statements, we may need to run mental simulations to decide whether we can trust them. Take 5.9. We may have an established belief that private motor cars contribute to global warming, by emitting greenhouse gases, and hence agree with 5.9 without much thought. Or we may study the question a bit more carefully. The speaker suggests that if the use of private cars is not controlled—presumably by legislation—then global warming will accelerate. But this supposes that without such controls, individuals will go on and on burning more fuel in their cars. On reflection, other factors may mitigate this, one of which is education about the risks of global warming and the exercise of restraint. Another, which may be more influential, is the reduced supply and increasing cost of oil and all its products such as petrol. In the summer of 2008, for example, following a period of sustained increase in world oil prices, U.S. motor manufacturers reported large reductions in sales of new vehicles, especially those consuming gasoline at the highest rates, such as four-wheel drive sports utility vehicles and pick-up trucks. In fact, sales of Ford SUVs in the United States were down more than 50%. On this basis, we might infer that the contribution of private motor cars to global warming is set to decrease, in the absence of any legislative controls. A person without this actual knowledge of the car market could still come to doubt the truth of 5.9 by hypothetical thinking and reasoning. This requires them to imagine factors other than legislative control that might curb private motoring. Such reasoning requires understanding of causal relationships, such as the way in which economic costs influence human behaviour.[20]

The meaning of conditionals

A slightly different question is what does it *mean* to believe a conditional statement? To clarify, take the case of a conditional bet. Suppose on visiting a taverna in Crete, you are unlucky enough to encounter a Greek philosopher who offers you the following wager at even money. He proposes to draw a card at random from a pack of normal playing cards and bets you that:

'If the card drawn is a King then it will be a spade'.

It seems evident that the bet is 3:1 in your favour as only one King in four will belong to the spade suit so you take the bet. The philosopher then draws a card, which turns out to be the seven of hearts. Much to your dismay, he then demands that you pay up. From his perspective the wager was 49:3 in his favour. What is going on?

Logic textbooks have long promoted the idea that a sentence of the form 'if p then q' means the same as 'not-p or q', an interpretation known technically as *the material conditional*. It is false when you have p and not-q but otherwise true. Understood this way, you undertook to pay the philosophers when the following statement was true:

'Either the card is not a King, or it is a spade'.

This second statement is clearly true for all cards in the pack except the kings of clubs, hearts, and diamonds. But would anyone other than a logician think that this was what was meant by the original conditional bet? The key issue is whether you think that the statement is true when a card that is not a King is drawn from the pack. Most ordinary people think that the statement is irrelevant and so the bet must be cancelled.

Most philosophers and psychologists now agree that the ordinary conditional statement, as we understand and use it in everyday language, is not the material conditional of the logic textbooks.[21] What it means to believe a conditional statement 'if p then q' is to believe that q is probably true, when we suppose that p is.[22] Whatever we may believe about situation in which p is *not* the case, is irrelevant. Thus, we naturally assume that the probability that

'If the card drawn is a King then it will be a spade'.

is 1 in 4 and not 49/52! And when we evaluate a statement like 5.7, we only think about what will happen *if* the president is a Democrat: our beliefs about Republican presidents are neither here nor there. Thus conditional predictions encourage us to imagine some condition and then calculate its consequences. The same is true for many other kinds of conditional statements. Consider conditional advice, as in

5.11 If you go out drinking tonight, you will fail your exam tomorrow.
5.12 If you leave by 4 pm you will avoid the rush hour traffic.

These sentences also invite you to imagine a condition and consider its consequences. 5.11 is a warning, intended to discourage you from going out drinking, whereas 5.12 is a tip, intended to encourage you to leave early. We can also use conditionals to express threats and promises such as

5.13 If you turn up to work late again, I will fire you.
5.14 If you finish your homework, you may watch TV.

Of course, whether such conditional advice and inducements actually change our behaviour, depends on many factors. First, the statement has to be credible and here the same kinds of factors apply as for conditional predictions. Is the person advising us to be believed? Does this person normally carry out their threats and promises? Are there obvious counterexamples that come to mind? Also relevant are the goals that we have.[23] Consider 5.11. which might be stated by a mother to her teenage son. If the boy had simply been overconfident and unthinking the advice may be effective. But if he had done no work and expected to fail the examination anyway, he might well ignore the advice.

Reasoning with conditionals

When we reason with conditional statements, we are affected by what we believe about the relevant events and the extent to which we can imagine counterexamples to our inferences. [24] Consider an apparently very simple inference, known as Modus Ponens. For example:

If the card has an A on it then it has a 3 on it.
The card has an A on it.
Therefore, the card has a 3 on it.

In an abstract context like this, the inference seems blindingly obvious and is endorsed nearly 100% of the time, when given in experiments. In fact, so rapidly and routinely is this inference made, that it appears to belong more to the realm of intuition than reflection, perhaps delivered by the rapid process of language comprehension. This is one of several conditional inferences that have been extensively studied by psychologists. In this section, I consider just a brief example of how our beliefs can influence such reasoning.[25]

In discussing belief bias earlier, I showed that an invalid argument may appear valid when presented in a realistic context. The converse can be shown with conditional inference. Even the very obvious Modus Ponens may be resisted when the conditional statement goes against a person's beliefs. Take the following argument:

> If capital punishment were reintroduced into the UK then the murder rate would drop.
> Suppose that capital punishment were reintroduced.
> Does it follow that the murder rate would drop?

Given this problem, most people who are opposed to the death penalty would be reluctant to endorse the conclusion of the argument. Suppose, however, that we tell them that this is an experiment in logical reasoning, and that they must assume for the sake of the experiment that all the information given is true and draw conclusions on that basis. Now many more participants will say the conclusion follows, especially those of higher general intelligence. This is similar to findings noted with the belief bias effect earlier. Thus while the reflective mind can be influenced by thoughts and beliefs that come to mind, blocking the 'easy' inference of Modus Ponens, we can also use reflection to *inhibit* such beliefs and reinstate the logical answer. As with the belief bias, however, such inhibition is not easily achieved. It only seems to occur reliably when participants of high ability are given very strong and clear logical reasoning instructions.[26]

Two general tenets of the two minds hypothesis are (a) that reflection is much more effortful (and time consuming) than intuition and (b) that reflective thinking is more effective in those of higher cognitive ability. Research on deductive reasoning has provided much evidence for these claims.

The Wason selection task

One of the most famous problems used in the psychology of reasoning is the 'selection task', invented by the British psychologist, Peter Wason in the 1960s. Wason is considered to be one of the founding fathers of the modern psychology of reasoning and I was fortunate enough to have him as my own PhD supervisor. His famous task involves the logic of conditional statements and is notoriously difficult to solve, despite its apparent simplicity. An example of the task in its standard from is shown in Figure 5.2 and you may attempt to solve it before reading on.

There are four cards lying on a table. Each has a capital letter on one side and a single digit number on the other side. The exposed sides are shown below:

The rule shown below applies to these four cards and may be true or false:

If there is an R on one side of the card, then there is a 5 on the other side of the card

Your task is to decide those cards, and only those cards, that need to be turned over in order to discover whether the rule is true or false.

Fig. 5.2 An abstract form of the Wason selection task.

Participants are trying to decide which cards to turn over in order to decide if the statement 'If there is an R on one side of the card then there is a 5 on the other side of the card' is true or false. Note that they are told that each card must have a letter on one side and a number on the other. Thus the J card indicates that there is not a letter R and the 2 there is not a number 5. Common choices are R or R and 5, but the correct choice is R and *2*, which few participants find. The reason is that only a card which has an R on one side and does not have a 5 on other would disprove the statement. Hence, only selection of these two cards could find such a counterexample case. You cannot actually prove the statement true. For example, you might turn over R and find a 5, which would be consistent with the rule. But if there an R was discovered on the back of the 2, it would still be false for the cards as a whole.

Very early in my research career, I discovered something very curious about the abstract form of the task.[27] Take the problem above and just add the word 'not' to the rule, so that it reads:

If there is an R on one side of the card then there is *not* a 5 on the other side.

With the same four cards, R, J, 5, and 2, what now is the correct choice? The answer is R and 5 because only a card with an R on one side and a 5 on the other could prove the rule false. The curious thing is that nearly everyone gets this version of the task right. What is more they can give you the correct logical explanation for why it is the right choice. But the same participants, then given a standard form of the problem without the negation, will get it wrong again.

I called this phenomenon 'matching bias' because people seem to choose the cards R and 5 that match those stated in the rule, whether the negative is there or not. Matching bias is a powerful influence of the intuitive mind that makes us think about these particular cards. Somehow the rule is *about* the R and 5, with or without the negative. Recent research has shown directly that people do indeed focus their attention mostly on the matching cards, looking at these and thinking about them to the exclusion of the others.[28] This shows a very important way in which the intuitive mind can bias and influence our reasoning: it can direct our attention selectively to parts of the information presented. The evidence suggests that reflective reasoning is still engaged on the selection task, but only directed at the cards attended[29]. People tend to find a 'good' reason to choose J and 5 whether it is on the standard task, where it is logically incorrect, or on the negated task, where it is correct! Matching bias operates rather like the misdirection employed by professional conjurors. We look at what they want us to see, reflect on what they direct us to think about.

One of the most striking cases of matching bias influencing real world thinking occurred in November 1973, when President Richard Nixon, beleaguered by the Watergate scandal, famously said in a television interview, 'People have got to know whether or not their President is a crook. Well, I'm not a crook.' These words were quoted over and over and contributed to his downfall and eventual resignation about six months later. In saying that he was *not* a crook, Nixon merely called attention to the possibility that he was exactly that. Next to admitting that he was a crook, it was about the worst thing he could have said. In general, we use negatives in everyday language to deny presuppositions. As Wason once pointed out, to say that 'a whale is not a fish' seems quite acceptable whereas to say that 'a horse is not a fish' is entirely anomalous. It is plausible to assume that your listeners might confuse a whale with a fish, but hardly a horse. So by saying 'I am not a crook', Nixon inadvertently implied that there were reasonable grounds for supposing that he was!

Matching bias is so powerful on the standard selection task that very few people can overcome it; in many studies, no more than 10% or so of undergraduate students choose the logically correct combination of cards. We now know that this small minority are those of exceptionally high general intelligence. However, the problem can be made a great deal easier when it is cast in real world contexts, as in Figure 5.3. Here there is a social rule that relates permission to drink alcohol to the age of the drinker. Most people shown this problem correctly choose the person drinking beer and the one who is under the age of 18 as those requiring further investigation. Furthermore, success on problems like this has little relation to cognitive ability.[30]

Why should this be? The answer is that on the standard problem the intuitive mind is prompting the wrong answer and obstructing the efforts of the reflective mind to solve the task with logical reasoning. By contrast, on some realistic versions, the intuitive mind is prompting the correct answer and taking the pressure off the reflective mind. Most people will have encountered something like the drinking age rule before and know that violators have to be underage drinkers. So little if any *reasoning* is required to choose the correct cards. Hence, good reasoners—people with high IQs—have little advantage.

Research on the selection task shows that although you do not need to have encountered precisely the same rule before, you do need to have knowledge of a similar rule in order for the task to become easy. One famous demonstration that knowledge could make the task easy was run in London in early 1970s. At that time the UK Post Office charged a lower rate for mail where the envelope was unsealed rather than sealed: a rather odd and non-obvious rule. When students were given a version of this rule using envelopes rather than cards, most solved it easily, turning over sealed envelopes and those containing lower value stamps. Of course only a sealed envelope with the lower value stamp could break the rule: the post office would not object if you put a higher value stamp on an unsealed envelope! However, later studies showed that when this task was given to students in countries (e.g. the United States) who had never had such a rule, they were unable to solve the task.[31] When relevant

You are a police officer observing people drinking in a bar. You must ensure that the following rule is being obeyed:

If a person is drinking beer then that person must be over 18 years of age

The following cards represent four drinkers. One side of the card shows what they are drinking and the other their age

| Beer | Coke | 22 years of age | 16 years of age |

Your task is to decide those cards, and only those cards, that need to be turned over in order to discover whether the rule has been broken

Fig. 5.3 A realistic form of the Wason selection task.

knowledge does not spring to mind, people have to rely on the same (ineffective) reasoning effort that they apply on the abstract selection task.

It would be a mistake, however, to think that putting problems in a realistic context improves logical reasoning. Earlier in the chapter, we saw that real world knowledge can also create a belief bias that interferes with logical reasoning. A more plausible account is that the intuitive mind dominates choices on the selection task. The selections it prompts are much more influential than any reasoning of the reflective mind, except for a very small number of individuals with high IQs. Research also shows that prior knowledge does not always prompt the correct answer. Suppose a mother says to her young son:

If you tidy your room then you can go out to play.

If cards are used to represented what happened, they can show these events.

A. Tidied room
B. Did not tidy room
C. Went out to play
D. Did not go out to play

If people are asked to turn over cards to find out whether the mother followed the rule, then they make what appear to be the logical choices: A and D. The rule would clearly be broken if the son tidied his room and was not then allowed out to play. But if they are asked instead to check whether the *son* obeyed the rule, they now turn over B and C. This is neither the logical answer not the matching one, but something different. People assume instead that the child would be disobeying the rule if he were to go out to play without first tidying his room. Thus the same problem has two perspectives. The mother and son have a social contract and they can each violate it in different ways. In fact, the choices seem quite appropriate in both cases, but they show that it is not some general process of logical reasoning that is being encouraged by the context.[32] So powerful are these kinds of effect that some evolutionary psychologists have even claimed that the ability to solve realistic versions of the selection task reflects an innate Darwinian adaption to detect cheaters.[33]

Research on the selection task and other kinds of reasoning problems shows that abstract logical reasoning is not at all easy. We are not very good at it, and only people with high IQs making a big effort to follow instructions seem to perform well in these experiments. Given the manifest intelligence of our species, this suggests that logical reasoning is not as important to human intelligence as many philosophers and psychologists have traditionally assumed. Any conscious, reflective reasoning that we engage in is limited by context, so that the intuitive mind also seems to dictate the agenda for our reflective reasoning. If our attention is directed to the wrong information—as in matching bias—we have little chance of solving the problem.

Reasoning with probabilities

I concluded the previous chapter by pointing out that our intuitions about probability are very unreliable and may lead to biases and errors in decision making. Psychologists have also studied directly how people reason about probabilities. Probability theory and logic are related in ways that might not be immediately obvious. The following argument is obviously invalid:

> X is a man.
> Therefore, X is a man who smokes.

And the following obviously valid:

> X is a man who smokes.
> Therefore, X is a man.

Logically, there cannot be more men who smoke than there are men. It is a logical possibility[34] (though a factual falsehood) that all men smoke, so in the most extreme case there could be as many men smokers as there are men, but never more. The logical relationship here seems so obvious. If you select a person at random, it could never be more likely that they were a man and a smoker, than that they were a man. In fact, for any two events, A and B, the probability of A and B can never be greater than the probability of A.

Why am I bothering to labour this obvious logical point? The reason is that when asked to reason about probabilities, people sometimes violate this simple logical principle. This was famously demonstrated using the 'Linda' problem.[35] Participants are given this description:

> Linda is 31 years old, single, outspoken, and very bright. At University, she studied philosophy. As a student, she was deeply concerned with issues of discrimination and social justice, and also participated in anti-nuclear demonstrations.

They are then asked to judge how likely it is that Linda is.

1. A bank teller
2. A feminist
3. A feminist bank teller

There is a strong tendency for people to rate 3 as more probable than 1, even though this is logically impossible for the reasons given above. The effect is known as the conjunction fallacy. If Linda is a feminist bank teller, she is also a bank teller. So even if you believe that *all* women like Linda who are bank tellers are also feminists you could only justify 3 being as likely, not more likely than 1. The conjunction fallacy appears to be a clear case of an intuitive error.

Linda does not sound very much like a bank teller (cashier) but she fits much better to the stereotype of a feminist. No surprise then that almost everyone rates 2 as more probable than 1. Although it is logically impossible for 3 to be more likely than 1, the intuitive mind supports this choice more strongly with some 'feeling of rightness' because of the fit of Linda's description to the feminist stereotype.

The experiment can be run in different ways. For example, the statements can be included in the same list so that participants see all of them. When this is done, people of high ability may resist the fallacy. A likely interpretation is that while these individuals also experience the intuitive prompting to rate 3 as more likely than 1, they are able to override this by logical reasoning. When the choices are rated by separate groups, who see only 1, 2, or 3, the bias is still present: the group given 3 rate it higher than the group given 1 but now there is no relation to cognitive ability.[36] Why is this? Essentially, there is no means available to calculate the correct answer to the problem, so when separate groups are used, all anyone can go on is their intuitive feeling. Only when a person is about to rate A&B as more likely than A, do they have the opportunity to see the logical problem it creates.

There are some clear parallels here with the study of belief biases in deductive reasoning. In both cases, an intuitively compelling response is suggested by the intuitive mind. A believable conclusions feels right, as does a choice consistent with the feminist stereotype. In both cases, the bias that results can be resisted by people of high general intelligence, but only if there is some transparent means for logical reasoning to be applied. In the case of syllogistic reasoning, they must be told to reason logically in order to have some resistance to belief bias. In the case of the conjunction fallacy, they must see their choices side by side so that their logical relationship can be noticed.

Here is another famous problem involving probabilities that the reader might like to attempt before reading on:

> A city has two cab companies, Blue and Green. The Blue company runs 85% of the city's cabs and the Green company runs 15%. A witness identifies a cab involved in a hit-and-run accident as green. Under tests, she is shown to be 80% accurate in identifying cabs of either colour under the same viewing conditions. Is the cab more likely to be green or blue?

Most people give the answer green, whereas the correct answer is actually blue.[37] If asked to give the probability that the cab was green, many set it to 80%, the reliability of the witness, whereas the actual probability is 41%. If there were no witness statement, it would be apparent that the probability that the cab was blue would be 85%, which is the *base rate* frequency of blue cabs in the city. However, once we have an individual witness statement, then for many individuals the base rate apparently becomes irrelevant. However, this information cannot be ignored. Suppose that the city has exactly 100 cabs, 85 blue and 15 green. If the witness saw a green cab, there is a 20% chance she mistook it as blue. So out of 85 blue cabs, she would declare 17 to blue. If she saw a green cab, she would correctly identify it as green 80% of the time. So out of 15 blue cabs, she would have said blue on 12 occasions. This means the odds are 17:12 in favour of the cab being blue when the witness describes it as green![38] See Figure 5.4.

Ignoring (or seriously undervaluing) the base rate in problems like these is known as the base-rate fallacy and is a very important finding. On the standard form of the problem, high-ability participants do no better than low-ability ones. As with belief bias and the conjunction fallacy, they need some help in the way the problem is presented.[39] Consider the following version of the cabs problem:

> A city has two cab companies, Blue and Green. There are equal numbers of blue and green cabs in the city. However, 85% of the cabs involved in accidents are blue. A witness identifies a cab involved in a hit-and-run accident as green. Under tests, she is shown to be 80% accurate in identifying cabs of either colour under the same viewing conditions. Is the cab more likely to be green or blue?

Many participants now switch their answer to blue, especially those of higher general intelligence. Statistically, the problem is equivalent to the first one. The difference is that the base rate is now *causally* linked to accidents. Blue cab drivers have a lot more accidents, suggesting that the Blue company

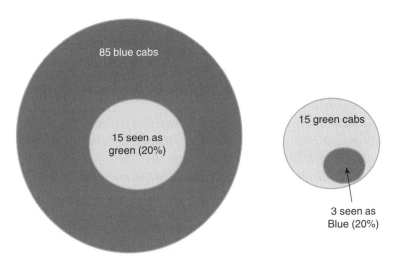

Fig. 5.4 Illustrations of the probabilities in the cabs problem.

employs careless or reckless drivers who cause accidents. With this clue that the base rate is relevant after all, participants can attempt to balance the base rate information against the reliability of the witness. Combining the two is very hard, however, and still requires high cognitive ability to achieve.

The base rate fallacy has huge practical implications. The example discussed suggests one area of real life application: the role of eyewitness testimony in criminal trials. It is well known that juries tend to place too much reliance on eyewitness testimony and that they may be relatively unimpressed by statistics provided by expert witnesses. However, it is not just eyewitness testimony to which base rate evidence is relevant. Another example is known as the prosecutor's fallacy.[40] Suppose police conduct a mass DNA screening of suspects in a murder case and find an individual with a match. Only one person in 100,000 has a DNA profile that could show the degree of match found to the sample. The prosecutor wants to argue that this means that the accused (against whom there is no other evidence) has a 0.99999 chance of being guilty. In doing so, he commits exactly the same fallacy as the participant who thinks that there must be an 80% chance that the witness was right about the colour of the cab.

If the murder occurred on the street in a large city and the body was dumped in a random site, there might be as many as a million men with the same degree of access to the murder victim as the accused, in which case 10 of these could be expected to match the DNA profile. So how can we possibly conclude that our suspect has only a 1 in 100,000 chance of being innocent? Clearly we cannot. Another very important area where base rate neglect can be a serious problem is in medical diagnosis. Take the case of mass screening of women over 50 for breast cancer. The false-positive rates for mammograms are substantially higher than the base rate of the condition being tested for. This means that the majority of the women called in for further investigation will actually be healthy. The statistical relationship involved is well understood and explained the UK's National Health Service guidelines. However, misunderstanding of the probabilities has apparently led to inappropriate treatment decisions in other countries.[41]

Most medical schools do not teach the Bayesian statistics that are needed to take proper account of base rates. Studies on the intuitive judgements of medical students and professionals suggest that they are susceptible to the base rate fallacy when making diagnostic judgements. In fact, as their training develops, they become more focused on the individual patient and *less* likely to take account of base rates![42] This can lead to bad decisions. For example, patients presenting with certain tumours who are young, have no relevant family history, or exposure to environmental risks may have favourable base rates, meaning that it is statistically very unlikely to be malignant.

In such cases, a risky biopsy would be medically ill-advised, but may be carried out if base rates are ignored. However, another bias comes into play here, especially in the United States, which has a strong tradition of litigation against doctors. In such a context, doctors may be inclined to conduct hazardous investigations (to which the patients must assent) rather than risk being sued should a serious condition be missed.

There is much other research on reasoning with probabilities which I do not have the space to discuss here. The conclusions they suggest are similar, however. Statistical reasoning is not something to be left to intuition, which can seriously let us down. Decisions made in criminal courts, by doctors and in many other real world contexts may rely on accurate understanding of probabilities and statistical relationships that are far from intuitive. It follows that doctors, lawyers, and other experts need to be trained in good statistical reasoning as part of their basic education. We know that people can acquire formal understanding of probability through appropriate training and apply this in the real world. But the reflective mind needs help through appropriate education to achieve this: a matter far too important to be left to chance.

Conclusions

Reasoning is particularly important when we are confronted with novel problems, or ones that require explicit consideration of facts and rules. In such cases, the intuitive mind, with its reliance on experience-based learning, may let us down badly. Explicit reasoning is the domain of the reflective mind and one of its most important functions. This is why study after study shows that reasoning problems (in general) are better solved by those of high general intelligence. IQ, in fact, is predominantly a measure of the ability to engage in abstract reasoning about novel problems.

The relation of intelligence to reasoning is complicated by several factors, though, as I have shown in this chapter. Sometimes the intuitive mind will assist us in solving a reasoning problem by providing helpful intuitions. This is most likely to occur when we have relevant prior experience, as on some realistic versions of Wason's selection task. Intuition is often a false or fickle friend, however. When it directs our attention through matching bias, for example, it may lead us to the right or the wrong answer, depending on how the problem is phrased. It may also lead us to belief biases in deductive reasoning, or to stereotypical thinking that ignores the logic of a problem phrased in terms of probabilities.

Successful reasoning with novel problems is very difficult for most people and seems to depend on several factors. One certainly is general intelligence, but studies show that intelligent people may also be prone to biases and fail to apply their reasoning ability, according to how the task is presented to them. If the need for logical reasoning is not transparent, they will show no advantage. Another issue is education and training. For example, most doctors are highly intelligent but still make substantial and important errors when reasoning about probabilities. The evidence strongly suggests that experience alone does not lead them to understand the theory of probability or the principles of Bayesian inference. Formal education and training can, but it must be provided for the expert groups that require it.

Notes and references

1 For a recent discussion of a range of attempt to provide a logic for inductive inference, see Kyburg (2008).

2 Lee, Goodwin and Johnson-Laird (2008).

3 The great majority of studies of human reasoning use university students as their participants. And yes, this does limit the generality of the findings. We know that the ability to engage in logical reasoning is related to general intelligence and that this participant group are above average for the population. Surprisingly, however, recent studies show very wide variation in the reasoning ability of students (Evans, Handley, Neilens, and Over, 2007; Newstead, Handley, Harley, Wright, and Farelly, 2004).

4 For detailed coverage of the 'mental logic' approach, see Rips (1994) and Braine and O'Brien (1998).

5 For application of mental model theory to a wide range of reasoning problems, see Johnson-Laird and Byrne (1991).

6 See Evans, Barston and Pollard (1983) and for a recent replication of their findings, Klauer, Musch, and Naumer (2000).

7 Evans et al. (1983), p. 298.

8 Direct evidence for this claim is provided by Evans et al. (1983).

9 For relevant studies, see Sa, Stanovich and West (1999), Stanovich and West (1997), and Gilinsky and Judd (1994). Note that although IQ scores are calculated to remain constant across the life span, raw score performance does decline in old age.

10 Research suggests that belief bias is mostly a tendency to reject unbelievable conclusions. By default, people tend to accept conclusions that are neutral or believable.

11 Evans and Curtis-Holmes (2005) and de Neys (2006).

12 Lord, Ross and Lepper (1979).

13 Fugelsang et al. (2004).

14 Goel (2005, 2008).

15 Particularly relevant are studies by Goel and Dolan (2003), De Neys et al. (2008), and Tsujii and Watanabe (2009).

16 Evans et al. (1983).

17 Evans and Over (2004).

18 I have written a scholarly book on hypothetical thinking as well (Evans, 2007).

19 Stevenson and Over (2001).

20 For an argument that causality is fundamental to hypothetical thinking, see Sloman (2005).

21 See Bennett (2003), Edgington (1995), Evans and Over (2004).

22 Evidence for this claim has been reported in a number of recent experimental studies (Evans, Handley, and Over, 2003; Oberauer & Wilhelm, 2003; Over, Hadjichristidis, Evans, Handley, and Sloman, 2007).

23 In a recent study (Evans, Neilens, Handley, and Over, 2008) we showed that people find such advice credible depending on not just the link between p and q, but also the costs and benefits of relevant actions and consequences.

24 See Evans and Over (2004). Chapter 6.

25 The psychological literature on conditional reasoning is reviewed in detail in my recent scholarly books (Evans, 2007; Evans and Over, 2004). The findings in this literature are also consistent with the two minds theory, but a description of them here would add little to the points made in the chapter. I do, however, discuss another finding on conditional reasoning in Chapter 8.

26 See Evans et al. (in press).

27 Evans and Lynch (1973). For a review of the many experiments that were published in consequence, see Evans (1998).

28 Evans, Ball, and Lucas (2003).

29 Evans and Ball (2009).

30 Stanovich and West (1998).

31 The postal rule problems was first published by Johnnson-Laird, Legrenzi and Legrenzi (1972) and the first demonstration that it was culture-specific was that of Griggs and Cox (1982).

32 There are a number of published demonstrations of this kind of perspective effect. The example is taken from one of the earliest: Manktelow and Over (1991).

33 This claim was first made in a paper published by Cosmides (1989) one of the advocates of the massive modularity hypothesis discussed in Chapter 2. This paper proved hugely controversial both for its methodology and for the form of evolutionary argument it proposed. One difficulty is that while it might have been adaptive for our ancestors to have a mechanism for detecting cheaters, that provides no kind of guarantee that such a mechanism, in fact, evolved (Fodor, 2000). Another obvious problem is that young children are taught social rules of behaviour, so a tendency to identify and dislike cheaters could easily be acquired in development.

34 Logical possibilities include anything that can be imagined (however improbable) that does not violate the laws of logic. Some philosophers also add the constraint of the laws of physics.

35 First demonstrated by Tversky and Kahneman (1983).

36 Stanovich and West (2008b).

37 This problem was another first devised by Kahneman and Tversky. The base rate fallacy has been heavily researched since their major paper on this topic (Kahneman and Tversky, 1973).

38 The problem seems much easier to understand here once actual frequencies, rather than probabilities, are given. Gigerenzer and colleagues have made much of this difference, arguing that probabilities are arbitrary and that people are more likely to encounter frequencies in a natural environment (Gigerenzer, 2002). However, this position is highly controversial (Barbey and Sloman, 2007).

39 See Stanovich (1999), Stanovich and West (2008b).

40 For discussions, see Gigerenzer (2002) and Evans (2005).

41 See Gigerenzer (2002).

42 There are many published studies on this (for example, Casscells, Schoenberger, and Graboys, 1978; Eddy, 1982; Heller, Saltzstein, and Caspe, 1992).

Chapter 6

Thinking about the social world

Humans are intensely social animals. In comparison with other social species, our high intelligence coupled with the unique powers of human language has allowed us to build the most complex kinds of social structure. With modern technology, however, we could in principle survive and flourish in relative isolation from one another. It would be much more cost-effective and 'green' for office workers to stay at home than for everyone to travel into work on a daily basis, as they still do in millions in cities all over the planet. Clearly, it is much cheaper and more energy-efficient to send people the information they need to work on. But it may be hard to engineer this switch in the habits of society. Many people find home working lonely and isolating and need the social contact. It is not surprising, then, that solitary confinement is considered such an effective form of punishment in prison systems, a practice condemned as torturous and uncivilized by the great nineteenth century psychologist, William James.

We have been a socially organized species for a very long time and it is more than likely that much of the basis of our social behaviour is hardwired into our old minds by evolutionary processes.[1] It is certainly plausible that our old minds have built-in procedures for thinking and acting in the social world. In any event, there is much research in social psychology that supports the two minds hypothesis. Much of our social behaviour is caused by factors other than what we are conscious of believing and intending to do.

Social psychology and the two minds hypothesis

Social psychology is a huge field of study and one that is largely separated in practice from the field of study of cognitive psychology discussed in Chapters 3 to 5. Academics, like everyone else, have a limited capacity for learning and also a somewhat tribal nature. On the whole, social and cognitive psychologists tend to read different journals and attend different conferences from one another. Hence, surveying research in social psychology is extremely useful for our present purpose, providing a largely independent source of evidence for the two minds hypothesis. It is true that dual-process theories in social psychology were influenced by research in cognitive psychology, especially the study of automatic and controlled processes. However, the major dual-process theories of reasoning and decision making (Chapters 4 and 5) arose mostly from separate roots, such as the attempt to understand cognitive biases. Until recently, there was little cross reference or mutual citation between these literatures.[2]

Social psychologists study behaviour in a social context. Some focus on group processes like leadership, conformity, and deviance. A big field of study is that of social attitudes and closely linked with this are the topics of stereotypes and prejudice. Social psychologists also study the mechanisms of social influence, persuasion, and attitude change. Above all, social psychology is concerned with the *self*, the social person. It follows that social psychology deals with the same topics as folk psychology both in the everyday and more technical use of that term. For example, we all hold beliefs about *other people's* beliefs, attitudes, and motives, a form of meta-representation (see Chapter 2). When we say that Laura is lazy, Paul is aggressive, or Sue is sociable, these are concepts which help us to predict or understand how they will behave in various situations. Laura may fail her examinations, Paul may get into fights, and Sue will need little excuse to organize a party.

We, ordinary people, may also invoke folk psychology to explain 'social influence' with such comments as 'Peter has always been susceptible to peer pressure' or 'Mary is a different person since she got religion'. Similarly, we explain or predict people's behaviour with reference to their attitudes when we say, 'Mike takes lots of exercise because he is health-conscious' or 'Martha will never buy a fur coat: she is in favour of animal rights.' Like professional social psychologists, we also recognize the distinction between core beliefs that are close to someone's identity and peripheral ones that are not. For example, we expect that a Jehovah's Witness will refuse a blood transfusion, even if it puts their life at risk. By contrast, we think that someone will easily abandon a mistaken belief in the meaning of an unusual word, when presented with evidence of their error.

This correspondence with the domain of folk psychology makes social psychology more vulnerable to the influence of common sense than other fields. For example, people have few intuitions about the way in which the visual system works, but many about the ways in which people influence each other's behaviour. There is a strong evolutionary argument (see Chapter 2) that folk psychology is a built-in feature of the human mind that developed as a Darwinian adaptation. Hence, we are generally adept at 'mindreading': figuring out other people's beliefs and intentions unless we were born autistic. But just because folk psychology has adaptive value, it does not necessarily mean that it is a good basis for any kind of *scientific* psychology. Social psychology may have to do a good deal more than formalize these intuitions: it may need radically to rethink them.

From the viewpoint of the two minds hypothesis, we should expect social behaviour broadly to exhibit the same features discussed in earlier chapters. A basic idea is that there are two forms of knowledge—implicit and explicit— and correspondingly, two forms of decision making. One is fast and intuitive, drawing upon habits and other forms of implicit knowledge while the other is slow and reflective, drawing upon explicit knowledge and reasoning. If this is right, it should be reflected in the social domain. For example, we might expect that we will have implicit social attitudes towards individuals and groups that might influence our actions directly through the intuitive mind. We should also have explicit attitudes and beliefs that affect our behaviour through the reflective mind and the two may come into conflict. And if the intuitive mind dominates behaviour, the reflective mind will confabulate an explanation for it.

In fact, this is *exactly* the direction in which social psychology has been moving for some time now, switching its focus from explicit to implicit processes. That this has happened quite independently of the research in cognitive psychology that I have discussed to date provides powerful evidence for the two minds hypothesis. There has actually been a major revolution in the thinking of social psychologists over the past 30 to 40 years. Prior to this, it was generally assumed[3] that people held beliefs that consciously controlled their social behaviour, in line with folk psychology or the single mind view. From the 1980s onwards, evidence has amassed for an opposite point of view: that we, conscious persons, are neither aware of the basis of our social behaviour nor in intentional control of it. Much of our social knowledge is implicit. We may think we hold one attitude towards a social grouping, but really have another. We may believe we are egalitarian but at an unconscious level hold a stereotype, which affects the way we behave.

Over the past 20 years or so, there has been an explosion of dual-process theories in social psychology.[4] I will not attempt to describe and review these here, but a few points should be noted. One line of work emphasizes two modes of processing, assuming that people process social information in relatively deep or shallow ways. I will discuss this approach later in relation to studies of persuasion. Other theorists focus on the idea that there are two kinds of knowledge, implicit and explicit, a central assumption of the two minds theory laid out in Chapter 3, but applied specifically in the social domain. A particularly well-developed theory of this type was proposed by Smith and DeCoster in 2003.[5] There is a huge amount of published research in social psychology, and much of it with a dual-process orientation. In this chapter, I can only hope to provide a flavour of the topics that social psychologists study and the kinds of results that have moved researchers towards a two minds approach.

Forming impressions of people

First impressions are important, according to popular culture. But how exactly do we form impressions of other people? The ones that concern social psychologists are not the physical aspects of a person that we perceive, but rather their psychological characteristics or *traits*. Are they intelligent or stupid, extravert or introvert, friendly or hostile? A lot of research suggests that such impressions are formed rapidly and fairly automatically, sometimes from a single glance, an apparent function of the intuitive mind. But sometimes we are consciously seeking to gain an impression of someone with our reflective minds. When we do so, are we really in conscious control of the impressions we form?

Suppose that you are sitting on an interview panel, trying to appoint a computer programmer. Your task is to put together information from qualifications, work experience, references and the interview performance to evaluate each candidate. Perhaps the most predictive information is already there even before you interview the candidates. And probably the most useful aspect of the interview is the information that the candidate provides in answer to your specific questions. But as soon as you meet someone and start talking to them, the automatic mechanisms of impression formation kick in. You may find them attractive (or not), interesting, or dull and so on, all of which might sensibly influence whether you think they are the kind of person you might ask around for dinner or enjoy sharing an office with, but which may have very little relevance indeed to their competence as a computer programmer. Worse still, the impressions you form may be implicit, so that you are not aware of how they are affecting your thinking and your decisions. It is not surprising, then, that the predictive value of job interviews has been questioned by many academic researchers. Nor that a range of non-verbal factors have been demonstrated to predict interview success, including physical attractiveness, positive personality traits, and even the firmness of a handshake![6]

A great deal of social psychological research shows that people spontaneously and involuntarily attribute traits to people (sometimes just photographs of them) even when this is quite irrelevant to the task they are set.[7] Some research, however, suggests that when people form impressions deliberately, this produces different results. For example, in one study[8] participants were judged to be high and low in aggression, from a self-report scale. They were then asked to read a series of statements describing other people's behaviour in social situations, which were ambiguous with regard to their hostility. The study found that aggressive participants tended to see the behaviour as hostile, but this bias disappeared when they were instructed to think carefully about the reasons for their behaviour. In this case, it appeared that the reflection removed a bias in the intuitive mind. Is it generally the case, however, that automatic social judgements can be overridden by reflective and effortful thought? This is clearly a very important question.

It is likely that initial impressions will generally be very influential. First, in most situations we will not be trying consciously to form impressions, and so the automatic processes will take over. Second, there is also much evidence that impressions can be implicit, so that we are not even aware that they are affecting our judgements and behaviour. In one study,[9] participants were shown pictures of three young women with long hair and three with short hair. In one condition, the long-haired women were all described as being kind and the short-haired women as capable. In the other condition, the descriptions were reversed. After a filler task, participants were shown four more pictures (of different women) and asked for two of them to judge kindness and for the other two to judge capability. In each case, one woman had long and the other short hair. The study showed that participants were now biased in their impressions by the hair length. However, interviews conducted after the experiment was completed showed that participants had not consciously noticed the relationship between the descriptions and hair length. These findings are similar to those shown generally for implicit learning tasks (Chapter 3). When asked to justify their choices, participants also confabulated reasons for their answers, commenting that women had 'those typical eyes of the dependable person' or 'the sharp gaze of a bright person' and so on.

Studies of impression formation support some of the central assumptions of the two minds hypothesis set out in Chapter 3. That is, there are two kinds of learning, two kinds of knowledge, and two routes to the control of our judgements and other behaviours. We may try, and to some extent succeed, in forming impressions of people by conscious reasoning about what we notice and attend to. However, the evidence also shows that we spontaneously, indeed compulsively, attribute traits to people without any conscious effort to do so. Moreover, the basis of this automatic judgement can be that of association with incidental variables such as length of a haircut that we would never consider to be relevant by any conscious process of reasoning. Not only are we are unaware of these implicit impressions and their effect on our behaviour, but we are likely to invent rational sounding explanations for the intuitive feelings they elicit.

Attitudes, stereotypes, and prejudice

A classic problem in social psychology is the dissociation between what we think, what we feel, and what we do. Technically, these are described as cognitive, emotional, and behavioural components of *attitudes*. The cognitive level belongs to the new mind and the emotional to the old. What we do may be controlled by either or both. An attitude always has an object, such as an individual person or a social group. Consider the profiles of three young people who grew up in a region of the UK with a high British Asian population, comprised mostly second or third generation immigrants from the Indian subcontinent (see Box 6.1). John is a racist through and through and it shows in every component of his attitudes to racial groups. He believes such groups are alien and should be deported, feels anger and disgust towards them, and attacks them verbally and physically when he gets the opportunity. In this case, cognitive, emotional, and behavioural components of his attitudes are all aligned. Many cases are not so clear cut, however. Mike, for example, is a racist only in cognitive terms. He has no particular emotional response to Asians and even quite likes some individuals in the group. He does not behave aggressively or negatively towards them. Sarah would appear not to be a racist at all if you talked to her, but she has an automatic and uncontrollable emotional reaction when surrounded by individuals of a different racial group.

In terms of the two minds hypothesis, emotions reside in the old mind and may reflect either ancient evolutionary processes or learnt reactions. They are quite distinct from the explicit attitudes and beliefs held in the reflective mind, which form the basis of the statements we make as well as our conscious reasoning. Behaviour, however, is a complex function of the two minds working in co-operation or competition with each other. John, for example, who is a racist in both his minds behaves aggressively towards Asians and may even physically attack them. Of course, this requires other facets of his personality than racism, such as a violent nature and an indifference to social norms. Mike appears to be a cognitive racist. His racism seems to be restricted to his reflective mind, rather like a scientific theory. It has no emotional basis and is reflected only in his verbal behaviour. This profile is probably quite rare now in contemporary Western societies, but is certainly psychologically plausible. Such cognitive attitudes to race and gender were commonplace when I was growing up in England in the 1950s. Sarah's profile is far from unusual. Her emotional reactions stem from her old mind and conflict, uncomfortably, with her explicit beliefs and attitudes held in the new mind. Her behaviour is somewhat affected also, since the old mind often wins control of our actions when such a conflict occurs.

Box 6.1 Three kinds of racist attitudes

Here are profiles of three young people who grew up in the East Midlands of England, an area with a high population of British Asians.

John

John hates Asians. He will tell anyone who listens that they should be 'sent home' are 'taking our jobs' and that it is time for whites to take control of England again. When he sees an Asian person he feels anger and loathing. He is a member of a neo-Nazi right wing political party. He frequently yells insults at Asians in pubs and other public places and on occasion goes out with his mates looking for victims of this group that they can beat up.

Mike

Mike believes that British Asians are not British and should not be living in England. He often expresses these views in private to people who share his opinion. However, when he meets Asians, he feels no particular emotion towards them and is generally civil and polite. He is even quite friendly with one or two Asian colleagues at work, although that does not change his view of the group as a whole.

Sarah

Sarah prides herself on her liberal attitudes and always votes for left-of-centre political parties. When asked, she will argue that British Asians are as British as everyone else and strongly object to racist arguments. However, when she finds herself in the company of Asians, particularly if they are in the majority, she feels very anxious and uncomfortable. She avoids going to locations that are frequented by Asians even though she hates herself for doing so.

Could racism have an evolutionary basis? There are certainly some authors who think so. One interesting hypothesis is that as well as evolving a physical immune system, we also evolved a *psychological* immune system.[10] The old mind is not in the least politically correct: there is strong evidence that we experience discomfort at the sight of people with facial disfigurement or obvious disabilities and may avoid their presence. We also have negative reactions to other major deviations from morphological norms such as extreme obesity or thinness. This could reflect an evolved behavioural defence mechanism designed to protect us from contagious diseases. This argument can be extended to fear of foreigners and races that look different from ourselves. Contact with alien cultures also entails exposure to microbes against which we may not have developed adequate defences. Of course, our ancestors could have had other reasons to fear alien tribes who might well be hostile. Finally, people who look like us are likely to carry more common (and selfish) genes. This may explain why people of the most liberal and egalitarian (explicit) beliefs may still feel uncomfortable or apprehensive when surrounded by a different racial group.

How should social psychologists go about measuring people's attitudes?[11] The problem is complex because what we think with our reflective minds may not correspond with what we feel with our intuitive minds. And the way we behave may be determined by either or both of our minds. Outside of the academic world, it is often assumed to be straightforward: you just need to ask people. Market researchers, for example, send out questionnaires with rating scales, so that people can tell them how much they like particular products and what they want them to do. These methods do have some value. People can certainly self-report their behaviour with reasonable accuracy such as what they watched on the television last night. This only requires an accurate personal memory of what you were doing and a disposition to answer the question honestly. Self-report of attitudes, especially social attitudes, is a more complex business, however; at best, people can only tell you what they *believe* to be the case. They can only pass on the explicit knowledge accessible to their reflective minds.

Racial prejudice is a particularly big issue in the United States where most social psychological research is conducted. Traditional methods of measuring attitudes are similar to those of market researchers and opinion pollsters. In this approach, people are given a list of statements and asking the extent to which they agree with them. Such questionnaire methods can be very direct, using statements such as A: 'black people tend to be lazy' or B: 'women can do any job as well as men', or more subtle using statements like C: 'bussing school students is a good thing', or D: 'companies should actively attempt to recruit more women'. However, even such less direct questions are fairly transparent. If you believe the results of such questionnaire methods, then Americans have been becoming progressively less racist and sexist over the past 40 years. However, there are two potential drawbacks to this approach.

First, people may give you the answers that seem to be socially desirable. This is not necessarily a conscious bias. People have a self-concept, a set of beliefs which they hold about themselves, which might include positive attributes such as being egalitarian and liberal minded. They probably will not want to see themselves as prejudiced. Campaigners for political correctness in the Western world have succeeded to a large extent in establishing the cultural norm that it is a bad thing to express views that could be seen as racist, sexist, homophobic, etc. In countries like the United Kingdom, this movement has been backed by legislation that makes it a criminal offence to incite hatred, by written or spoken statements, on grounds such as race, religion, or sexual orientation. In the United States, minority groups have been protected by a number of favourable court settlements where individuals have claimed wrongful dismissal and other forms of discrimination. So even if campaigners have failed to change attitudes, individuals will be much more wary of expressing them.

The other issue, more pertinent to the two minds hypothesis, is that while conscious attitudes have in many cases genuinely changed over the past 40 years, people might still retain stereotypes at an implicit level. The all too conscious prejudices expressed in the 1960s and 1970s might simply have gone underground, persisting in the intuitive mind. Such implicit stereotypes and prejudices may still affect our behaviour. For example, a personnel manager may have an unconscious preference for candidates who are white, male, and middle class, and appoint disproportionately from this group. In any particular selection decision, however, he will always construct good reasons in terms of qualifications and experience for the decisions made, with which to convince both himself and others.

Measuring implicit attitudes and stereotypes

How could social psychologists check whether *implicit* attitudes are in play when people make judgements, or whether they exist at all? Methods evidently need to be indirect and subtle. One method, called *priming*, has been borrowed from a field of cognitive psychology, the study of implicit memory. Suppose the participant is asked to study of list comprised of words and non-words, which are pronounceable strings of letters. In each case, they need to press a key to say yes it is a word or not it is not. Compare the following sequences:

A. Callot stemp trick plast horse donkey.
B. Callot stemp trick plast house donkey.

In each case, the correct answers are no, no, yes, no, yes, yes. The only difference is that the penultimate word in A is 'horse' and in B is 'house'. What happens in experiments like this is that the final word 'donkey' will be recognized significantly quicker in the A list than the B list. The reason is that the immediately preceding word in A, 'horse' is closely related in meaning to 'donkey' while the word 'house', in B, is unconnected. Hence, 'horse' is said to have *primed* the response to 'donkey'. The theory is that words of similar meaning are stored in a related way in the brain, in what is known as a *semantic network*.

A stereotype is a collection of concepts attached to a social group, which sounds quite like a semantic network. If there are stereotypes in the brain, then we may be able to activate the relevant neural circuits by presenting people with a word or picture related to that group. Then we can check whether features of the stereotype will be primed. There are many studies showing exactly this. One that applied this method to the study of race prejudice in white American adults, proceeded as follows.[12] Because they did not want participants to know that the task was about race, they presented the prime words 'black' or 'white' *subliminally*, that is in such a way that they participants were not aware they had been presented at all.[13] Following the prime, they were presented either a string of letters (non-word) or a word that were clearly visible. The participants' task was simply to decide whether the letters made up a word or not. Hence, they had no idea that the experiment had anything to do with race, or even social psychology, for that matter!

In this study, published in 1997, the words to be identified were either stereotypical of white or black Americans. Both stereotypes have positive (flattering) as well as negative (derogatory) aspects. Positive features for blacks include 'athletic, religious' while negative ones include 'lazy, violent'. Positive features of the while stereotype include 'intelligent, successful' while negative ones are 'greedy, materialistic'. The object was to see whether the prime word— black or white—would help people to identify words more quickly when they conformed to the stereotype, compared with a neutral prime. Any such effect would, of course, be wholly unconscious. The results did indeed show priming effects but in a very disturbing pattern. The word 'white' primed responses, but only to positive words in the white stereotype words like intelligent or successful. Conversely, the word 'black' primed responses only to *negative* words from the black stereotype like lazy or violent. This suggests that the stereotype is more than purely cognitive. The white participants also seemed to have a positive emotional attitude towards white and negative attitude toward blacks.

The fact that such stereotypes continue to exist in the mind after years of campaigning to eradicate them from modern society is worrying. Perhaps, though, they are just semantic networks reflecting our knowledge of what the stereotypes are supposed to be. After all, most people can state the stereotypical features if asked, even though they may claim not to endorse them. That would not explain the difference between positive and negative words in the above study, though. Nor is it easy to explain away the results of the Implicit Association Test (IAT), which is often used to demonstrate implicit prejudice.[14] In this task, people are shown words on a computer screen and are required to classify them by pressing keys. For example, you might be shown a list of first names and asked to classify them as male and female by pressing a key with the left hand for one, and the right hand for the other. Or you might be given a list of concepts and asked to classify them as good or bad by the same method. The clever part is that you are then asked to perform both tasks at once, using the hands say as follows:

A. Male, good (left)   Female, bad (right)
B. Male, bad (left)   Female, good (right)

People who implicitly associate men with good and women with bad will perform task A quicker. Those who have the opposite association will perform task B quicker. Although somewhat more transparent than subliminal priming, research has shown that the IAT is very difficult to fake. The method can be used to test any association between categories, attitudes, and stereotypes. And of course, it does not simply show that you know a stereotype. It shows that you *like* some social groups and *dislike* others. Thus people who are consciously convinced that they lack negative attitudes to those of another group are quite likely to discover that they do, according to the IAT.

Research using these implicit methods tells us that prejudice is alive and well in the politically correct contemporary Western culture, no matter how egalitarian our conscious attitudes and beliefs may be. Readers may find this conclusion depressing and disturbing. Some social psychologists have suggested optimistically that we can become aware of our implicit stereotypes and inhibit their influence on our judgements. A survey of this field of work by an eminent and highly respected social psychologist, John Bargh, takes a more pessimistic view in which he labels the implicit social cognition as a 'cognitive monster' within us.[15] Bargh claims that we have little ability to control implicit stereotypes and that to argue otherwise is wishful thinking. However, there is some evidence to suggest that people *can* suppress the influence of implicit attitudes by conscious effort, rather as they can suppress belief biases in reasoning (to an extent) when given strong instructions to reason logically (Chapter 5). One such study was conducted by Tim Wilson and his colleagues.[16]

In this study, participants listened to a tape-recorded description of an unpleasant person (a convicted sex-offender) as well as a likeable one (the prosecutor who was responsible for his capture). The descriptions were accompanied by photographs of the two men being described. The participants were then told that the experimenter had made a mistake and had accidently switched the photographs. The person they thought as the sex offender was really the prosecutor, and vice versa. Thus having formed initially strong positive and negative attitudes to the individuals portrayed, participants now needed to reverse these impressions. The experiment showed that when people were given plenty of time to rate their attitudes towards each person, they successfully corrected their ratings. However, when put under time pressure, they reverted strongly to the original attitude that was formed before they were told about the switch. Thus the original impression persisted unless they were able to correct it by conscious effort. In this case, the competition between the intuitive and reflective mind seems to operate in social judgement in a similar way to that already observed in the cognitive psychology of reasoning and decision making, discussed in the previous two chapters. Intuitions dominate unless the reflective mind intervenes by conscious effort.

Persuasion and attitude change

Measuring attitudes and trying to *change* them by persuasion is a major activity of modern society. There is a massive amount of resource committed to opinion polling, market research, focus groups, etc. in order to find out what we think and believe about everything from soap powders to political candidates for election to major public office. There is an equally enormous amount of resource devoted to changing our attitudes, in the form of advertising and political campaigns, as well as through religious and formal education. As we shall see, some of this effort is directed at changing attitudes in the reflective mind, but may be more effective when it is aimed directly at changing our behaviour directly via the intuitive mind. And although we may feel as though we are in conscious control of what we do, the evidence time and again suggests that when the two minds come into conflict, the intuitive mind will usually win.

In general, the more powerfully behaviour is controlled by the intuitive mind, the less effective will be arguments and campaigns, directed towards the reflective mind, in changing it. As an example, a very large and expensive advertising campaign was undertaken by the UK government in the 1980s with the aim of changing sexual behaviour in the light of the developing AIDS epidemic. The main slogan of the campaign 'Don't die of ignorance' doubled up as the common sense psychology underlying it. The assumption was that if people were educated about the risk of AIDS and how it is transmitted, then behaviour would change. The campaign emphasized the risks of casual sex and multiple partners as well as urging universal use of condoms as a barrier to infection. It was directed as much at heterosexual as homosexual practices. The campaign succeeded in reducing ignorance by increasing explicit knowledge, but had much less impact on actual behaviour. For example, a survey of British adolescents in the early 1990s[17] showed that awareness of AIDS and how to avoid it was fairly good, but that most of the youngsters perceived themselves to be at low risk and that condom usage was alarmingly low. One difficulty that has emerged is that condoms are thought to be appropriate for casual relationships but not 'serious' ones. Requests to use a condom might be interpreted as lack of trust in a valued partner. However, relationships interpreted as serious might last only for a few months and so an individual over a period of years could be exposed in this way to unprotected sex with many partners.

Studies of AIDS awareness suggest that perceived self-risk is the critical factor in changing behaviour but that these perceptions may be unrealistically low. People are resistant to statistical evidence of risk as was observed with smokers when studies first confirmed the risks of smoking to long-term health. I suspect that this resistance might be in part due to the tendency of our reflective minds to invent reasons for what our intuitive minds want to do. Given the strong urges involved in sexual behaviour and a chemical addiction like cigarette smoking, we may deceive ourselves about the risks. Also, people seem to have genuine difficulty in applying statistical probabilities to individual cases, like themselves. Of course, one of the groups at highest risk from AIDS, homosexual men, did eventually change their behaviour, but not on the basis of theoretical information about risks. It took gay men dying in their thousands for individuals finally to understand the risk to themselves.

The effect of communications in persuading us depends quite critically on whether we process them in a reflective or intuitive manner, as demonstrated in a number of early studies of dual processes by social psychologists.[18] Much advertising depends upon the assumption that we will process the communications in a shallow, intuitive manner without critical or reflective thinking. A good example is the use of famous and/or attractive people to endorse products. For example, golf stars like Phil Mickelson play with a specific brand of golf ball, which is linked to a sponsorship contract, and may appear in advertisements on television, recommending this product.[19] Superficial processing with the intuitive mind will usually have the desired effect. Advertising is a Darwinian process: the methods which fail to work quickly get dropped, as there is no commercial return to pay for them. Sponsorship by the famous and glamorous works, or it would not persist.

When people apply their reflective minds to such communications, the results are much less predictable. For example, you might think, 'this must be a good golf ball because otherwise Mickelson would not recommend and play with it himself' which is positive. But you might also think 'Mickelson is only playing with and recommending this ball because he is being paid a large amount of money to do so. It does not necessarily mean the ball is better than other leading makes.' Or worse still, you might think 'Using high profile stars like Mickelson means that this advertising campaign must be very expensive. I just want to pay for the manufacture of the golf ball, not all this expensive promotion.' So effortful processing could lead to the *opposite* effect to that intended by the advertiser.

A number of factors influence whether people engage in reflective thinking about communications. Much depends on context, but also on individual personality. Some individuals seem to enjoy analytic thinking while others like to rely on intuition: something that social psychologists can measure using a test called Need for Cognition. So depending on your circumstances and the kind of person you are, you might process communications in a more or less reflective manner. To give another example, consider political advertising intended to promote candidates for election. One method is to present serious arguments, statistics, etc. for a party or candidate, explaining policies and their benefits in the hope of engaging the reflective mind. Another is to 'press buttons' by showing the candidate with an attractive looking family, or mentioning their heroic war record. Such a superficial approach can easily make positive but hard to verify assertions, such as claiming that the candidate was a brilliant lawyer before entering politics. This latter approach has dominated U.S. politics for many years and has also become much more prevalent in British political campaigns in the past 20 years or so. If it works, it is because people spend little time and effort thinking about political advertisements, probably a fair assumption. Where audiences can be targeted, however, advertisers may vary their approach. An ad for a 'heavy' newspaper, for example, will contain much more in the way of arguments and evidence than one aimed for a tabloid audience.

You might think that more intelligent people would require more intelligent arguments to persuade them; for example, those which consider both sides of an issue. A recent study of informal reasoning suggests otherwise, at least when strong emotions are involved. Students in an American university were divided into two groups according to their views on the emotive topic of abortion: anti-abortion or pro-choice.[20] They were asked to rate the quality of arguments for and against abortion. Each text actually contained four arguments which could be either pro or anti. Examples of the arguments used were:

The fetus should not be destroyed due to the mother's mistake (anti).
Abortion reduces respect for human life in general (anti).
Killing human beings is wrong even though it is only a fetus (anti).
It is better to limit the births of unwanted children than those who are wanted (pro).
The fetus is not hurt by early abortion (pro).
Women should be able to decide whether to go through with something that affects them as much as pregnancy and childbirth (pro).

The texts were put into four categories according to whether all the arguments were anti, all were pro, had two anti followed by two pro, or two pro followed by two anti. The quality ratings of the two groups are shown in Figure 6.1. They show two different cognitive biases. First of all, notice that the anti-abortion students were most impressed with anti-abortion arguments, whereas the pro-abortion students were most impressed with the quality of

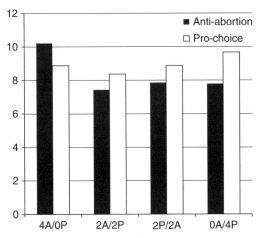

Fig. 6.1 Rated quality of arguments as a function of their content - number of arguments anti-abortion (A) or pro-abortion (P)—and the prior position of the participant. Data from Stanovich and West (2008a).

pro-abortion arguments. This is known as *myside bias*. When we hear someone arguing for a point of view we already agree with, their claims seem to be more cogent and well-founded. Notice also in the figure that one sided-arguments, whether anti or pro abortion were rated as better than balanced arguments. In this study, which used large numbers of participants, these biases were equally marked in students of high and low intelligence. People's preferred processing style (need for cognition) also had very little effect on the judgements.

These results are quite surprising. We might expect that people of higher intelligence would be less prejudiced by their own position and more appreciative of balanced arguments, but this is evidently not so. This seems to be another case where the intuitive mind dominates. Arguments that agree with our own views give rise to positive feelings whereas those against produce negative feelings. Even if people reflect, they will probably construct a justification for what their intuitive minds are telling them, a process of confabulation that I discuss further in Chapter 7. It also shows that while those of higher intelligence can engage in more effective reflective reasoning, there is no guarantee that they will do so. However, the study did provide a clue as to what may underlie these biases. When participants were grouped according to the *strength* of their belief on the issue, clear differences arose. Both myside bias and one-sided bias were only present for those held strong beliefs on the subject, whether pro or anti. Hence, these biases only operate when beliefs are strongly held, and given the topic, almost certainly arouse strong emotions.

The studies discussed in this section clarify the role of the two minds in persuasion. Much advertising and political campaigning is directed at influencing people with superficial cues through the intuitive mind. This must be largely effective or the interested parties would not pay for it. However, people *can* engage their reflective minds and when they do so, the communications can have very different effects from those intended. Some people enjoy critical thinking more than others and this predicts to some extent how they will process persuasive arguments. However, once strong emotions are involved, people are inclined simply to approve or criticize arguments only the basis of whether they already agree with the view being argued. In such cases, the intuitive mind dominates.

Social influence, conformity, and obedience

What we believe and think is not just a function of education, advertisements, and other forms of communication. It also depends on our social identity and the groups to which we belong. The way in which our own views are affected by those of other people around us is known as *social influence*. Some psychologists like to portray children and the adults into whom they develop as if they were scientists, developing hypotheses from observations of the world around them and gathering evidence to test and change their theories of the world. This is far from reality. To put it simply, the main reason that people believe things is because *other people believe them as well*, especially when those other people are members of the same social group.

Social influence is the foundation of our education system. If you do see yourself as a scientist, you may be shocked that powerful groups in the United States campaign for children not to be taught evolutionary theory (which is founded on massive scientific evidence) or to be taught 'intelligent design' as a rival 'scientific' account, even though it is contradicted by equally large amounts of evidence. If you are a person with a strong religious belief you may believe equally strongly that children should be brought up to share your beliefs and values. You may also be worried about the fate of children who are brought up in another culture and taught some alternative set of cultural or religious beliefs. The truth is that children (and adults) mostly believe what they are told and hence reflect the culture and social groups around them. The view that education should be based on science and observable evidence is itself a belief system, no matter how well founded its advocates believe it to be. And even within this system, much has to be taken on trust. For example,

I believe that Australia exists, although I have never actually been there to check it out for myself.

Much of what we know about the world comes to us only through watching television, reading newspapers, or listening to other people. This is both adaptive and in some ways problematic. The fact that we can learn in this way—collecting beliefs in our explicit knowledge system for use by the reflective mind—gives us an immense evolutionary advantage over animals that can learn only by direct experience. However, it comes with a cost. Most beliefs are not based on personally verifiable observations or founded in universal, evidence-based science. On the contrary, people all around the world hold strong but mutually inconsistent sets of beliefs derived from their peer groups: religious beliefs being an obvious case in point. It amazes me that powerful political leaders in the twenty first century can apparently believe a number of things which are flatly contradicted by scientific evidence. They believe them because people they know, like, and trust believe the same things. Social influence also has to be taken into account in the legal definition of sanity. If someone in isolation believes that God is going to destroy the world next Wednesday, she will probably be considered a paranoid schizophrenic with delusions. If someone else believes the same thing because he is a member of a religious sect who has somehow deduced this prediction from their established dogma, then he is likely to be legally sane. If simply believing something without good evidence was marker of insanity, most of the world's population could be regarded as mentally ill!

As much social psychological research shows, norms of our peer groups provide a very strong basis for our beliefs and our behaviours. Most people conform to these norms most of the time. It is more than likely that normative influence is deeply rooted in our old minds. The philosopher Peter Carruthers, for example, argues that people are unique among other animals in having developed a cognitive module for normative behaviour.[21] Other animals have social rules that are enforced by peers, but only humans, claims Carruthers, have internalized control, such as feelings of guilt. If he is right to call this a 'module' (see Chapter 2) then we might expect it to be detachable part of our (old) minds that is absent in some individuals. This does seem to be the case for people known as psychopaths or sociopaths. These terms are misused in popular culture as not all psychopaths are serial killers or even criminals. In fact, psychopathic personality is much more common than is generally realised. Individuals of this type feel no guilt or concern for the feelings of others and tend to be highly manipulative and good liars. They are very disruptive and of little value in building cohesive and supportive social groups. This helps to make Carruthers' argument. In a species whose evolution is so strongly built around social organization, a normative module would be highly adaptive. Individuals who deviate strongly from social norms tend to get ostracized, of course, something which could well have had fatal consequences in the environment of evolutionary adaptation.

Some of the most dramatic demonstrations of social influence concern our tendency to comply with authority. Obedience is very important in certain groups and organizations, an extreme case of which is the military. Soldiers are heavily trained, conditioned perhaps, to obey orders without hesitation. Yet in spite of this, both society and military authorities from time to time hold people to account for doing precisely this. The war crimes trials conducted in Nuremburg after World War 2, principally to prosecute German Nazis, raised a debate about personal responsibilities of soldiers. Should 'I was only following orders' be considered a legal defence for the most heinous of acts? This debate led to important psychological research as we shall see. However, the issue is still very much with us. The contemporary code of the U.S. military states that failure to obey an order by a superior officer is a military crime, subject to military discipline. The code also contains a get-out clause (for the military authorities): the order has to be *lawful*. A soldier, for example, is not required to obey an order to shoot unarmed civilians. The question is whether this puts an unrealistic burden of responsibility on a soldier who may have limited education, have been subjected to several years of a regime in which obedience is habitual, and is operating under stressful conditions in a war zone. The military authorities apparently do not accept this argument as a defence. A recent example is the prosecution of several junior U.S. soldiers, following the revelations of prisoner abuse in the Abu Ghraib jail in Iraq, which came to light in 2004.

In fact, we have known for many years that the compulsion to obey authority is strongly ingrained in us, even under much less severe circumstances than that faced by soldiers operating in war zones. Would you imagine that you could inflict great pain on another person and put them at risk of death, just because someone told you to do so? Not someone with a gun at your head, but simply a professor in a psychological experiment? Most people think not, unless they have read of the experiments of Stanley Milgram, arguably the most famous in the whole history of psychology.[22] Milgram's studies were inspired by the prosecution of leading Nazis for war crimes in the Nuremburg trials and the research was specifically designed to test the credibility of the defence to such charges of 'just following orders'. Milgram was Jewish and partly motivated by a desire to understand the Holocaust.[23]

The basic experiment involved an experimenter, a real participant—the teacher—and a stooge participant (an actor) who played the part of the learner.

The learner was learning word-associates and was to be given an electric shock by the teacher every time he made a mistake. The shock level started at 45 volts but was increased with each mistake. The scale was marked with warnings about dangerous and eventually potentially lethal shock levels. The learner would cry out in pain, and as the shock levels increased, would bang on the walls, plead to be released and complain of a heart condition. In spite of this most participants continued to increase shock levels to 300 volts or more. (No actual shock was administered.) Typically, the teachers, the real subjects of the experiment, protested strongly, but were told constantly that the experiment required them to continue and that the experimenter would take the responsibility. The original experiments were run on male subjects, but later females were tested as well. Although they showed more distress, the compliance levels among women were just as high.

It is impossible to run modern replications of these experiments because of the strict ethical controls that are now in place. The procedure was extremely stressful for the participants and could potentially cause them long-term emotional damage. However, there are many less dramatic ways of showing that people will carry out actions against their conscience and will when confronted with strong authority. Milgram's experiments shocked the world when they were published and cast doubt on the validity of war crimes trials. They showed that ordinary people, not conditioned to obedience, not operating under warfare conditions, will nevertheless carry out appalling actions simply because an authority figure tells them to do so.

The implications for the two minds hypothesis are fairly clear. First, it is evidence of the illusion that we, conscious persons, are in control of our behaviour, acting according to our explicit beliefs and values. Most people, if asked, do not think that they would give high levels of shock in the experiment, but most people, in fact, would. We are actually much more subject to social pressures, such as peer-group conformity and obedience to authority that we believe ourselves to be. Second, it shows that we can become aware of two minds conflict, as I illustrate with some other examples in Chapter 8. Participants in Milgram's experiments did not *want* to administer the shocks but they felt compelled to do so. They were very much aware of the conflict and very stressed as a result.

Social identity, in-groups, and out-groups

A major factor in social influence is *social identity*. A person's social identity is given to them by virtue of the groups to which they belong. In fact, all of us have multiple social identifies. For example, I am, among other things, a psychologist, a man, a golfer, a father, a musician, a Brit, a sports fan (generally), and an Arsenal fan (particularly). Our various group memberships define *who we are* from a social point of view.[24] Some of these identities seem very central and important. I have noticed, for example, that when we are discussing applicants for positions in my department, colleagues get uncomfortable if the candidate has a foreign name that provides no clue to their gender. Of course, we are not sex prejudiced (or so we think) but somehow we just need to know this aspect of someone's identity. On the other hand, I could know someone for a long time and never think to ask what religious beliefs they may or may not hold. Not so if you grow up in Northern Island. I am told by friends who have that you absolutely have to know whether someone is a Catholic or a Protestant. No matter if they are a Jew: they must be either a Catholic Jew or a Protestant Jew.

Occupation must be one such core identity, because when strangers meet, the question 'What do you do?' seldom takes long to surface. And of course, gender, ethnicity, and religion are core social identities. Whether or not they are salient in the everyday context may depend on whether you live surrounded by the in-group or not. For example, if you are white, middle class, and vaguely Christian and most other people you meet on a daily basis are the same, the importance of these identities may not be apparent. Members of minority cultures, however, such as Arab-Israelis or female surgeons may experience the consequences of being in someone else's out-group on a daily basis. Social behaviour may also be influenced by reference groups, ones that we do not yet belong to, but aspire to do so.

Group membership affects not just the way we behave but the way we *think*. A classic finding is that we think of members of our in-groups are individuals who vary considerably in their social traits and behaviour, but those of out-groups as much more similar to one another: *we* are individuals, but *they* are all the same. You might think that this makes sense for major stereotypes, such as racial prejudice. When you label a member of an out-group as stupid or violent, for example, you are somehow assuming that they are all the same. But social psychologists have shown that this is a much more subtle effect that applies to in-groups and out-groups within otherwise essentially similar populations. For example, you would hardly expect a Princeton undergraduate to think that his colleagues would behave differently from those in a rival (similar) university, would you? But they do.

In one study, Princeton students watched another student, the target, make three simple decisions on a videotape.[25] For example, the target might be asked to choose to listen to classical or rock music in a (supposed) psychological experiment on auditory perception. Having observed the decision made, they were then asked to estimate the percentage of other Princeton (or Rutgers) students who would make the same decision. Where participants had little expectation of what the decision would be, they were strongly influenced by the group membership in making their estimates. Princeton students thought Rutgers students would make similar decisions to each other, whereas Princeton students would vary a lot more. When the study was run on Rutgers students, the precise opposite trend was observed. In both cases, the in-group was seen as more individualistic than the out-group. Needless to say, both universities recruit students of high cognitive ability and from relatively similar population groups.

These differences in perception of people in in-groups and out-groups are very robust and general. For example, males think that females are more similar to each other than males are and vice versa. The same conclusion applies to natural social groupings of all kinds.[26] As is usual, social psychologists have come up with many different theories to explain why this might be so. The key factor, of course, is the self. We see the world from our own perspective and we, by definition, are members of the in-group. Some theories see the effect as fulfilling a social need, our need for individuality, perhaps, or the need to be able to predict the behaviour of out-groups. Others take a more cognitive orientation: we have more detailed information about in-group members, know more individuals, and have more chance to perceive their variability.

Research on social identity and social influence suggests to me that 'we', conscious persons, are very much the prisoners of the genetic programming in our old, intuitive minds. We do not, in fact, have the freedom to think, believe, and act as we wish, independently of the social and cultural context in which we find ourselves. We have a fundamental tendency to form ourselves into in-groups and out-groups, which provide our social identities, as well as many of our core beliefs, and which shape our attitude and behaviour towards those on the inside and the outside. Sadly, our hard-wired social psychology provides the basis not just for prejudice, but for conflicts, wars, and brutality of various kinds. Historically, propagandists have exploited our intuitive minds by labelling out-groups as evil and inhuman and in no way like us. People may be hated and persecuted for no other reason than that they were born a member of a different racial, religious or ethnic group.

Conclusions

Common-sense psychology holds that while some processes may be unconscious, when it comes to the big decisions, 'we' are in charge. That is, conscious persons who make conscious decisions, in accordance with explicitly held beliefs. Social psychologists used to think this way as well, until research over the past 30 years forced a change of view. In this chapter, I have briefly surveyed a wide range of phenomena that are studied by social psychologists: obedience, conformity, impression formation, stereotypes, persuasion, and attitude change. In each of these domains, we find evidence for the two minds hypothesis. In fact, it is almost impossible to understand many of the research findings unless we entertain the idea that there are dissociations and conflicts between knowledge and intentions that are consciously accessible and those that are not.

In addition to the research discussed here, social psychologists have taken a leading role in considering the question of what forms of thinking can be conscious. They have examined the notion that much behaviour can be controlled automatically without intervention of conscious reflection, argued for the illusion of conscious will, and proposed that we often confabulate or invent explanations for our behaviour. They have even investigated the basis of volitional behaviour in the brain. The role of consciousness in control of our behaviour is a central concern for the two minds hypothesis. The contribution of social psychologists as well as philosophers, cognitive scientists, and neuroscientists to these questions will be discussed in the next chapter.

Notes and references

1 Certainly many evolutionary and social psychologists believe that this is the case (Buss, 2004; Forgas, Williams, and von Hippel, 2003; Cosmides and Tooby, 1992).

2 Hopefully, this situation is changing. In a recent project, the philosopher Keith Frankish and I persuaded social psychologists, cognitive psychologist, philosophers, and anthropologists to come together in a single conference to exchange ideas, followed by an edited volume (Evans and Frankish, 2009) to which scholars of all these disciplines contributed.

3 Stewart et al. (2008).

4 A well-known collection of papers on this topic is edited by Chaiken and Trope (1999). For recent reviews which relate dual process theories in social psychology to those in cognitive psychology see Evans (2008, 2009) and Smith and Collins (2009).

5 See Smith and DeCoster (2000). They also provide a review of a large number of dual-process theories in social psychology, which they attempt to integrate within a single framework.

6 See, for example, Caldwell and Burger (1998); Stewart et al. (2008).

7 See Uleman, Blader, and Todorov (2005).

8 Zelli, Cervone, and Huesman (1996).

9 Lewicki (1986).

10 Schaller and Duncan (2007).

11 For a recent review of research on attitudes and persuasion, see Crano and Prislin (2006), and for a recent collection of chapters Crano and Prislin (2008).

12 Wittenbrink, Judd, and Park (1997).

13 These words were shown briefly on a computer screen, followed by a 'mask', that is a pattern in the same position as the word. Such masks are known to delete any conscious perception of the word.

14 For a recent review, see Nosek, Greenwald, and Banaji (2007). Readers who wish to try the test on themselves can do so at the following website: https://implicit.harvard.edu/implicit/.

15 Bargh (1999).

16 Wilson, Lindsey, and Schooner (2000).

17 Ford (1992).

18 The earliest dual-process theory in social psychology seems to be the 'elaboration likelihood model' or ELM for short (see Petty and Cacioppo, 1981; Petty and Wegener, 1999), which was specifically concerned with deep and shallow processing of communications and the effect this had on their persuasiveness. Closely related is the heuristic-systematic theory of Chaiken and colleagues (Chaiken, 1980; Chen and Chaiken, 1999).

19 The world's most famous golfer (and sportsman) Tiger Woods attracted immense levels of sponsorship income prior to the well-publicized scandal about his private life that broke late in 2009. This shows how powerful this form of advertising can be. Note also that the mass defection of his sponsors subsequent to the scandal shows the importance of the emotional aspect of intuitive processing. Clearly, his prowess as a golfer was unaffected.

20 Stanovich and West (2007, 2008a).

21 See Carruthers (2006).

22 Milgram's experiments were first published in the 1960s, but he ran many variants, which he later summarized in a book (Milgram, 1974). So important was this work that editions of the book remain in print to the present day.

23 For discussion of the history of Milgram's research and personal motivations, as well as the impact of his work on psychology and society, see Benjamin and Simpson (2009).

24 For review and discussion of social identity and the self, see Ellemers et al. (2002).

25 Quattrone and Jones (1980).

26 For a review see Ostrom and Sedikides (1992).

Chapter 7

Consciousness and control

Consciousness is one of the most baffling phenomena in all of science. Each of us is locked into our own little world of private experience, not knowing why we should be us rather than anyone else, or indeed why we should exist at all. For all we know for sure, we might be the only sentient being, surrounded by persuasive robots. Everything we individual people know, believe and feel about the world ultimately comes down to a conscious experience, like a memory, an image or an emotional feeling. Psychologists can, and often do, forget this. We can actually study people behaviourally, neurologically, and *phenomenologically*, that is in terms of their mental experiences. The traditional approach of academic psychology is to study behaviour, at least from the twentieth century onwards. Scientific psychology hence has a similar appearance to physics. While physicists study the behaviour of physical objects and theorize about cause–effect laws to understand and predict their behaviour, psychologists do something similar with human beings (as do sociologists and economists at a higher level of abstraction). This is a science and a useful one. We can learn to predict much about how people will behave in particular situations, especially if we are well informed about their prior learning and motivation.

As shown a number of times in this book, the behavioural approach is now being frequently supplemented by neurological methods. In this sense we can 'look inside people's heads' to see what is happening in their brains while they are thinking or performing some cognitive task. Such studies have yielded a wealth of data, so that we are now becoming ever better informed about which parts of the brain are responsible for which mental functions. We know a lot about where—in the brain—language and speech are controlled, sensations are recorded, perceptions are developed, memories of different kinds are stored and retrieved, emotions recognized and processed, and so on. Everything that makes us *function* as people can be studied through our behaviour and ultimately located within our brains. But the one thing that defines us subjectively as people—our conscious experience—remains frustratingly inaccessible to these methods. In this sense, we cannot look inside people's heads at all.

The phenomenological approach takes people's internal mental states and experiences as the subject for study. Unfortunately, this is very difficult to do in a scientific way. The traditional method, handed down from philosophers, was for the scientists to study their own mental processes via introspection. As noted in Chapter 1, introspectionism never really recovered from the attacks of the behaviourists. Cognitive psychology allows information processing to occur between stimulus and response, while neuroscience studies the corresponding neural activity. But neither of these is the same thing as the flow of mental experiences through consciousness and neither relies on introspection. If we want to study conscious experience, it seems we can only do so indirectly, by asking people to describe these private mental events. But is this part of the enterprise of modern experimental psychology with its emphasis on behavioural measurement?

Try as we may, experimental psychology cannot in fact ignore the concept of consciousness. One of the major fields of study, perception, depends on the assumption that people can report or otherwise signal their mental experiences. Take the basic topic of what are known as perceptual constancies. The brain is highly adept at interpreting the information arriving at our eyes in ways that are useful to us. For example, when you recognize someone's face, it is their identity that is usually important. Their face actually looks very different, in purely visual terms, if it is seen in different light, at a different angle or at varying distances, but we still perceive the same person. When someone walks away from you, the image on your eye shrinks. But when viewed in a natural context, you will see the person remaining the same size but moving away. Only under trick viewing conditions, like an Ames room, will they seem to change size.[1] Similarly, a piece of coal under good lighting may be as bright an object on your retina as piece of white paper in poor lighting, but the former will still appear to be black and the latter white.

In order to study a phenomenon like perceptual constancy, the psychologist needs to know what you are *seeing*. To measure brightness constancy, for example, she may want you to judge the brightness of familiar objects under different lighting conditions. How could you do this? One method, perhaps, might be for you to adjust a patch of grey on a computer screen until it looks equally bright as the object under study. This seems like good scientific experimental psychology. Very precise measurements of apparent brightness can be made by providing the participant with a finely tuned device for adjusting the appearance of the grey patch. But no precision of measurement can remove the underlying introspectionism of the method, here. Although the participant is not giving a verbal description of their inner experience, their knob-turning is effectively an introspective report. We can only make sense of the setting on the basis that they are responding to an instruction to adjust what they are seeing.

What this means is that *phenomenal reports*, whether conveyed by language or by other behaviour, are an inescapable part of experimental psychology. And what this means in turn, is that psychology arguably is not *just* like physics, chemistry, biology, or geology, for all its use of the experimental method. Rocks, for example, do not think or feel things and nor can they be instructed by geologists to report these experiences.[2] Nor can we pretend to be just like geologists studying rocks, in the manner of radical behaviourists, with any real hope of predicting behaviour. As I pointed out in Chapter 1, without knowledge of someone's *personal* intentions or current goals, behaviourism ultimately fails. Habitual behaviour shaped in the old, intuitive mind can and often is overridden by intentional actions in the new and reflective mind, of which the conscious person may be aware. At least some of our behaviour is conscious in some sense. Discovering exactly what that sense is, however, is the main purpose of this chapter.

Some philosophical issues

Philosophy of mind is a discipline more than 2,000 years in age. The problem of what consciousness is and what it does has been a major preoccupation. What was traditionally termed the 'mind–body' problem is now probably better thought of as the 'mind–brain' problem, but no easier to solve. A basic issue is the nature of conscious experiences, which appear to have special subjective qualities, or *qualia* as philosophers call them. These do not appear to be physical in nature. Moreover, they have the remarkable property of being *about* something other than themselves. I may see someone's face, wonder if my cat is happy, or plan what I am going to eat for dinner. Each of these thoughts has an object: the face, the cat, or the dinner. As philosophers have pointed out, no objects in the physical (non-mental) world have this property of aboutness.[3]

What are mental experiences, if not physical objects? Even granted that they are something generated by the brain, they do seem to have a clear physical location, as other objects do. It is not clear that they are limited to the brain, or even the body. For example, suppose someone steps hard on my foot (one hopes) by accident. In neurological terms, what happens is straightforward. Pain (as well as touch) receptors in my foot are stimulated, sending messages via a series of synaptic connections to a relevant area of my brain. The normal result, if I am conscious, will be an experience of pain. The pain would not be felt if I had major nerve damage in my leg so that the signal failed to get through to my brain. So *where* exactly did I feel the pain? In my head? In my brain? Or in my foot?

Speaking for myself, when someone steps on my foot, I feel the pain there, in the foot. I may feel that the reflective part of 'I', the part that knows I am having the pain, feels to be somewhere in my head, but the pain itself is in the foot. Of course, you might think that is ridiculous, I could not *really* feel it in my foot. I really felt it in the brain and if it feels like the foot, this is an illusion that my brain created. But in making this argument, you are already crossing philosophical boundaries, and begging questions about the mind–brain problem. And even if you do *really* feel it in your head, how does that make it any less mysterious? Can a neurosurgeon or neuroscientist look inside your brain and locate this feeling?

The problem gets worse when you think about your visual experience of looking out of a window, say. The scene that you see is perceived again, not as being in your head, but *out there* in the world.[4] Does this mean that your visual consciousness extends outside the body and across the street? While this may sound mystical, some philosophers have argued for such an extended mind[5], while also maintaining the mainstream position (in contemporary philosophy) called materialism (or physicalism). Materialists believe that the mind can ultimately be reduced to an account in terms of the brain. This position is also sometimes described as monism, in contrast with dualism, but the philosophical distinctions do not end there. The term 'dualism' is usually intended to refer to mind–body or *substance dualism*, as famously proposed by Descartes, in which there are two kinds of material in the universe: physical matter and 'mind stuff'. Very few contemporary philosophers and cognitive scientists are dualists in this sense. However, not all are reductionists either. There is a form of non-reductive physicalism called *property dualism*, in which it is maintained that while the mind is a product of the brain, it has properties that cannot be reduced to a description in terms of brain processes. Hence, property dualists argue that subjective conscious experience is not *just* the same thing as brain activity. For example, no alien scientist studying our brain activity could infer the nature of these experiences.[6]

To illustrate why the mind-brain problem is far from trivial, consider the (hypothetical) case of the intelligent robot.[7] It is conceivable that if the disciplines of robotics and cognitive science continue their rapid advances, at some distant point in the future, it will be possible to build a robot that can fully simulate a human being. Such a robot would be capable of performing all the same cognitive functions as us (perception, language processing, memory retrieval, etc.) and would behave in all situations exactly like a person. The question is, would it have consciousness? Would it *feel* anything? If you are a reductive materialist, then you have to say yes, because consciousness is just part of intelligent function. The problem with this is why does the robot *need* to have consciousness? At what point in the development of its intelligence would it arise? All we are doing is building up more and more complex programs for its computer-brain to run. And if the robot must be conscious, is that true of any information processing device? A thermostat, for example? A leading researcher in consciousness studies, Max Velmans, has considered this question in detail. One of his interesting conclusions is that while the robot may or may not have consciousness, there is no way we could ever tell.[8] Of course you could argue this about other people too, what is known as the 'other minds' problem. But if consciousness is in some way biological, it is conceivable that while other people have it, intelligent robots do not. The potential philosophical divisions are endless.

While materialism is the dominant position in contemporary cognitive science, substance or Cartesian dualism was popular in former times. One explanation for this popularity is the religious belief, which certainly influenced Descartes, that we have a soul that survives the death of the body. Another, however, is the compelling intuition of conscious minds as causal agents that is provided by folk psychology. In fact, I contend that the folk (ordinary people) are generally dualists, whether or not they hold religious beliefs.[9] How else could Hollywood market movies based on the premise that a person can wake up inside another person's body, as several successful films have done? But of course there is no generally accepted scientific evidence to support the idea that the mind is really separate from the body. On the contrary, there is a mass of evidence from clinical neuropsychology that people are, in some sense, a direct function of their brains, because when brains are damaged, it changes the person. In addition to impairing functions such as speech, vision, or memory, brain damage can radically alter personalities.

Fascinating though many philosophical issues concerning consciousness are, dwelling on them will not advance the current project very far. I am happy to leave such intractable questions as what consciousness is, how we could have evolved it and whether robots have it for philosophers to debate for another 2,000 years or so. I ask only that the reader accepts that the conscious person is a construction of the brain. What is more relevant to this book is the question of what consciousness *does*. In the two minds theory, consciousness, at least in its *reflective* form, is clearly associated with the new mind. Many authors have linked the stream of consciousness with the contents of working memory and associated concepts such as global workspace in the brain,[10] which is a key feature of the new mind, as discussed in Chapter 3. And dual-process theories in cognitive and social psychology often assign conscious, intentional, and controlled actions to what we are calling the reflective mind, while the workings of the intuitive mind are regarded as unconscious and automatic.

In this chapter, I will use the term 'reflective consciousness' to refer to conscious thinking, which involves active manipulation of information, as opposed to simply feeling or perceiving, which I term phenomenal consciousness. However, as we shall see, this does not mean that all the processing within the reflective mind is conscious, and certainly not that it can be accurately introspected upon. In fact, there are great difficulties in describing consciousness as though it had some causal role in our thinking. Is reading this book, for example, a conscious process? You might say yes, because you made a conscious decision to read it, can only do so while conscious and are conscious of what it is saying. Ok, but first of all the conscious decision you made to read the book may mean only that you were conscious *of* making the decision. We are often unaware of the reasons for decisions that seem conscious. And as to the process of reading the book being conscious, what exactly does this mean? You are certainly not conscious of the low level processing in the brain that allows that marks on the page to be interpreted as letters, words, and extracted meaning. In fact, by the time you become conscious of the meaning of my words, all relevant cognitive processing has been completed. The same has to be true of any 'conscious' cognitive act.[11]

In neurological terms, we have known for some years that conscious experiences lag behind the underlying events in the brain. For example, some famous studies by Libet[12] have shown that conscious experience may be delayed by up to half a second beyond the sensory stimulation. Moreover, Libet has shown that the experience is referred back in time to the point where the stimulus actually reached the sensory areas of the brain. What this means in practice is that 'conscious' intentional control of fast actions is purely illusory. For example, tennis players who return a fast service often report that they saw the direction of the serve and intentionally played the return to a particular area of the court. In fact, the timing is such that the action of returning serve must have been initiated, (via the dorsal visual system) *prior* to the perception of the service registering any conscious experience at all. If the action is 'intentional' then the intention itself must be *preconscious*.

While Libet's findings have been available for some years, more recently it has been shown that brain activity can anticipate much slower processes such as apparently free choice decision making. In one ingenious study,[13] participants are asked to make a free choice at any time to press a key with either left or right index finger. A sequence of random letters is displayed on the screen, one at a time, and the participant is asked to indicate which was present when they made their decision to press a key. This gives the timing of the 'free choice' in the person's consciousness. The researchers were able to show that the anticipatory brain activity for the left or right hand response was present up to 10 seconds in advance of this. Even with the time lag of the fMRI trace, the researchers often knew themselves seven seconds before the participant what decision they were going to make. So much for the idea that free will is exercised by the conscious person. Why do we feel, then, as though we have conscious control of our actions? I deal with this question later in the chapter.

Thinking and feeling: two forms of consciousness

The majority of dual-process theories in psychology appeal to the distinction between conscious and unconscious processing. In Chapter 1, however, I cautioned against the use of this distinction in defining the two minds hypothesis. I suggested instead that *both* minds have aspects that are conscious and unconscious. With the benefit of the material reviewed in Chapters 2–6, it is time to expand further on this idea. In Chapter 2, I reviewed the evidence from anthropology, archaeology, evolutionary psychology, and neuroscience to support the idea that the intuitive mind is in essence an *old* mind. Its neurological and psychological foundations date back to earlier animals, as well as apes and hominids, from which we evolved. Some forms of perception and learning represented in the human brain, for example, are to be found also in fish, birds, and reptiles. The same is true of basic emotions. The reflective mind, by contrast, is associated with the evolution of speech and language, as well as the massively developed frontal regions of our brains, which evolved so recently and distinctively in modern humans.

Consider this paragraph:

> Martha is very attached to Henry. When Henry comes home, Martha usually rushes out to greet him. She appears jealous when he tries to work at home, often distracting him and seeking his attention.

Let us take it that Henry is a grown man. Who is Martha? She might be his young daughter, but she might equally be a pet dog. The passage describes emotions and consequent behaviours. If Martha is a four-year-old girl, we will assume that she has conscious experiences of these emotions: she loves her father, she is happy when he comes in, she feels jealous and neglected when he ignores her. If Martha is a dog, is there any reason to revise any of this? I cannot see any. The behaviour is the same and doubtless physiological measurement would provide similar indicators of the emotional state. Moreover, we and dogs at some distant point had a common ancestor in evolution, so why should not the old mind of the human share some of the characteristics of the dog's mind, including what it *feels*. Suppose, however, I modify the passage as follows:

> Martha is very attached to Henry. When Henry comes home, Martha usually rushes out to greet him. She appears jealous when he tries to work at home, but understands that his work is important and tries not to distract him.

Now we know that this is a person and not an animal that is being described. The emotional response is the same, but Martha can *reflect* on it, understand the situation and inhibit the behaviour that the emotion demands. It is true that a dog can be trained to inhibit unwanted behaviours, such as begging at the table, but only by the use of old-mind learning systems. What it cannot do is mentally represent the situation, reflect upon it, and understand it. Both child and animal have sensory perception; both can see and recognize Henry, and each can feel and respond to emotions. So unless we want to deny any form of consciousness to animals, we need to say that they possess, in common with the old, intuitive human mind, what is known as *phenomenal* consciousness. At the very least, this is comprised of sensory experiences and emotional feelings. What human beings seem to have in addition is *reflective* consciousness, the ability to think as well as feel. We are not born with this: it emerges with the development of language. But again, who would want to deny the reality of emotional experience in infants?

In earlier chapters, I have made a good deal of use of the terms *implicit* and *explicit* in allocating systems and functions to the two minds. Do these terms not suggest unconscious and conscious respectively? Not necessarily so. Explicit knowledge is accessible to the reflective mind and hence what is often termed reflective consciousness. It can be articulated and described in language. Implicit systems can, however, register at the level of phenomenal consciousness. Consider, for example, the nature of implicit stereotypes revealed by the research of social psychologists. Such stereotypes are, by their nature, not available for conscious reflection, so in a sense we do not 'know' that we possess them. However, they can certainly impact on phenomenal consciousness. For example, a young white person with no consciously accessible beliefs of race prejudice may still have an implicit stereotype of black people that includes the idea of them being dangerous or violent. Such a person approaching a group of black men on a lonely street may then experience a feeling of fear disproportionate to what would be experienced were the men white. This experience is certainly conscious, if baffling and disconcerting to the politically correct new mind that reflects upon it.

I have argued that there are two kinds of learning: memory and judgement. We acquire implicit and explicit knowledge by different means and access the former when we make intuitive judgements and the latter when we make reasoned decisions. But again, intuitive decisions are not *unconscious* decisions; they are rather based on feeling instead of reflection. When we 'go with our gut', we choose to do what *feels* right. Psychologists often describe people as 'cognitive misers', meaning that they will not expend more cognitive resources than are necessary.[14] Reflective thought is a slow, cognitively expensive, and tiring process. Intuition and feeling are fast and easy bases for a decision. But such decisions are not wholly unconscious, because they are based on at least some feeling of knowing or rightness, if not stronger emotions. And of course, we have to be conscious, in the sense of awake and alert, to be able to do anything at all other than sleep, breathe, and metabolize. So the mere presence of conscious experience is not a decider between old and new mind.

Emotions are a product of the old mind, at least those known as the *basic* emotions: pleasure (or happiness), anger, fear, disgust, and sadness.[15] These are known to be mediated directly by subcortical brain areas, including the limbic system, which are evolutionarily old. The organs here exist or have direct correspondences with those to be found in the brains of fish, birds, and reptiles as well as other mammals. Such emotions have clear adaptive value and have played a major role in the evolution of animal species, as Darwin recognized, devoting a book to the topic.[16] Complex emotions such as ambition, pride, and compassion are only possible in humans who also possess a reflective mind; however, they are still characterized by *feelings* linked to these basic emotions. Such feelings are part of our phenomenal consciousness, which we (arguably) share with both preverbal children and other animals, together with other sensory experiences, such as those generated by vision and hearing. In fact, all phenomenal consciousness can be regarded as sensation: in the case of emotion, the sensations are generated internally by bodily processes. It is reasonable to regard phenomenal consciousness as primary and human reflective consciousness as secondary. Hence, some authors directly link emotion with the evolution of consciousness.[17] Of course, this does not make the associated qualia any less mysterious.

Emotions and motivational states are the essential tools of the selfish genes that control our behaviour for their own ends. All emotions have valence: they are positive or negative. In accordance with what Freud called the pleasure principle, we seek pleasure and avoid pain and other forms of displeasure. Most mothers strongly love their babies and protect and nurture them at all costs, with direct benefit to the genes. Sexual love and lust can, and often do, override rational reasoning and good sense delivered by the reflective mind, to the obvious benefit of the genes, and sometimes at catastrophic cost to the individual. Organisms need to survive and must learn to avoid what is dangerous, hence the basic and powerful emotion of fear, including all the forms of anxiety that humans can manufacture. We know from many studies that an old organ in the brain, the *amygdala*, is involved in both emotional learning, such as fear conditioning, and emotional processing, such as correctly identifying someone's emotional state from their facial expressions. Hence, there is a direct link between emotional processing and social cognition.

Perceiving other people's emotions is a basic part of our folk psychology whose survival value was discussed in Chapter 2.

If the idea of the old mind as unconscious is deeply flawed, so too is the description of the new mind as conscious. Consider the case of the explicit memory discussed in Chapter 3. Explicit memories are not what we are conscious of right now, but what can *potentially* be brought to mind and reflected upon. In fact, our stores of explicit knowledge vastly exceed our capacity for apprehension at a given time. These memory systems must be part of the reflective mind, in a two minds story. But in themselves, they operate unconsciously and automatically. For example, one form of explicit memory we have is for words: we know many thousands in our native language and can call these to mind and reflect upon their meaning and usage. The psychologist Don Norman famously posed the question: is MANTINESS a word?[18] Of course not, you say at once. By why of course and why at once? How do you know that it is not a word with such confidence and speed? There is no obvious cue from the letters. The letter patterns of MANTINESS are common in English and the string of letters is easy to pronounce. So did you search through all the thousands of words you know and check them one by one? Well no. So how did you do it? The fact is that you, the conscious person, have no idea at all.

As we think reflectively to solve problems and make decisions, our thinking is all the time *contextualized* with relevant knowledge and belief. For example, suppose my wife suggests to me that we take a last minute holiday in France. In considering this, a number of pieces of explicit knowledge will come to my mind. Perhaps it is springtime, and I recall that our previous holiday in France at this time of year was ruined by poor weather. However, I also recall that this holiday was in the north of France, whereas my wife is suggesting a location in the south, where I know the climate is more reliable. Other knowledge comes to mind: the pound is currently weak against the euro, so the holiday will be expensive. This again may be countermanded by recalling that I had a recent windfall of unexpected cash. The point here is twofold. First, such reflective decision making is aided by relevant knowledge supplied rapidly and effortlessly to working memory. Second, the process by which these explicit memories are retrieved from our vast store of such knowledge is completely unknown to the conscious person. Just how the brain is able to select such *relevant* knowledge with such ease is also a great mystery in cognitive science.

So while the intuitive mind is not wholly unconscious; it has emotions and other feelings that are conscious so the reflective mind is not wholly (or even mostly) conscious either. It relies upon fast and automatic access to (relevant) bits of (vast amounts of) explicit knowledge. But the points raised earlier apply also. I suggested that we can only really become conscious of any mental act, such as reading and understanding a passage of text, when all relevant information processing has *already occurred* in the brain. But surely we can make decisions that we, conscious persons, are in control of? It certainly feels that way, but the psychological evidence suggests otherwise. First, the feeling that we do things because we consciously intend to do them has been shown to be a powerful illusion. Second, we can and do confabulate explanations for our own behaviour, giving ourselves and others false introspective reports of the reasons for our actions. On the face of it, these findings pose a challenge for the two minds hypothesis, as some psychologists have moved so far from folk psychology as to propose that *everything* is done automatically. I will first consider the issues, starting with the problem of conscious will, and then try to untangle the complex web of issues they weave for the two minds hypothesis.

The illusion of conscious intention

Please perform the current action while reading this book: raise your left arm in the air, clench and unclench your fist. Never mind why, just do it! Ok, if you complied with my instruction, how exactly did you do it? What you will feel happened is something like this. You decided to comply with my instructions and so *willed* your left arm to raise and make a fist. If you did not comply, you probably felt that you consciously decided not to obey me. You *willed* yourself to resist, and to keep your arm in place. This concept of conscious willing is deeply ingrained in our folk psychology. But things are not as they seem. The experience of willing is a *consequence* of our intentional actions and not a cause. The contrary view is a compelling but false belief created by our brains.

The psychologist Daniel Wegner has devoted an entire (and very readable) book to this topic, entitled *The Illusion of Conscious Will*.[19] He points out that voluntary actions are normally accompanied by an experience of willing, a feeling that we caused the action by some internal mental force. Such feelings are part of our phenomenal consciousness and reinforce our folk psychological belief in ourselves as conscious agents. But this feeling must be an illusion. I have already pointed out one reason: the conscious experience of intentional actions and decisions may lag well behind the action itself. Thus our feeling that a conscious intention preceded the action must be illusory. Under some circumstances, this feeling of willing can be detached from actions that are normally regarded as voluntary. For example, patients with brain damage may have a rogue hand with a 'mind of its own' that appears to do things that the patient neither intends nor wants to do. Under hypnosis, or post-hypnotic suggestion, people will similarly do things which appear to them quite involuntary. The converse situation can also arise in which people have an *illusion of control*, believing they are controlling something which they are not. This can occur in gambling, for example, where a succession of winning throws of the dice creates the illusion that the gambler is controlling random events.

Illusion of control is closely linked with superstition. Superstition is the false belief that our actions have causal relevance when they do not. Professional sportsmen seem to be very superstitious and often develop rituals in preparations for events, such as Tiger Woods' famous predilection for wearing a red shirt in the final round of a golf tournament. In fact, superstitious *behaviour* is a product of the old mind, as the behaviourist B. F. Skinner demonstrated many years ago. If pigeon is given frequent reinforcements (delivery of food pellets) unrelated to its behaviour, it will nevertheless be subject to 'operant conditioning': learning to repeat what has been rewarded. Hence, behaviours it just happened to be performing when the food first arrived, e.g. turning its neck, will be repeated. Because the rewards keep coming, this behaviour becomes *superstitiously* conditioned. To demonstrate the effect in humans you can use a simple computer task in which, say, you ask people to control the presence of a blue flash on the screen by pressing a key. In fact, the flash occurs on 75% of trials at random. The participant will press the key frequently, often accompanied by the flash. Unlike the pigeons, we can ask them whether they feel in control of the flashes. People generally report experiencing a large degree of control, even though they have none at all.[20] This effect is just as strong when people are warned that there may be no connection between their behaviour and the event, either prior to performing the task or prior to rating their degree of control.[21] So the effect appears to be combination of old mind conditioning together with new mind confabulation.

The notion of free will is strongly featured in folk psychology. We say things like 'I didn't mean to say that—it just slipped out.' It is not always easy to tell if the actions of someone else are intentional or not, but as good folk psychologists we do our best to figure it out. So we say 'She doesn't know what she is saying, she is so upset' or 'he doesn't mean to be rude, but he is so thoughtless' and so on. Free will is also assumed by the criminal justice systems used in Europe, the United States, and many other parts of the world. In order to be convicted of a criminal offence, the defendant has to be considered to be responsible for their actions. Legal defences based on lack of responsibility might include being too young to understand the consequences of what you are doing, temporary insanity, or being hypnotized or drugged without your knowledge. However, *voluntary* use of alcohol and drugs is no defence, even if they change your behaviour. And while we might accept *weakness of will* as a reasonable explanation of a friend's inability to quit smoking or lose weight, the law will not accept it as a defence to impulsive shoplifting, let alone more serious offences.

Folk psychology and the law strongly endorse what I called, in Chapter 1, the chief executive model of the mind. While certain behaviour may be accepted as automatic and not requiring conscious acts of will, say an experienced driver changing gears, there is nevertheless a conscious person inside the brain who is *in charge*, and responsible for whatever behaviour is observed. This person has free will, because if they acted in a way that was illegal, or otherwise meet with social disapproval, they could have chosen to do otherwise. Thus if they transgress norms, society has the right to punish them. As the social psychologist John Bargh has observed, psychological research has strongly undermined the basis for this folk belief in free will.[22] First, many of our actions can be shown to be controlled unconsciously and 'automatically', far more than was suspected even 20 years ago. Second, actions which appear to everyone, including the participant, to be under voluntary control can be determined by the circumstances in which people find themselves.

If people had free will, it is hard to see how we could do experimental psychology. The experimental method is this: we compare behaviour under two conditions, which vary in only one respect. For example, we randomly allocate people to two groups, and give them all a communication intended to change their attitude to drink-driving. One group get statistical evidence, the other a graphic description of particular incident where drink-driving led to a fatality. Research like this generally shows that while statistical evidence has more predictive value, people are more impressed by graphic descriptions, the so-called 'vividness' effect. So the second group will show more of the desired attitude change against drink-driving. Because there was no other difference between the two groups, we conclude that vivid communications *cause* attitude change more than statistical ones. If a person was in the first group and unimpressed, it is likely that had they been assigned to the second group, they would have been more impressed. Note that this happens in spite of the fact that people are *reflecting* upon the communication given. So reflective cognition is predictable from known causes. The person did not choose to change their attitude, it was the vivid nature of the material that did it for them. Experimental manipulations are just as effective in causing the behaviour of 'controlled' as 'automatic' thinking, so in what sense does the former enjoy free will to determine itself?[23] Experimental psychologists still rely on folk psychology, however, when it comes to obtaining ethical clearance for their studies. Great emphasis is placed on the use of volunteer participants who have given informed consent to the procedures.

I am not going to enter here into philosophical debate about whether there are ever circumstances under which an individual can be said to be exercising free will. However, a little reflection will show why the feeling that we do things because we intend to do them must be an illusion. Take the case of a group of friends having a conversation. Is each person's contribution to be considered an intentional, voluntary action? It would seem so, but what exactly does this mean. Do I, the conscious person, intend to say what I say before I say it? How can I, when what I say just comes straight out of my mouth, in response to what my friend just said? Of course, on occasions we may rehearse what we intend to say, using inner speech, as when preparing for a job interview. But as intentional actions, these inner speech events have exactly the same problem. How do we know what they are to will them in advance? Our intention to speak cannot reflect the content of what we say, unless every rehearsal is itself rehearsed in an impossible infinite cycle. The best we could say really is that our speech acts reflect our general goals, such as to be polite, impress a visitor, or to communicate some information. And even then, a skilled experimental psychologist could demonstrate that a number of these goals were not in the conscious awareness of the speaker.

To understand why we believe in conscious will, consider first a simpler illusion: that of perceived causes. Generally, the brain will perceive a causal link between two events when they co-occur in space and time.[24] The causal event must happen just prior to the caused one. Illusory causation is exploited in cartoon animations and in video games. A simple example of the latter is the 'bat and ball' games that appeared on the earliest PCs. The bats consisted of short vertical lines on either edge of the screen, which could be moved up and down via controls accessible to two opponents. The ball moved across the screen and could be intercepted by a bat, which would reflect it back into play. The ball would also appear to bounce off the floor and ceiling represented by horizontal lines. Of course, the ball was not actually moving: it was just a sequence of pixels being alternately switched on and off to create an apparent motion across the screen. Nor can the 'bats' possibly strike the ball and influence its movement. But because the ball deflects immediately after impact with the 'bat', 'ceiling' etc, it is perceived as being a causal event. (Sound effects may be used to enhance the illusion.) The complex and realistic graphics of contemporary games still require this basic illusion for them to work. In the same way, experienced computer users feel as though there is some direct and simple link between the movement of the mouse and the pointer on the screen.[25]

Wegner suggests that the illusion of conscious will is produced in a similar way. When the brain generates 'intentional' actions, these (normally) result in conscious thoughts of intention at the same time. The association leads to a feeling of causation. Let us analyse this a bit more deeply. When the events are external, like the video bat and ball, their perception is available in phenomenal consciousness, or whatever state of sensation such consciousness corresponds to in the brain. However, as with emotions, internal events in the form of 'feelings' may also be placed into phenomenal consciousness. All such events are then accessible to the brain for further processing, with or without reflective consciousness.[26] We may reflect on events which are both internal sensations and external perceptions in reasoning about the world and constructing our beliefs. In this case, the assignment of cause (intentional feeling) and effect (action) probably reflects a built-in mechanism; the tendency to see the world in terms of causal relations appears to be 'hard-wired' into the brain.[27] In any case, it seems that the repeated co-occurrence of intentions and actions is sufficient to generate a belief of a causal link, such that it appears that our conscious thoughts *caused* an action. But in reality, they did not.

The reader might think I am arguing *against* the two minds hypothesis here. Does the hypothesis not include the idea that while some cognitive acts are automatic, others are volitional and controlled? Yes, it does. I am merely trying to distinguish between volitional cognition and the conscious experience of willing something. We know that cognition can be volitional, because people can follow instructions and do things they would otherwise not do. Just as well, or we could not run any psychological experiments on them. We also know that people can have goals and intentions that are explicit and reportable. As discussed in Chapter 1, there is also much research on so-called *executive processes*, which are known to be associated with frontal lobe activity, and hence the new mind. So yes, in some sense, the reflective mind does perform intentional acts. But this does not mean that there is a conscious person in charge of our behaviour, nor that the conscious beliefs we form and hold about ourselves and our actions are necessarily correct. The evidence suggests instead that the reflective mind posts a feeling of willing into phenomenal consciousness *as a result of* carrying out an intentional act, which is often but not necessarily an indication of the actual intention.

I admit all this seems very strange when first encountered. If not the conscious person, then exactly who or what is in control of 'controlled' cognition? The answer is more a what than a who. First, *everything* we do from breathing to deciding to marry someone is somehow controlled by the brain. Second, barring mysticism, the conscious person itself *must* be a construction of the brain. What else could it be? I and others believe it to be an internal narrative closely linked to folk psychology. But just as folk psychology does not need to be an accurate scientific psychology to serve its purpose, neither does the story of our lives as told by the reflective mind need to represent the actual way in which the brain allocates resources and makes decisions. In fact, the evidence suggests that this story is substantially fictitious. I turn to this next.

Self-knowledge and confabulation

Psychological treatments of consciousness have focussed mostly on two aspects. One is the notion of conscious, volitional control; the second is the notion of *access*. Unconscious mental processes are, by definition, inaccessible to the conscious person. A number of scientific psychologists have, however, gone along with the folk psychological belief that there are also conscious mental processes that are both controllable and accessible, that is reportable by the person. The evidence that they are wrong on both counts has been amassing over the past 30 years or so, much of it in the field of social psychology.

There is a large opinion polling industry that relies for its existence on folk psychology. In the case of political polls, pollsters ask two different kinds of questions designed to obtain intentions and reasons, respectively. The former question is usually 'for whom do you intend to vote in the forthcoming election?' People can answer this question with reasonable accuracy. Such opinion polls have quite a good record of forecasting election results, provided that the contest is not really close and that there are no 'late swings' of opinion. Is this evidence for folk psychology: does it mean that people can indeed report conscious intentions? Actually, no. What it shows is that people can often *predict* their own behaviour. We can do this because we (that is, our brains) formulate *theories* of what we do, which are accessible to the reflective mind. Because we have many opportunities to observe our own behaviour, these theories are often (but by no means necessarily) accurate. For example, if we have always voted for a particular political party, it is likely that we will do so again. If our friends are all talking about a particular candidate, we may decide that likely we will vote for her as well, because we normally do what our friends do. And so on. As the reader will by now appreciate, the fact that we *feel* we exercising free will and expressing conscious intentions is no evidence that we are doing so.

The other type of question that pollsters ask is much more problematic. They stretch folk psychology beyond its competence when they ask us to explain the *reasons* for our political preference. For example, they may present us with a list of political issues and ask us to rate the extent to which each is influencing our voting preference. Such polling has no scientific value because people cannot answer such questions with any accuracy. To paraphrase the title of a famous psychological paper[28] on this topic, we are asking people to tell us more than they can know. How can a multimillion dollar industry like opinion polling rely on such false testimony? That it does so is testament to the power of folk psychology. The companies, newspapers, and political parties that commission such polls are all convinced by their intuition that people know the reasons for their actions and can report them. That science shows the opposite to be true does not seem to have penetrated far into the everyday world.

The issue here is that of introspective access. Along with the issue of conscious will and conscious control comes a belief that we have access to the working of our minds. Because we, conscious persons, are in charge and calling the shots, so we, conscious persons, are evidently aware of how and why we do things. In fact, we have no such self-knowledge, as I realized very early in my career in a paper published in 1975.[29] In Chapter 5, I described a reasoning problem known as the Wason selection task. In the basic, abstract form of the problem, as I described earlier, participants are strongly influenced by a 'matching bias'. That is to say, they tend to select cards that are explicitly mentioned in the statement. If they are testing the rule, 'if there is an A on one side of the card then there is a 3 on the other side', people usually choose A and 3, which is wrong. If instead they are given the rule, 'if there is an A on one side of the card then there is NOT a 3 on the other side' they still choose A and 3, which is now right. The question that Peter Wason and I asked in this collaborative work was 'Do people know that their choices are influenced by matching bias?' The answer was an unequivocal 'no'. When asked to give reasons for their choices, no participant *ever* said that they chose a card because it was explicitly mentioned in the rule. Similarly, people never report belief bias, overconfidence, hindsight bias, or any other cognitive bias as a reason for their actions. If asked, they give an explanation which seems plausible given their choices and the instructions of the task. They are not lying, but they are confabulating.

There are many similar findings in the psychological literature.[30] One famous one is where participants were asked to choose between four identical pairs of nylon stockings laid out in a left to right order. Candidates showed a marked preference for the pair on the right of the display. But when asked to explain the reasons for their choice, no one mentioned the position in the display, the actual causal factor in the decision. What experiments like these show is that people do not have access to the causes of their choices. However, this does not prevent them from answering the question put to them by the experimenters. Instead of saying 'I have no idea' people give you a plausible explanation, which is in fact an invention of the reflective mind. Thus folk psychology is reinforced. If it is a professional opinion poll, the pollsters will always have reasons and explanations from the folk to report back to their clients.

There are many different studies of self-insight or self-knowledge to be found in the psychological literature, all yielding similar conclusions.[31] You might think that experts, at least, would know the basis of their decision making. You would be wrong. For example, most people are overconfident in their judgments: experts too. So because you know more, it does not mean that you know more about what you know. And experts are no better at explicating the reasons for their decisions than anyone else. Some years ago, I supervised studies of general practioners to find out how they decide to prescribe medication for individual patients, in a computer-simulated task.[32] For each imaginary patient, we gave them quite a long list of relevant medical evidence. Doctors typically told us that they made use of 7–8 pieces of information in drawing their decisions. Statistical analysis of their choices showed that they only actually used about 2–4 of these. Moreover, they were equally confident that they had made use of each piece of information, whether they had or not.

An expert is someone who knows a lot. Expertise can be implicit, in the intuitive mind, or explicit in the reflective mind. Normally, experts have a combination of both. But there are no experts in *self*-knowledge. What makes the problem so difficult is that while people do not know the causes of their behaviour, they *think* they do. Of course, sometimes people do give the correct explanation of their actions and this has been the cause of some confusion for dual-process theorists including, in the past, myself. The difficulty is this. We know that people often confabulate reasons for their actions, and these confabulations must be a property of the reflective mind. But we do not want to say that this is *all* the reflective mind does, as it would hardly have had enough reason to evolve. There must be genuine volitional cognition. In writing an earlier work on dual processes, my colleague David Over and I were clearly struggling with this problem when we said '…we do not regard explicit thinking as simply serving to rationalize behaviour, and believe that decisions and actions can result from explicit processes.'[33] We were implying here, in common with other authors, that while one function of the reflective mind is to confabulate, another is to take true volitional actions. I now think this is a false disjunction.

My current view is similar to that of the philosopher Peter Carruthers, who has laid out his argument very elegantly in a recent scientific paper.[34] Carruthers is a keen advocate of the idea that folk psychology reflects the evolution of a cognitive module for 'mindreading'. We routinely interpret other people's behaviour using the concepts of folk psychology: we attribute to them mental states such as feelings, beliefs, and motives to explain and predict their behaviour. Carruthers argues, supported by much psychological evidence,[35] that we turn this mindreading facility on ourselves. In other words, we theorize about our own minds, in the same way that we do about other people's. Much of the data is common; we can observe our own behaviour and the situation in which we find ourselves. But there are two important differences in this process of self-interpretation. First, we are quite expert about our own behaviour, because we get to see so much of it. Second, we have access to the sensations in our phenomenal consciousness. For example, if we have an emotional experience, say anxiety in particular situations, we know this first hand. With another person, we might need to be sensitive to subtle cues to notice their anxiety.

What these two added factors mean is that our theories of our own behaviour will tend to be more accurate than those we hold about others. Of course, we often get it wrong as well, as psychologists keep showing. But when we say that someone is rationalizing or confabulating, all we mean is that they are getting it wrong *on this occasion*. What we should not be suggesting is that on other occasions people have true access to their mental processes. They do not: they simply have a good theory. To put it another way, *all* introspection is self-interpretation, whether accurate or not. This is what Over and I got wrong in the above quote. Actions can be volitional and goal-driven without the person necessarily being aware of the actual reasons for these actions. Hence, we must not confuse intentional action with self-insight.

Let me try to put all this together. First, there *is* such a thing as voluntary, intentional, or volitional cognition. We (organisms) can, and do, adopt goals within the reflective mind, which may successfully compete with and override habitual behaviours in our intuitive minds. This is core to the two minds hypothesis. However, this does not happen in the way that folk psychology would have us believe. 'We' are not conscious persons in control of our behaviour and the reflective mind does not equal a conscious mind. The conscious person is a construction of the brain, an illusory narrative that accompanies us through life. In a phenomenological sense, it is 'us', but in no sense is it an accurate record of either mind. Intentional, voluntary actions originate in the brain some time before any conscious experience of intention is registered. You can make an argument for free will, if you want, but only if it is *preconscious*. The explicit beliefs that we form about ourselves, that we can call to mind and reflect upon, are no different in principle from those we form of other people. We (conscious persons) have no access whatever to the processes that underlie our actions. We only have access to the theories which our mindreading module has helped us to construct.

This all may seem very scary, if you are encountering it for the first time. I have been living with this knowledge for a long time now and it is not really a problem for me. As a scientist, I think and write these things because the evidence for them is overwhelming. As a person, I live in the world of folk psychology just like everyone else. I don't go around thinking, 'I didn't really decide that, my brain did.' In any case, it is a false distinction. There is no 'I' that is separate from my brain. As an individual, I do make decisions. The fact that my consciousness gets to learn about them some time later and with invented reasons is really neither here nor there!

Neural correlates of reflective consciousness: dispelling the zombie

As I mentioned in the previous chapter, social psychology has progressively moved away from a folk psychological approach. Many dual-process theories have been developed in this field, but so too has the evidence for 'automaticity', limited self-insight, and confabulation. This has led some social psychologists towards a position that the social neuroscientist, Matt Lieberman, describes as the 'psychological zombie' hypothesis.[36] A zombie, in these terms, is a person in whom consciousness is an irrelevance that can safely be ignored.[37] If everything is automatic, the zombie can manage quite well without (reflective) consciousness. For those who have made the full journey it looks like this:

Folk psychology	$\rightarrow$	Dual-process theory	$\rightarrow$	Automaticity
(one mind)		(two minds)		(one mind)

In other words, what was a one mind story (folk psychology, reflective) became a two mind story, and then at the other end, a one mind story again (now automatic, unreflective).[38] Of course, I agree with Lieberman that we are not zombies, or I would not be writing this book.[39] I would prefer not to talk, as he does, as though reflective consciousness itself was the cause of our behaviour. I would rather say that neurological *correlates* of reflective consciousness are what actually underlie our deliberative judgements. In fact, I would prefer not to define the two minds hypothesis in terms of consciousness at all. Nevertheless, the evidence that Lieberman gives for his case is helpful, and I will describe it shortly.

The zombie version of the one-mind theory is as inadequate as the folk psychology version. In many ways, it is folk psychology in reverse. Folk psychology puts conscious awareness, intention and control together in one package. Zombie theory throws them all out in one package. Because, as we have seen, conscious will is an illusion and reported intentions are confabulations, some authors draw the conclusion that there cannot be any such thing as volition, or intentional behaviour. But as I pointed out just now, we don't have to throw out the baby with the bathwater. We can have controlled as well as automatic cognition; in fact we *must* have, if we look at the evidence. We just should not confuse it with the folk psychological theory of the conscious mind.

As a brief reminder, the evidence that I presented for the two minds hypothesis in Chapters 3–6 was based on experimental studies of learning, decision making, reasoning, and social cognition. The evidence for the reflective mind does not depend in any way upon introspectionism or the folk concept of consciousness. Let me remind the reader briefly of some of that evidence. There are distinct implicit and explicit systems for learning and remembering, a conclusion strongly backed by experimental and neuropsychological evidence. When people rely on fast, intuitive processes for reasoning and decision making, they often fall prey to cognitive biases. When they engage in reflective thinking, these biases can often be overcome. This is more likely to happen if participants are of high intelligence, are allowed more time, or are given instructions that encourage careful reflection. Intuitive processes tend to dominate when people are given little time or required to occupy working memory with another task. Similarly, in the field of social psychology, there is much evidence that systematic, effortful processing in the reflective mind can produce different behaviour and different beliefs than reliance on fast, automatic processes in the intuitive mind.

Lieberman himself adopts a dual-process position, arguing for a distinction between reflexive (old mind) and reflective (new mind) cognition. He has developed a theory of the neurological systems that underlie this distinction in social cognition, although it seems to me to work just as well beyond the social domain. He distinguishes between the X system (refleXive) and the C system (refleCtive), each comprised of a number of identified brain regions[40] (see Table 7.1). Without going through the function of each region in detail, we can note that in general X system areas are older in evolutionary terms than C system areas. Already mentioned in this book are the basal ganglia, involved in conditioning and implicit learning, and the amygdala, which is involved in emotional learning and processing. Unsurprisingly, the C system includes a number of parts of the prefrontal cortex, as well as the medial temporal lobe, which includes the hippocampus, the key organ in forming explicit memories (see Chapter 3).

The regions which Lieberman lists are essentially those already known to be involved in implicit and explicit social cognition. In itself, this is no evidence for their being *systems*. The critical evidence that they are such is the same as that which Lieberman offers against the zombie hypothesis. The argument goes like this. C system areas are already known to be associated with reflective

Table 7.1 Lieberman's (2007b) assignment of brain areas to the X (reflexive) and C (reflective) systems

X system	C system
Orbitofrontal cortex (OFC)	Lateral PFC
Basal ganglia	Medial temporal lobe
Amygdala	Posterior parietal cortex (PPC)
Lateral temporal cortex (LTC)	Rostral ACC
Dorsal ACC	Medial PFC
	Dorsomedial PFC

PFC, prefrontal cortex; ACC, anterior cingulated cortex.

consciousness while X systems areas are not. Hence, activation of these regions provides the necessary neural correlates of (reflective) consciousness. The question now is whether this kind of consciousness *does* anything; whether it has a causal role in our cognition. According to Lieberman, the finding which can show we are *not* zombies is this: when activity is high in the X system it should be low in the C system and vice versa. In other words, when we are observing 'automatic' social cognition, the X system should be dominant, but when we are looking at reflective, controlled cognition, the C system should dominate.

The method to test this is simple in principle even if quite technical in practice. As a result of much experimental research, dual-process theories can stipulate cases where responding is automatic (intuitive, type 1) or controlled (reflective, type 2). Learning may occur implicitly or explicitly, attitudes can change with or without reflection, emotional processing can be done reflectively or automatically and so on. Sometimes one or the other mode of processing can be induced by appropriate instructions or by other manipulations. Sometimes it can be inferred from the response people make: as when they may go with either belief or logic when reasoning with belief-laden materials (Chapter 5). What Lieberman and his colleagues do is to examine tasks like these while simultaneously imaging brain activity using an fMRI scanner. They have now collected an impressive range of evidence to support the two systems theory. In general, C system regions are relatively active when people are processing tasks reflectively and the X system regions dominate when responding is non-reflective. In some cases, activation of one system leads to inhibition of activity in the other.

If we were zombies with non-functional consciousness, what would we expect to find in terms of brain activity? One possibility is that we become conscious when neural activity passes a certain threshold. For example, if we reflect on someone's emotions then activity in the brain area responsible for this function would increase compared with automatic processing. But according to Lieberman this is *not* what happens: instead activity switches to a different part of the brain. An alternative zombie hypothesis might be that a set of 'consciousness neurones' lights up when we have a conscious experience but actually do nothing. In this case, the region doing the work in automatic mode should still be active during reflective mode, as it is the real controller for this activity. But this is not what happens either. The two modes of cognition do appear to correspond with activation of distinct areas of the brain.

I do not wish to place undue emphasis on neuroscience in building the case for the two minds hypothesis. The brain is enormously complex and the methods of neuroscientists provide a range of methodological challenges. There is currently a huge amount of research using these methods and it will take time for a clear understanding of what it all means to emerge. However, the evidence so far is very encouraging. We cannot divide the brain in half— left-right, up-down or front-back—and say that half is the old mind, and that the new. It is nowhere near as simple as that. But the two minds distinction that has emerged from 30 years of research on dual process theories is now being consistently supported by studies of brain function. There are different regions of the brain corresponding with implicit and explicit memory, with emotion and reasoning and with reflective and non-reflective modes of cognition. In general, regions associated with intuitive cognition are older than those associated with reflective cognition, as the hypothesis requires. Lieberman's research programme, although at a relatively early stage, is particularly promising.

Conclusions

The problem of consciousness, particularly qualia, may seem intractable. However, the current project does not require us to wrestle with the deep philosophical questions. One of my main concerns has been to show that we should not think of the two minds as conscious and unconscious, even though a number of dual-process theories in psychology have attached these labels. Rather it appears that the two minds correspond to two different forms of consciousness. Phenomenal consciousness, that of sensations and feeling, is the product of the old mind, although its output is also accessible to the new mind. Reflective consciousness is distinctively human, requiring language and meta-representation, and an indicator of new mind activity.

Psychological treatments of consciousness have focused on two aspects: access and intentionality. Many assume, in line with folk psychology, that we both have access to conscious mental processes and are in intentional control of them. Hence, the popular use of the contrastive term 'automatic' to describe unconscious processes. But this is wrong too. There is no ghost in the machine, no person with a magical force called consciousness that can resume control from the automatic pilot. We are aware of our experiences and the fleeting contents of our working memories, but we are not aware of either the old or new mind processes responsible for posting these sensations. Nor are we, conscious persons, in control of what we do. The feeling that we are willing or controlling our actions is an illusion: everything that we experience is a result of prior brain activity, which has already initiated our 'conscious decisions'. We, conscious persons, are a construction of our brains. There really is nothing else that we could be.

The wrong conclusion to draw from this possibly depressing argument is that there is only one mind after all because everything is really automatic. In a sense everything really *is* automatic, in that there is no conscious controller. But the evidence still supports the case for two minds, even though both work through unconscious processes and each delivers a form of conscious experience. First, there is the evolutionary evidence that humans retain an animal-like form of cognition with the addition of distinctively human aspects. Then there is the considerable body of evidence for dual processing in learning, reasoning, decision making, and social cognition that I considered in Chapters 3–6. Finally, the neuroscience is in support as well. The cognitive activity that gives rise to reflective consciousness is neurologically distinct from that which does not. Reflective consciousness is experienced when we process explicit information though a limited and singular working memory system. Its presence is an indicator that the new mind is engaged on a task, no more and no less.

At this point, I shall assume that the case for the two minds has been made. What remains is to reflect upon how it is possible for human beings to operate as rational agents in a complex world with not one but two distinct systems available for organizing our cognition and action. Will they not come into conflict? Yes, sometimes they do. Will they not, in general, have to cooperate in a successful manner to enable individuals to live their lives, achieving many of their goals? Yes, they will. I turn to these issues in my final chapter.

Notes and references

1 The Ames room is designed to appear like a regular shaped room when it is not. By a trick of lighting and perspective, a wall may appear to run across the back of a rectangular room, when it is actually receding into the distance on an angle. Under these conditions, a person walking along the wall will indeed appear to shrink.

2 An apparent objection to this argument is that introspective reports are just pieces of verbal behaviour whose meaning cannot be taken at face value. Dennett (1991) coined the term heterophenomenology, as opposed to Cartesian phenomenology, to emphasize that introspections are not authoritative can be confabulatory as described late in this chapter. I agree that people can only describe the way things feel to them and not the workings of their brains. However, there are no means to access the conscious experiences of other people other than by their direct or indirect descriptions of them.

3 Traditionally, philosophers refer to this property of consciousness as 'intentionality'. I avoid the term here due to its easy confusion with the everyday use of this term. When I refer later to intentional acts, I use the term in the familiar sense of wilful or purposeful. Other mental states such as beliefs, desires, and intentions also have this property of aboutness, whether conscious or not. Although man-made objects can also have aboutness, e.g. a can opener is about a can, many philosophers argue that this is derived intentionality, and that only minds can have original intentionality.

4 There are a number of ways that visual images can be experienced. If we call to mind the face of someone we know, the visual experience of this feels to be 'in the head'. A vivid image experienced while falling asleep or waking up, however, may be seen as out in the world, even though we generally know it is not real. Schizophrenics or those under the influence of hallucinogenic drugs may see images that seem to be *really* out there.

5 See Clark and Chalmers (1998).

6 For a detailed argument for this position see Velmans (2000). Most cognitive scientists, however, are reductionists. My sympathy with property dualism will be evident in places in this chapter. For example, a reductionist would not refer, as I do, to the 'neural correlates' of consciousness. However, it makes little difference for the purposes of the two minds theory which position one adopts on this issue.

7 Thought experiments about robots are popular in philosophy and cognitive science. Recently, a whole book was devoted to the question of whether robots could or should have emotions (Fellous and Arbib, 2005). Related to this is the idea of a zombie: a molecular copy of a human being without consciousness. According to some philosophers, it creates problems for materialism if you can even *imagine* that a zombie could exist (Chalmers, 1996).

8 Velmans (2000) provides an excellent review of philosophical, neuroscientific, and psychological studies of consciousness and some very interesting analysis of the problems faced in this field.

9 Empirical evidence exists to support my intuition on this. See Stanovich (1989).

10 See Baars (1997) and Baddeley (2007).

11 See Velmans, Chapter 9.

12 Review by Libet (1996).

13 Soon et al. (2008).

14 See for example, Stanovich (2009c) who deals at length with the issue of why intelligent people can still make poor decisions.

15 This is a typical list, although there is some variation between authors in describing basic (or primary) as opposed to complex (secondary) emotions. For example, Izard (2009) divides basic positive emotions into interest and joy.

16 Darwin (1872).

17 See Izard (2009) for a discussion of this and a review of contemporary psychological research on emotion.

18 Norman (1969).

19 Wegner (2002).

20 This effect is observed under two conditions: (a) when acting to achieve reward, which actually occurs frequently or (b) when acting to avoid an unpleasant event, which actually happens rarely. In both cases, however, the events occur randomly without relation to the action.

21 Matute et al. (2007).

22 Bargh has written extensively on this topic. For good examples see Bargh (2005; Bargh and Ferguson, 2000).

23 See Bargh and Ferguson (2000) for a detailed presentation of this argument. In practice, there is always a lot of variability in behaviour within the best designed

experiment. So we never claim that our experimental manipulations are the sole cause of the behaviour we observe. In this sense, behaviour is never shown to be completely determined by external influences.

24 First demonstrated in a classical work by Michotte (1962).

25 Strictly speaking there is a direct causal link between mouse and pointer, albeit dependent upon complex hardware and software arrangements in the computer. My point is that the user experiences a much more direct connection between the two. Other aspects of modern computer interface exploit our facility for causal learning in the same way. For example, when we click on an icon, it appears to depress, suggesting that we have physically pushed a button. When the software fails to respond, users are likely to click the mouse button harder to get it to work!

26 Some authors, like Carruthers (2006), argue that the contents of phenomenal consciousness are subject to 'global broadcasting' throughout the brain. In this way, any specialized cognitive module that has a relevant contribution to make can respond to the input. Conceivably, there is a built-in module for causal induction that generates causal beliefs from contiguous events.

27 For a convincing argument that causal relations are pervasive in the mental models we form of the world, see Sloman (2005).

28 Nisbett and Wilson (1977).

29 Wason and Evans (1975); see also Evans and Wason (1976); Lucas and Ball (2005).

30 Described by Nisbett and Wilson (1977).

31 See Wilson (2002) for an engaging review and discussion of many such studies.

32 Evans, Harries, and Dean (1995; see also Harries, Evans, Dennis, and Dean, 1996; Harries, Evans, and Dennis, 2000).

33 Evans and Over (1996, p.160).

34 Carruthers (2009).

35 Wilson (2002).

36 Lieberman (2009).

37 This should not be confused with the philosophical zombie problem. The solution that Lieberman offers would not help the philosophers.

38 This is something of a simplification. However, the trend towards ever greater emphasis on automatic control of social behaviour is evident in a number of the chapters in the volume recently by Bargh (2006).

39 I mean to say the psychological zombie hypothesis is not compatible with the ideas of this book. Whether a zombie could write this or any other book is another question altogether!

40 For detailed description of these systems and their function, see Lieberman (2007b). For a wider review of social neuroscience, see Lieberman (2007a).

Chapter 8

The two minds in action: conflict and co-operation

Human beings are in some ways like other animals, but in others very different. In common with other mammals, we mate, reproduce, nurture, and protect our young, while gathering food and other resources needed to sustain life. Also like other animals, we are motivated by basic biological drives like hunger, thirst, and sexual desire. We are a socially organized species, but so are others, like chimpanzees, lions, and killer whales. In all of these basics, the old mind within us has a major role to play. It is the central claim of this book, however, that the ways in which we differ from other animals could not have been achieved simply by fine tuning and extending this old mind. With the distinctively human evolution of language and 'mind-reading' came the basis for the new, reflective mind. This is what enables us to be scientists and engineers, creators of literature and drama, designers of complex economic and social systems, and many other things, which no other species on earth comes remotely close to achieving. It is a greatly improbable feat of evolution, but it happened nonetheless, because here we are.

On the surface, human beings function most of the time as though we had a single mind in that we (mostly) live fairly orderly lives in which much of our behaviour is consistent with our personal goals and ambitions. Most adults of my acquaintance manage to earn their living by spending the requisite time engaged in appropriate activity at work, while also pursuing various hobbies, sustaining personal relationships, and keeping their finances in balance. Of course, this is not always the case—people may get fired, dumped by their partner, or find themselves in large amounts of debt. We are not invariably rational in achieving our goals. But the point is that most people who are sane, and of reasonably normal mental capacity can function quite well in the modern world. We achieve most of our goals, most of the time.

This observation creates a challenge for the two minds hypothesis. If we have two distinct minds of a very different nature, as argued in this book, then how come we (mostly) function as though we were of one mind? Why are we not constantly in turmoil and conflict as our two minds conflict and compete?

My answer to this is twofold. Our two minds often *do* conflict, but thanks to our powers of confabulation and self-deception, discussed in the previous chapter, we are largely unaware that this is happening. I will discuss some cases in this chapter where two minds conflict is so severe that we cannot rationalize it away. Second, since the new mind evolved with the old already in place, it was essential that the two would largely co-operate to produce effective behaviour. From a Darwinian perspective, the new mind simply could not have evolved in such a way as to disrupt behaviour and put us at a competitive disadvantage. In fact, the reverse must be true. Nevertheless, it behoves an advocate of the two minds theory to offer some explanation of how this happens in practice. I will do my best to supply such an account in due course.

Before we look in detail at how the two minds conflict and co-operate, it is necessary to understand what each mind is *trying to do*. This means we have to consider the topic of rationality. I suggest there are two forms of rationality, one practised by the old, intuitive mind and the other by the new, reflective mind. By understanding the difference between these, we shall be able to see how it is that the two minds normally co-operate but sometimes conflict with each other. The two minds pursue somewhat different goals by very different mechanisms. So let us start out by considering what it means to be rational.

Two kinds of rationality

Definitions of rationality in Western culture tend to favour the new mind. There is a long tradition in philosophy and literature of contrasting the terms *rational* and *emotional*. This tradition goes back to Aristotle and other Greek philosophers who regarded the mind as pure and the body as impure. In this mind–body dualism, the sensations and emotions were regarded as bodily functions. In this way of thinking, logical reasoning and reflection are what sets humans apart and denote their superior rationality. In popular culture, this idea was personified by Mr Spock, of the original Star Trek TV series. Spock, being a Vulcan, lacked human emotions but had superior reasoning ability. Both of these attributes were part of his assumed greater rationality, or 'logicality' as it was termed in the programme. As a counterpoint to this, his commander, Captain Kirk, was portrayed as a 'gut feeling' man, whose decision making was often guided by his rather transparent emotions. On many occasions, of course, Kirk's human intuitions were seen to triumph over Spock's Vulcan logicality. In the later series, *Star Trek: The Next Generation*, Lieutenant Data, an emotionless robot, played a similar role.

The equation of rationality with reasoning is also prevalent in much psychological writing on dual-process theories. One major author, Seymour Epstein, describes the two systems (equivalent to intuitive and reflective minds) as *experiential* and *rational*, respectively.[1] This terminology suggests that learning from experience does not make us rational, only reasoning does that. Other authors, including Stanovich,[2] have put great emphasis on the ability of people to find correct solutions to problems in logic and probability that can only be achieved by reasoning. If rationality is to be defined in this way, it has much in common with general intelligence, for it is people high in IQ who at excel at this kind of reasoning.

The corollary that emotions are somehow *irrational* seems to be expressed in some intuitive understanding of two minds conflict that is reflected in such everyday expressions as 'the heart rules the head.' Perhaps the popular belief is that emotions somehow muddle thinking and cloud judgement. But we are in two minds about this (!) as evidenced by our attitude to *love*. Few people in Western culture approve of marriages arranged for convenience or profit, as we still think love is the best motive. Romantic love features strongly in drama and novels, and provides a traditional basis for a happy ending. Even the heroines of Jane Austen's novels, who were required by circumstances to make 'good' marriages, that is, ones that brought financial security, were also required (by literary convention) to be mutually in love with their husbands by the end of the work.

Contrary to popular belief, I suggest that there can be no rationality *without* emotion. Carefully examined, the claimed rationality of Vulcan Spock and robot Data makes no sense. Both characters, for example, showed *ambition* in achieving senior officer status, a complex emotion. They were also motivated to save lives. But if we had no emotion, why would we care if we, or anyone else, lived or died? Data, in some episodes, is even portrayed paradoxically as *wanting* to have emotions. Both from an evolutionary and an individual perspective, rationality is 'instrumental': we are rational when we act in such a way as to achieve our goals. This idea underlies decision theory, discussed in Chapter 4, where it is assumed that people are (or should be) trying to maximize gains and minimize losses from their own point of view. Goals are always about achieving what we *want*, and avoiding what we do not want. And what we want is pleasure, happiness, and positive mood, while what we do not want is displeasure and unhappiness.

A confusion may occur here between rationality of purpose and rationality of process. Instrumental rationality is rationality of purpose: achieving your goals. However, in order to achieve goals, we must behave in appropriate ways. Sometimes the process may be very simple, as when we eat the food in front of us to satisfy hunger. The process of achieving other goals may be very complex indeed. Consider, for example, what was involved in achieving the goal, set in the 1960s, of landing a human on the moon. Simple human goals can be achieved, like animal goals, by following instinct and habits, but more complex goals can stretch the powers of the reflective mind to the limit. From an evolutionary point of view, both old and new minds must achieve instrumental rationality, or they could not have evolved. But there are very important differences between the two.

Old mind rationality

To understand old mind rationality, it is helpful to consider the behaviour of mammals, excluding apes and humans. Such animals may appear to have individual or personality rationality, that is, to behave in such a way as to achieve pleasure and avoid displeasure for themselves. As thousands of laboratory experiments in the behaviourist era of psychology showed, rats, pigeons, and other animals will learn to adapt their behaviour to the environments in which they are placed. If pressing a lever brings the reward of food pellets, they will soon learn to do it. If the reward is switched off, they will stop. Similarly, animals will learn to avoid pain, such as electric shocks, by doing what is required. It is a little more complicated than that, as I will point out later, but essentially their behaviour is *instrumentally* conditioned to reward and punishment.

The rationality we observe in animals, however, is not really personal. Animals behave the way they do because they were programmed by their genes to do so. And their genes, of course, were *selfish* in so doing. It is the genes that determine what is pleasurable and what is painful. The genes require that the individual survive long enough to reproduce and nurture the next generation, so that the genes can replicate themselves in another vehicle. For this reason, and only this reason, the genes motivate the individual to nurture itself by eating and to protect itself by avoiding pain. The genes decide what is pleasurable and unpleasurable for the individual. They also provided animals (not just mammals but much earlier ancestors) with a general mechanism for learning from experience. All else being equal, they (and we) learn to do what brings pleasure and not do what brings pain.

In the case of non-human animals, provision of basic emotions, drives, and habit learning is not always sufficient for the genes to replicate. So many animals are also pre-programmed by the genes with fixed, instinctive behaviour patterns. Examples would include the way in which the mother mammal will bite through the umbilical cord and eat the afterbirth, as well as both mother and offspring knowing (without learning) how to engage in the essential suckling of the young. As observed in Chapter 2, the evolutionary strategies of genes are ultimately not at all mindful of the welfare of the individual animal. Suffering and early death may be the fate of many who have served the genes' purposes. But animals obey their instincts because they can do no other. Their brains are computers following programs written by their genes. In so far as the old mind in humans shares the same history, its rationality too is primarily that of the genes and the not the individual.[3]

Old mind rationality is instrumental in a particular way that makes it distinctive from new mind rationality, discussed below. It is entirely driven by *past experience*. It is rational to repeat behaviour that was rewarded in the past, and to avoid that which was punished. When instincts override this habit learning system, as they often do in non-human animals, then the same applies in the lifetime of the species, rather than the individual. Instincts evolved because they embody behaviours that helped the genes reproduce *in the past*. This has some very clear implications and severe limitations. Individual animals behave as they do because they *must*, given their experiential learning and instinctive programming. They are not free to vary their behaviour for any other reason. If they encounter hazards that were not present in their environment of evolutionary adaptation, the results are often disastrous. For example, few animals have any protection against the hazard of fast moving vehicles on human-built roads. They may even have counterproductive evolutionary strategies, such as running in a zig-zag pattern before a moving car: a behaviour designed to confuse the pursuit of a predator, heavier, and less manoeuvrable than themselves. And unlike a child with language, a cat or dog cannot be at all easily taught to avoid such hazards.

Animal behaviour, armed only with old-mind rationality, is inevitably vulnerable when environments changes. Polar bears, for example, are endangered by global warming because they are programmed to hunt for food in an environment that is disappearing. They cannot revert to their brown bear days and go hunting in the woods, because the change is too rapid for natural selection to cope with. While selfish genes crave immortality, none may ultimately achieve it. The vehicles they create can only, by the mechanism of natural selection, be adapted to past environments. That is in the nature of the process, as is its relatively slow development of new adaptations. Species die out and new ones are created. The same will probably apply to the human species but it appears that our reflective minds confer some unique advantages. First, we can and do design and adapt environments to suit our needs. Second, we can anticipate and plan for the future. This suggests that the new mind has a different kind of rationality.

New mind rationality

In *The Robot's Rebellion*,[4] Keith Stanovich argues eloquently that there is a division between genetic and individual rationality: both are instrumental, but the ownership of the goals differs. He asks us to consider that both genes and individuals have goals, some in common but others in conflict. He argues, as I have above, that the goals which the old mind seeks to fulfil are predominantly those provided by the genes, and that old mind rationality is thus essentially genetic rationality. However, in the new mind, we often pursue goals that serve us as individuals but do not serve our genes. This seems undeniable. For example, we crave long, healthy, and happy lives which, if achieved, serve no benefit to our genes. They need us only to live long enough to reproduce and raise the next generation so that they can do the same. The genes gave us sexual desire and pleasure, but when we pursue this as an end in itself, using contraception, we clearly obstruct the underlying genetic rationality. The genes gave us hunger and the desire to gather and consume food. But they did not give us the desire to eat in gourmet restaurants, sipping a classic wine.

Human behaviour seems infinitely more complex than that required by genetic rationality. How does it serve the purpose of the genes, for example, that we developed mathematics, science, and engineering? There is, perhaps, a basic emotion of curiosity, which creates complex motivations in the new mind, underlying our desire to understand the world, the universe, and our own history. But the genes did not give us curiosity for this reason. It must have had some basic survival value, like making sure that our nomadic forebears explored new and possibly better environments. Other human achievements, such as the motor car, television, and the Internet similarly serve no obvious genetic purpose. All of these things make us humans very different indeed from any other species on the planet. And of course, none of them would be possible without the reflective mind.

As I said in Chapter 2, we know that the uniquely human developments of language, meta-representation, and large forebrains were all *necessary* to create the reflective mind. We do not understand the evolutionary pressures that caused these developments. The reflective mind itself is probably an accidental product of evolution to quite a degree, and a dubious one from the viewpoint of the selfish gene. Stanovich suggests, in effect, that the genes blundered by giving us 'long-leash' cognition, the ability to think for ourselves. The idea in *The Robot's Rebellion* is that whereas the reflective mind may initially have had some benefit to the genes, in allowing us to think flexibly and solve problems in novel and unforeseeable environments, it also enabled us to rebel. We can and do pursue our own goals, and not just those of our genes. My purpose here is to explore the consequences of the fact that the new, reflective mind did, by whatever means, become exclusively developed in our species.

New mind rationality, like that of the old mind, is instrumental. But it differs in two very important ways. One is in the kinds of goal that it pursues and the other is in the mental resources that it directs to this end. The new mind is mostly motivated by complex, not simple emotions. The goals it seeks are set in the future, sometimes a long way in the future. Long-term plans are the preserve of the new mind. When a student gets out of bed early on a cold winter morning to attend a lecture, she may be motivated by an ambition to get a good degree in two years' time to become a professional lawyer in five years' time to achieve success, status, and material comfort in 10–20 years' time, and even a comfortable pension and retirement 40 years hence. (She may even enjoy learning for its own sake!) The reflective mind can also pursue much shorter term goals. Cooking a good dinner, for example, may require our detailed attention right now this minute, at a critical stage of the process.

Long-term goals and complex emotions seem to have an essential basic ingredient of old mind emotion and motivation, much elaborated and refined by new mind knowledge and reflection. But it is not just the motivation that is different, but the mechanism for its achievement. Unlike old mind rationality, which is driven by the past, new mind rationality is driven by the *future*. It is safer to anticipate the future than simply rely on the past but old, intuitive, animal-like minds do not do this because they *cannot*. The new mind, by contrast, can imagine possibilities, make suppositions, and simulate future events. It does this by using its special resources—explicit knowledge, working memory, meta-representation, and the ability to engage in novel thinking and reasoning. But because the new mind seeks to achieve goals in a different way, it can also come into conflict with the old mind. By forming plans and pursuing long-term goals, the new mind is often required to suppress short-term desires and established habits formed in the old mind. But the intuitive mind can also assert itself, frustrating new mind rationality, as I will show later.

The potential power of new mind rationality is enormous and gives us a huge advantage over other species. Other animals have little warning when their environment changes and little ability to adapt rapidly to it when it does. In the dangerous period of the late twentieth century known as the 'cold war', there was great political tension and conflict between the powers of East and West, each of which possessed a nuclear arsenal powerful enough to destroy the planet many times over. The catastrophe of nuclear warfare was, of course, only possible in the first place because of the intelligence in the reflective mind that enabled the atomic science and technology required to build such horrendous weapons. But the disaster of nuclear warfare that has (so far) been avoided was also only possible because of new mind rationality. The only actual use of nuclear weapons in history was against an enemy unable to reply in kind. While government leaders and military commanders have throughout history used the strongest weapons available against their enemies, so far this has not happened between two nuclear powers. This can only be due to our ability to imagine the future and reflect on the consequences of our actions.

This is not to say, of course, that new mind rationality generally triumphs. It is very much an issue at present as to whether the human species will successfully avoid the disastrous consequences of climate change. We seem at least to have passed the lengthy period of global warming denial that held up world co-operation, as people continued to be motivated by past reinforcement of traditional industrial and economic practice, rather than by anticipation of the future consequences of continuing in their familiar ways. But like nuclear warfare, global warming is not something we can learn to avoid by experience. In the worst scenarios, few members of the human race may survive to learn anything. It is important, then, to study what happens when the two minds come into conflict and how that conflict may be resolved.

The two minds in conflict

How can we have two minds without being aware of the fact? The answer to this lies in the issues I discussed in the previous chapter. First, folk psychology evolved not because it is a correct account of the workings of our brains, but because it enabled us to understand and predict the behaviour of others to a useful degree. It is a simple, one mind theory.[5] Second, the conscious person is a construction of the brain and a narrative of interpretation in which folk psychology is turned inwards to account for our own behaviour. So well is the story told that most of the time we are unaware of the operation of the old mind. Even when the goals of the old mind trump those of the new, as they frequently do, the new mind quickly supplies a rational theoretical explanation.

Since the two minds are trying to do different things in different ways, it is inevitable that they will sometimes conflict. The conflict can be so extreme that everyone becomes aware of it. I consider two examples below. First, I consider why people gamble at all, and how they can become pathologically addicted. Second, I discuss some anxiety disorders that typify two minds conflict and show how the most effective treatment of these conditions is a two minds therapy.

Normal and pathological gambling

From evidence discussed earlier in the book (Chapters 4 and 5), it appears quite clear that nature did not equip the old mind with reliable intuitions about probability, chance, and randomness. Random events are perceived as non-random and vice versa. And when we rely on intuition to solve laboratory problems involving probabilities, we can make serious mistakes, resulting in such biases as the base rate and conjunction fallacies, discussed in earlier chapters. This may help, to some extent, to explain to answer the curious problem of gambling. Why is it so popular? Research indicates that around 80% of those in Western culture indulge in gambling to some extent, a significant minority of whom gamble quite regularly. A much smaller, but still relatively large proportion of the population, around 1–2%, develop into *pathological* gamblers, for whom gambling appears to be an addiction and a compulsion.[6] Curiously, the bulk of this gambling is on games of chance, such as lotteries, fruit machines, and roulette, where the gambler is guaranteed long-term losses. Even where an element of skill is perceived to exist, as in betting on the outcome of horse races and other sporting events, this is largely illusory. Almost everyone who gambles does so in the face of persistent financial loss. And yet participation in state lotteries is enormously popular, and many millions of visitors fly into Las Vegas alone every year[7] to try their luck in games of chance on offer at the casinos.

Normal gambling, let alone pathological gambling, is hard enough to understand. First, you do not need to be a mathematical genius to understand that the odds are rigged against you. If a fruit machine pays out 80%, then you are going to lose around 20% of what you stake over a run of bets. Similarly, most roulette players surely know the wheel is designed to yield a healthy profit for the house. But if the reflective mind cannot figure it out in advance, surely the intuitive mind should do so, given some experiential learning? Not so, it seems. Many people persist in gambling in spite of regular losses. Why? First, this is definitely another case of the old mind overriding the new. But why should it encourage us to gamble away our money? Learning theorists have proposed some answers. First of all, when people gamble they receive intermittent reward. Learning theorists have known for a long time that 'partial reinforcement' leads to very stubborn habits. If a pigeon gets a food pellet every time it pecks a key it keeps pecking. If the reward is turned off, it soon stops. If instead it gets a reward now and then, at random intervals, which is later turned off, it keeps on pecking for a long time. Behaviours thus learnt under 'partial reinforcement' are very hard to extinguish.[8] But as learning theorists point out, there are also other rewards for the gambler, such as the excitement involved in following and cheering on a horse that is riding with your money. It also helps you to acquire the habit if rewards are frequent and delivered quickly. This makes Internet gambling, a huge growth industry, particularly addictive. So in a sense it is rather similar to a physical addiction like smoking cigarettes. The reasons for starting to smoke, drink, or gamble are typically social: a desire to do what friends and colleagues do. But once people start, they find it is habit-forming and self-sustaining.

From an evolutionary perspective, there is no reason to think we should be born with good explicit theories of chance and probability for our reflective minds to access. However, like other animals, we should be good at learning from probabilistic or 'noisy' environments, and we might expect this facility to be present in our old, intuitive minds. Not much in the actual world is deterministic. Suppose that certain species of tall trees, which can be seen from a distance, are often (but not always) found next to small bushes with edible berries. If the probability of food is high enough, then it is worth the foraging animal's while making the trip to investigate. It would not be adaptive in the real world to require 100% reward in order to learn an association. So we may well have some built-in procedures in our old minds for learning from noisy environments. However, the world in which we evolved would not have the special properties of casino games. In particular, studies show that people have great difficulty understanding that casino wheels have no memory. They have a compelling intuition that previous outcomes on the casino wheel influence future ones.

So it seems likely that persistent gambling is due to inappropriate application of old mind learning procedures that evolved for a different purpose: a case of old mind irrationality. However, gambling also involves a lot of *new* mind irrationality. A lot of roulette players, for example, bet using systems that are designed to beat the odds. They cannot. They are all based on the fallacy that additional bets can compensate for previous losses, whereas every individual bet has an expected loss.[9] Gamblers also believe in luck, that they can have a lucky streak or be 'on a roll'. However, luck can only be judged after the event; luckiness is not a state that you can be in. Some gamblers believe that they can exercise skill in games of chance by influencing or predicting future outcomes of random processes. And of course, many false beliefs incorporate the gambler's fallacy, that somehow the history of previous outcomes can influence the future.

A common view in the academic literature is that these kinds of false beliefs drive the gambling habit. However, an alternative view is that the reflective mind is confabulating reasons to justify the behaviour driven by the intuitive mind. There are many psychological experiments that show just this kind of process, some of which have been mentioned in this book. Justifying gambling behaviour in this manner is similar to the way in which an alcoholic might argue that they are a 'social drinker', or the manner in which people work around phobias, discussed below. For example, a person who has a fear of flying may not like to admit it to themselves or others. They might take on a long and expensive train journey, not apparently because they want to avoid flying, but because it is the best way to see the country. In the same way, someone who is socially anxious might find that they are always too busy with work to attend a friend's party. But as we shall see below, anxiety disorders can become pathological so that is apparent to the individual and those around them that their behaviour is out of control. The same applies to gambling.

Pathological gambling is a serious problem, which is nowadays regarded as a compulsive disorder. Interestingly, it has a close link to a personality trait called *impulsivity*, which is the tendency that some individuals have to act spontaneously, without prior thought or self-control.[10] It is also linked to a personality disorder known as attention-deficit hyperactive disorder (ADHD), in which impulse control is severely lacking. In terms of the two minds hypothesis, the implication is quite clear. Compulsive gamblers are people whose intuitive minds tend to dominate their behaviour, without effective control being exerted by the reflective mind.[11] Pathological gamblers are more prone to hold delusional beliefs about chance and probability and there is some evidence that cognitive therapy, aimed at undermining these false beliefs, can be effective in treating the condition.

I have chosen gambling as an example because it is a purely psychological or behavioural form of addiction, thus more starkly demonstrating a two minds conflict. Of course, addiction to alcohol and other drugs, as well as other behavioural addictions (e.g. to video games) create similar problems and issues for the individual. Any of these compulsive behaviours severely disrupt the lives of the individual and their families, hence frustrating the goals held in the reflective mind. It commonly occurs that an individual *wants* (in their reflective mind) to quit smoking, drinking, gambling, excess eating, or whatever, but finds that they cannot do so, at least not without help. When the impulses and emotions of the old mind are strong enough, they will take control.

Phobias and their treatment

Fear is one of the basic emotions that we share with other animals. The old mind provides not only this emotion but an operant learning system that enables us to learn to avoid unpleasant and dangerous situations. While basic, this is quite a clever adaptive system. Suppose we and other animals were just programmed to avoid pain. Hence, if we touched something hot, we would withdraw our hand quickly. But pain avoidance in itself will not stop an organism from repeating a dangerous action. The solution the genes came up with to protect their vehicles was *fear*. When something bad happens, fear is conditioned to the situation and felt when it recurs. The fear has to be aversive in its own right. So when an animal encounters a situation it has learnt to fear, it runs away, thus avoiding the potential danger. However, learning by punishment is more problematic than learning by reward. In particular, it can be difficult to unlearn a fear response, and animals as well as people can become neurotic.

The term 'anxiety' covers a wide spectrum of human emotion and behaviour. There is an important distinction between normal anxiety and that which is pathological, also known as clinical anxiety. Consider normal anxiety first. In humans, with their reflective minds, anxiety is often experienced as a complex emotion. Much human anxiety is *anticipatory*. We worry that we will fail our examination, not be able to pay the electricity bill due at the end of the month, make a fool or ourselves at a dinner party, and so on. New mind rationality is built upon complex emotions and anticipatory anxiety can certainly be regarded as a rational mechanism. That is, it helps us to achieve our goals. For example, we worry about giving a public lecture and so prepare it better and achieve our goal of good performance.

Anxiety disorders, in which pathological anxiety is experienced, are another matter altogether. There are a number of these that are distinguished in clinical classification systems including phobias, panic disorder, obsessive-compulsive disorder, and post-traumatic stress disorder.[12] Simplest from a psychological (and treatment) point of view are what are known as specific phobias, in which a person develops a fear of some particular object or situation. An individual with an untreated phobia may be able to live a relatively normal life, although at some cost to their personal freedom. With the help of the reflective mind, such a person may be able to organize their life quite well to avoid flying or using lifts or whatever their phobia is attached to. Avoidance can, however, result in two minds conflict when a powerful motive in the reflective mind cannot be achieved. If you want to visit a dying relative on another continent you *have* to fly, of if you want to attend an important business meeting on the 40th floor of a skyscraper you *have* to take the lift. A phobic person in such a situation will be more than aware of the conflict. The goal of their reflective mind is likely to be frustrated by an overwhelming fear response that they are unable to control. This is the main reason that a phobic patient will seek treatment, rather than applying their own solution of avoidance. The phobia is stopping *them* from doing what *they* want to do. But of course the phobia is part of them as well, part of their brain, rooted in the old mind.

Agoraphobia is more complex and difficult to treat than specific phobias. In fact, it is these days normally regarded as a common feature of *panic disorder*, rather than an example of a specific phobia. Panic disorder is an extremely distressing and disabling condition in which the patient experiences both panic attacks and strong anticipatory anxiety concerning their recurrence. Panic attacks can recur in the absence of any obvious external threat, although the patient may feel safer in some situations than others. They are extremely unpleasant to experience, and while usually no physical harm is done, patients often report that they think they are dying. A 'cognitive' theory of panic attacks is that they are due to catastrophic misinterpretation of normal bodily sensations.[13] For example, a small rise in heart rate is noticed by the patient and interpreted as anxiety. Their fear of a panic attack then raises the heart rate further in a vicious positive feedback cycle until full panic is experienced. Agoraphobia normally develops as a patient seeks out a 'safe place' (e.g. home, office, car) in which panic attacks are less likely to develop or can be more easily contained. They then start avoiding situations like crowded public places or public transport where escape will be difficult.

Patients with panic disorder and generalized anxiety disorders are normally offered pharmacological treatment to control or ameliorate the symptoms. What is of interest here, however, is the kind of psychological treatment that is effective. Traditional forms of psychotherapy, which attempt to identify underlying psychological causes of mental illness, are of questionable benefit at best. On the other hand, cognitive-behavioural therapy (CBT), the preferred approach these days, works well in many cases. A recent survey has shown that CBT is very effective in treatment of a wide range of anxiety disorders as well as some forms of depression.[14] What is particularly interesting about CBT is that it is a *two minds* therapy. It combines behaviour therapy, directed at the old mind, with cognitive therapy aimed at the new.

Behaviour therapy comes from learning theory and is particularly effective in treating specific phobias. In a classic (if rather cruel) animal learning experiment a rat is placed in a shuttle box (see Figure 8.1). The box is divided in two by a barrier that the rat can jump over. Each half has a metal floor that can be electrified independently. There is also a light bulb in each half. Call the two sides A and B and assume the rat starts off in A. The A bulb lights up and a few

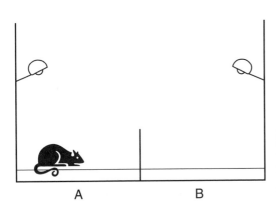

Fig. 8.1 Rat in a shuttle box. The electrified grid and lights in A and B can be switched on and off independently.

A   B

seconds later a painful electric shock is administered. The rat jumps the barrier from A to B to escape the pain. The procedure is repeated with the B bulb coming on followed by a shock, driving the rat back to A. And so on. Pretty soon the rat learns to jump the barrier whenever a bulb lights, without waiting around for the shock. In effect, the rat has acquired a phobic reaction to lights. Now what is interesting is what happens when the shocks are switched off. In the language of learning theory, 'extinguishing' the learning is a lot more difficult than when animals are trained for reward. In reward training, for example, a pigeon may learn to peck a key when it lights up to gain a food pellet. But if the food stops coming, the pigeon soon stops pecking.

In the shuttle box, however, turning off the shock is often not sufficient to extinguish the conditioning. The rat goes on jumping when it sees the light, maintaining its phobic reaction. Because it does not wait around in the dangerous situation, it has no way to know that the shock will not arrive. Hence, it cannot *unlearn* its phobia. If a barrier is brought down to stop the rat escaping, it will then experience the light followed by *no* shock. While the rat may be visibly distressed by being so trapped, it will soon learn that the light is harmless and lose its phobia. This simple experiment, and ones like it, are the essential inspiration for behavioural therapy treatment of specific phobias. Patients too must unlearn their fear conditioning, which can only be achieved by exposure to what they fear and not by the avoidance that they normally practice. To make this less traumatic, it is normally done in stages by a technique called 'systematic desensitisation' in which patients are gradually introduced to the object of their fear, initially at a safe remove.[15]

When a phobia is removed, the old mind stops dictating behaviour, and the new mind resumes its pursuit of complex goals. However, behaviour therapy is not enough on its own to deal with more complex conditions such as panic disorder and agoraphobia. Here, cognitive therapy is also needed. Cognitive therapy is delivered by conversation with the therapist and is aimed at controlling the patient's thoughts. It is hence a new mind therapy. For example, treatment of panic disorder would start with an effort to convince the patient that panic attacks, however awful they may feel, will not kill them or in fact do any lasting physical damage. This may not be sufficient, however. A person may have complete insight into the nature of their panic disorder but still be unable to control agoraphobic behaviour. The new mind may have the theory, but no one has told the old mind. The patient may then be taught the idea that panic attacks involve catastrophic interpretation of normally bodily sensations and to react differently, thinking the fear down, rather than up. Finally, the patient can be taught in effect to self-administer behavioural therapy when the situation arises. If they are travel phobic, for example, they may be persuaded to try making a very short journey in the company of someone they trust. So one form of cognitive therapy consists of teaching the patient the theory of behavioural therapy.

In summary, fear is an essential tool of the genes administered through the old mind. However, it is something of a blunt instrument that can create a range of neuroses and disorders. When this happens the conscious person will experience very direct conflict between the explicit goals of their reflective minds and the powerful emotions of their intuitive minds. They may be compelled, beyond their conscious volition, to perform actions and rituals (as in obsessive-compulsive disorder) or to avoid situations that provoke anxiety, as with phobias. Although people may to an extent confabulate explanations for their neurotic behaviour, it often becomes apparent to themselves as well as others that they, the conscious person, are no longer in control.

The two minds in co-operation

Typically, the intuitive mind deals with the habitual and the reflective mind with the novel. When we drive a familiar car on a familiar route to work every day, the process of driving the route is done mostly automatically, and the reflective mind is freed up, perhaps, to plan the day ahead or think about a tricky decision that will have to make. When we have a conversation with our boss, the intuitive mind tells us she is in a bad mood, and so the reflective mind decides to postpone discussion of the delicate matter we had planned. When I am writing this book, I reflect on what I intend to say, but the process of generating and typing in the actual words requires little or no attention on my part. In all of these cases, the two minds work in harmony and the individual achieves their goals.

Successful partnership depends upon the two minds dealing with the right tasks at the right time. The reflective mind has very low processing capacity and so routine tasks must, perforce, be left to the intuitive mind. This is fine, so long as the intuitive mind does not take over altogether, as in the case of some of the compulsive and neurotic disorders discussed above. Experts, for example, combine intuition with explicit knowledge and reasoning. Intuitive knowledge is very powerful, due to its speed and capacity. It is also a fickle friend, as I have pointed out a number of times, giving us feelings of confidence that may be misplaced and disguising a number of cognitive biases, which may influence our judgements. But we must largely rely on it, allowing our reflective minds to deal with novelty. Because we can reflect essentially on only one matter at a time, our attention must be focussed where it is most needed.

I will return shortly to the issue of which mind controls what behaviour. First, I want to deal with another important issue of co-operation: how knowledge is exchanged between the two minds.

The knowledge exchange problem

We have seen a lot of evidence in this book that there are distinct forms of knowledge: implicit and explicit, which I have claimed to belong to the intuitive and reflective minds, respectively. In Chapter 3, we saw that the acquisition of skills, habits, and procedural knowledge can occur without any explicit knowledge being available to the individual, other than knowing that they have learnt something. When I say 'I know how to play the piano', I really only mean that I (the conscious person) know *that* I can play the piano. All explicit knowledge is of the knowing that rather than knowing how kind. My reflective mind actually has no access at all to the motor programmes that my brain has developed to permit me, for example, to play a scale of C major. An amnesic patient may be able to speak a foreign language without knowing *that* they can do so. Only when they hear someone speaking the language do they realize that they can understand it. As we also saw in Chapter 3, studies by neuropsychologists and neuroscientists clearly show that implicit and explicit memories are located in different parts of the brain and function largely independently of each other.

In Chapters 4 and 5, we saw that decisions can be made by reflecting on explicit knowledge and beliefs about the world, and running mental simulations of future possibilities. They can also be made intuitively, relying on associations formed from prior experience. In Chapter 6, I discussed evidence from social psychology that we have both explicit and implicit knowledge of the social world and that these can differ. For example, we may have an explicit set of beliefs about ourselves in which we are egalitarian and liberal: these beliefs are reflected in what we say and to an extent in what we do. However, it appears that we also have implicit stereotypes that reflect the prejudices to be found in our culture and childhood, and that these also influence our behaviour and judgements through the intuitive mind.

For the two minds hypothesis, it makes sense that implicit and explicit memory systems are isolated from each other in the brain, without any direct means to communicate. It makes sense because the implicit systems are older and store information not only in different neural locations but in a different *format*. Consider a case where the two forms of knowledge seem to be in parallel. For example, I suffer from mild social anxiety, and while I enjoy hosting dinner parties, I get uncomfortable if my house is crowded with people in large numbers. This is true: my wife will tell you the same thing. So my intuitive mind reaction to parties—anxiety, grumpiness, etc—corresponds with my explicit knowledge. But the old mind 'knowledge' is really a disposition to react and behave in certain predictable ways in certain social situations, while my new mind knowledge is an explicit belief that I do so, supported by episodic memories of my behaviour in past parties. Moreover, while I have insight in this matter, others may not. Some people do not acknowledge their social anxiety and always find good reasons not to host or attend a party. The two forms of knowledge are not the same at all, and while they may correspond, they certainly need not do so. Nor do I *intend* to behave badly at parties, although I often do so.

In Chapter 3, I touched on the problem of *automation* of skills. This is the phenomenon by which skills which are practised under conscious control gradually become automatic, so that working memory and conscious attention is freed up for other tasks. Many authors write as though automation involves direct transfer of knowledge within the brain, from explicit to implicit forms. Critics of dual process theories in psychology have used this to question the idea that there are really two distinct systems for controlling our actions, or to suggest that there is a continuum between implicit and explicit knowledge.[16] However, as I explained in Chapter 3, there is no need to propose that explicit knowledge somehow transforms itself into implicit procedures by some mysterious brain transfer. Rather it is much more plausible that we use our reflective minds to *train* our intuitive minds. When we learn a new skill, we use our reflective minds to practise the actions required, intervening with volitional control of our actions. For example, for most of us, using a mouse to control a pointer on a screen is second nature and we may have forgotten that any effort was initially required to learn how to do it. If you happen to see someone who has never used a mouse, however, you will notice that it is far from immediate and intuitive.

What happens when you learn this skill is that you are told, or read, that moving the mouse will control a pointer on the screen. This is explicit knowledge. Using volitional cognition, which occupies the working memory store in the reflective mind, you move the mouse and observe the effect on the pointer. You practise doing this repeatedly. After a while, it seems to require less and less attention and eventually becomes automatic. What is actually happening, I contend, is that the deliberate movements are providing input–output information to neural networks in the associative learning system of the old mind. The reflective mind learns the rule quickly and explicitly while the intuitive mind learns it slowly, by experience. They are indeed separate systems of learning and memory. Moreover, it does not become a *skilled* movement until it is automated within the intuitive mind. The eventual hand–eye coordination achieved is far smoother and more accurate than the initial attempts under volitional control. Cognitive therapy, discussed earlier, is based precisely on the ability of the new mind to train the old.

If explicit knowledge can be transferred to the intuitive mind, does the converse apply with implicit knowledge? Yes and no. It is possible to acquire knowledge of your own intuitive behaviours, essentially by observing yourself. For example, my knowledge that I behave badly and feel uncomfortable at parties. The problem, as discussed in Chapter 7, is that when we do this, we engage in much inaccurate self-interpretation. We are, in fact, constantly engaged in theorizing about our own behaviour, as the reflective mind constructs the narrative that tells us who we are. When our behaviour originates in the intuitive mind, as it often does, we only have insight when our reflective minds hold a good theory. Thus a person with a mild phobia or social anxiety problem may avoid situations that make them uncomfortable but rationalize their reasons for so doing. If the anxiety becomes severe, then they may become aware of it, as no other explanation, including those more attractive to their self-concept, will deal with the facts.

In essence, the main reason that our two minds seem to co-operate so seamlessly (most of the time) is essentially for the reasons outlined in Chapter 7: the conscious person is a fictitious narrative, told with the concepts of a one-mind folk psychology. Only when the conflict between the two minds becomes extreme, does the storytelling break down.

Attention and relevance

I have talked much of the time as though we make our decisions *either* by intuition *or* by reflection. However, effective thinking and reasoning requires the two minds to co-operate, so that the reflective mind is thinking about the right things. Our attention must be focussed upon what is relevant so that our powers of reflection are used to maximum effect. What is relevant depends upon the whole context in which we are operating, including any internal goals and plans we may be pursuing. As has been long recognized in psychology, the locus of conscious attention must be determined by mostly by *preconscious* processes.

Major psychological theories of human reasoning and decision making rely on this distinction. In Chapter 5, I discussed the popular mental model theory of reasoning, proposed by Phil Johnson-Laird. When reasoning with statements, according to this theory, people formulate an initial *mental model* of the situation to which these statements refer. This process is rapid and automatic, as may be the drawing of a provisional conclusion. Only when people attempt to find counterexamples to a provisional inference is effortful, reflective reasoning involved, the kind which occupies our working memories. I prefer a somewhat different notion of mental models from Johnson-Laird, one which represents not just a situation in the world, but what we *believe* about it.[17] I provide an illustration using this type of mental model.

Suppose you are given this question:

> If Ruth meets her friend, they will go to the theatre.
> Ruth meets her friend.
> What follows?

Of course, people will say usually that they will go to the theatre. A mental model of the conditional statement might look something like this:

> Ruth meets her friend → (.9) they go to the theatre

Here the arrow suggests a causal connection between the two events and the number the degree of confidence that a person has that one leads to the other. This will typically be less than certainty (1.0) because we know from experience that plans can change or be derailed. This mental model is formed rapidly and intuitively without conscious reflection. Given the next statement, only minimal reflection is needed to draw the conclusion with high confidence. Now consider, this version, which would be presented to different participants:

> If Ruth meets her friend, they will go to the theatre.
> If Ruth has enough money they will go the theatre.
> Ruth meets her friend.
> What follows?

Many participants here now fail to draw the conclusion that they go to the theatre or draw it with less confidence.[18] From a strictly logical viewpoint, the second conditional should not change the inference. But of course it suggests a reason why Ruth may not be able to go to the theatre, a *counterexample*. The effect of this is to lower the confidence in the causal relationship. Perhaps it is only now .5 instead of .9. Confidence in the conclusion drops accordingly.

The actual suppression of the inference could be caused intuitively or reflectively. People may rapidly and unconsciously revise the original mental model, or they may reflect on the counterexample and decide not to draw the first conclusion that comes to mind. The psychological evidence suggests that either or both may occur.[19] The important point here is that even though this a problem in reasoning, the speciality of the reflective mind, the context for that reasoning is set intuitively, by rapid and preconscious mental processes. Our thinking is not confined strictly to the information given; in fact, it is very difficult for normal people to do so.[20] Whenever we have prior knowledge or belief relevant to the problem in hand, this is rapidly and effortlessly retrieved. Our thinking is always *contextualized*. In laboratory experiments, this may not

Table 8.1 Three problems

1. A bat and ball cost $1.10 in total. The bat costs $1.00 more than the ball. How much does the ball cost? _____ cents.

2. If it takes 5 machines 5 minutes to make 5 widgets, how long would it take 100 machines to make 100 widgets? _____ minutes.

3. In a lake, there is a patch of lily pads. Every day, the patch doubles in size. If it takes 48 days for the patch to cover the entire lake, how long would it take for the patch to cover half of the lake? _____ days.

help us, leading to belief biases on some occasions as discussed in Chapter 5. But in the real world, it is vital.

The amount of information that we can keep in mind at one time is very small, and limited by our working memories. But the amount of information stored in the brain is vast. For any given problem or decision that faces us, we are likely to have relevant knowledge. Making rational real world decisions depends critically upon our ability to access this knowledge when we need it. So like the chess players I discussed earlier in the book, the intuition which tells us what to think about, is at least as important as the reflective reasoning that we then engage in. In Gary Klein's studies of decision making in the real world, he was initially surprised to discover that rather little reflective reasoning was involved, especially when urgent decisions needed to be taken by such professionals as firefighters and doctors. Mostly what marks out such experts is their ability rapidly to retrieve and apply solutions to the present problem that are suggested by their prior experience. They do sometimes engage in slower, reflective reasoning, but only when the problem before them is unusually novel and puzzling in its presentation.[21]

Before reading on, have a look at the three problems shown in Table 8.1 and jot down your answers. I will discuss them shortly.

The intervention problem

It is clear from the above discussion that rapid, intuitive processing of problems and decisions must precede any engagement of reflective reasoning. Efficient and effective as this it, it also creates a problem. Our intuitions often suggest an immediate answer or decision that we may be tempted to accept without any serious reflection. After all, intuition is effortless and reflection is hard work. This suggested inference or action we call the *default* or intuitive response. Often this default is accepted and acted upon. However, the reflective mind can also intervene by overriding this default response and replacing it with one which is more considered, based on slower, reflective thinking.[22]

The problem is that we sometimes need this intervention to make a good decision, because the default intuition is faulty, and will lead us into a cognitive bias (see Chapter 4).

Although not all theorists agree, there are good reasons for thinking that the two minds interact in this way. The first is that the intuitive mind operates much more quickly and can process larger amounts of information. If the two minds worked on a problem in parallel, like a horse race, then the intuitive mind should always win, being that much quicker. But that is not what happens. When intuitive and deliberative judgements point in different directions, sometimes one wins out and sometimes the other, as numerous studies of reasoning and decision making have shown (see Chapters 4 and 5). Second, the reflective mind operates through a single, central working memory system, a precious but limited resource that can only properly manage one task at a time. It is also requires much higher effort than the intuitive system. It therefore makes sense that this system is recruited to deal with the most pressing task that is facing us at a given time. Most of the time our brains accept the default behaviour and judgements that are based on habit and intuition. But sometimes, the (reflective) cavalry are called to the rescue.

We actually know quite a lot, from the experiments conducted by psychologists, about when the reflective mind will intervene in decision making. This will happen more often when people are given strong instructions for rational thinking, for example to engage in logical reasoning and disregard prior beliefs. There will be less intervention when people are given little time to think about the problem, or are required to carry out another task at the same time that requires their attention.[23] People are also more likely to check out the first answer that comes to mind when they have less feeling of confidence in it. It appears that intuitions come with a 'feeling of rightness' that unfortunately is not necessarily an accurate predictor of whether we are actually right or not.[24] It also appears that those of higher intelligence may intervene more effectively on their intuitions, but the story here is more complicated than it appears at first sight.

I have already said that general intelligence, or IQ, is related to the workings of the reflective mind. People high in IQ are better at reflective reasoning, as numerous studies have shown. But there is more to being smart than having a high IQ, as Keith Stanovich has pointed out in a number of recent publications.[25] He has coined the term 'dysrationalia' to describe the phenomenon by which smart people do dumb things. There are a number of reasons why this can come about. First is education and culture. We can only think with the tools that our life experience has provided us with. A person of high IQ, for example, will be a weak chess player if they have come new to the game: however, they will probably learn to be a stronger player, with time, than someone of lower IQ. A brilliant physicist may be a poor social thinker, if they have never studied that domain and bring only prejudice to it. But most importantly, IQ is a resource that you have to apply to a problem for it to be of any use to you.

Take an analogy with motor cars. Some cars are designed for higher performance than others: they have more powerful engines, more responsive steering, better road holding, and so on. So all else being equal, a person driving a high performance car will be able to drive more quickly from A to B, assuming speed limits are not in force. But all else may not be equal: the person with the high-performance car may be a poor driver who uses his vehicle badly. Having a high IQ means that you have a high cognitive capacity: a brain designed for high performance. But you can still use it badly or inappropriately. So one cause of dysrationalia is that while a person of high IQ *could* reason well, they are actually failing to engage their reflective abilities. Instead, they are inclined by their personality or circumstances to rely on gut feelings and intuitions,[26] to be strongly influenced by prior beliefs (which may be false) or prone to social influence by peers (who may not be bright). This second factor in intelligence is called *rational thinking disposition*. People vary not only in their cognitive ability but also in their disposition to think critically about problems they face. This is an aspect of their personality which affects they way they think about problems. There is a positive correlation between IQ and rational thinking, but it is relatively modest in size.[27]

The three questions shown in Table 8.1 make up a short test of 'cognitive reflection' designed by Shane Frederick.[28] Each of them suggests an intuitive answer which will actually be wrong if the person accepts it. When people give the wrong answer, it is usually one of these default intuitions. For question 1, the default intuition is to say 10 cents. The tiniest amount of reflection will show that this is wrong: if the ball costs 10 cents, the bat must cost $1. But the difference between $1 and 10 cents is then 90 cents, not $1 as the problem requires. The correct answer is 5 cents. The intuitive answer to 2 is to say 100 minutes, but this is really silly if you think about it. The answer is 5 minutes. The intuitive answer to 3 is 24 days, whereas the correct answer is 47. Surely, smart people will not have difficulty with such questions? Well, they do. In Frederick's study, one group studied were Harvard University undergraduate students, a selected group of high IQ. Their average score was 1.43 out of 3, and only 20% managed to get all three questions right!

What is going on here? The actual arithmetic involved in solving these problems is fairly trivial and should not have proved a challenge for any of the participants. In any case, the author showed that mathematical ability was not a factor. The problem is that each of these problems provides a default intuition that is quite compelling: not because it is right, but because it *feels* right. So many people simply go with their gut feeling and do not engage in the fairly simple reasoning needed to check it out. When they do so, they discard the intuition and usually find the right answer. The study showed that performance was strongly linked to a standard test of rational thinking dispositions. However, Frederick also found that people who are patient do better on the task, while those who are impulsive do poorly, measured in several ways. For example, participants who did poorly were also willing to pay more than twice as much as high scorers to receive a book order from the web by next day delivery.

Recall that one of the key factors in pathological gambling is impulsivity. I interpreted that as meaning that people with very high impulsivity are unable to control the impulses emanating from their old, intuitive minds. Frederick's study, although very different in design and focus, suggests the same thing. Those who intervene on default decisions are exercising the reflective mind and overriding the intuitive mind. As with the gamblers, the people who *fail* to do this are impulsive. Their intuitive minds tend to dominate their judgements, even when their gut feelings let them down badly. And if they have very efficient reflective minds (high IQ) this does them little good, because these resources are not brought to bear on their problem solving. So basically, to do well in occupations, like science, where IQ is important, you need to have an analytic thinking style.

Summary and conclusions

You may have a different view of yourself than you had before picking up this book. Like most people, you may have assumed the common sense, folk psychological view of the mind in which a conscious person, a Chief Executive, sits at the top in control. The psychological and neuroscientific evidence discussed in this book overwhelmingly refutes this. There is a conscious person, a self, at the centre of life as human beings *experience* it. However, the focus of experimental psychology is the understanding of how and why we behave in the way that we do. It turns out that studying the experiences of the conscious person is of very little help in developing a scientific account of behaviour. Contrary to the folk beliefs that underlie practices such as opinion polling, we can by introspection give very little account of how our brains work, or even the reasons for our actions.

The psychology of learning, thinking, decision making, and social cognition has been marked by the proposal of numerous dual-process theories, especially in the past 20 years or so. But the idea of two kinds of thought is much older than that and can be traced back through hundreds of years of philosophical and psychological writing.[29] Both in the older and the more recent writing something is very striking. Different authors again and again propose similar distinctions, often without the knowledge that others have done so before them. Some of the theories are restricted to narrow domains and many use different labels but the dualities they propose have striking similarities. There are processes in the mind that are fast, automatic, high capacity, and intuitive (type 1) and there are others than are slow, volitional, low capacity, and deliberative (type 2). It appears that academic writers are continually discovering and rediscovering this division. This is important, because we are not simply talking about perpetuation of a fashionable idea or 'meme' that has taken on a life of its own.[30]

Some authors have proposed stronger theories that distinguish two systems, although theses have typically been restricted to particular domains: for example, there are two system theories of learning, reasoning, decision making, and social cognition. There are some difficulties with two system theories, however, not least of which is the definition of a 'system'. And then of course, we must ask why the same type 1/type 2 distinction seems to appear in all these different fields of psychology. And that is before we start, as I have done in this book, to make links with yet other fields of study, such as mental illness and compulsive behaviours. So in this book, I have chosen to explore the strongest hypothesis of all to which dual-process theories can lead us: the reason that similar dualities are constantly being discovered in different domains is because there are in fact *two minds* within the brain, responsible for them all. The two minds are ever present, interacting and competing, whether we study learning, thinking, social psychology, clinical psychology, or any other field of human behaviour.

In a two minds story, there are multiple systems within the brain, specialized for different purposes, but each belonging to one mind or the other. We have discussed many of these and everywhere we find dualities: dorsal and ventral visual systems, implicit and explicit learning and memory systems, intuitive and deliberative systems for judgment and decision making, implicit stereotypes and attitudes as well as explicit social belief systems. And these divisions are not just supported by the interpretation of psychological experiments. In all of these cases, there is neuroscientific and neuropsychological evidence, in some cases rudimentary but in others highly developed, to show that distinct and dissociable regions of the brain correspond to the type 1 and 2 version of each system.

In Chapter 2, I introduced the basic evolutionary arguments for two minds theory, and have referred to the role of evolution at numerous points within this book. It seems evident that in some respects we are very like other higher animals, but in others very different. The two minds hypothesis explains this on the basis that we have an old mind which has much in common with other animals. Indeed aspects of its function: the senses, the emotions, and the general algorithm for experiential learning are to be found not only in apes and other mammals, but in birds, fish, and reptiles. And this old mind is still a very powerful force within us as the discussion of neurotic disorders and compulsive behaviour earlier in this chapter illustrates. This old mind has continued to evolve and develop within human beings but not, anywhere near, to the point where it can explain the extraordinary and unique accomplishments of the human species.

We do not know exactly how and why the new mind developed. It is not entirely unique to humans: there is a rudimentary system of working memory and controlled attention in other animals that permits them to deal with novel situations. But it is uniquely *developed* in human beings. The evolution of language, folk psychology, and the ability to meta-represent (represent the thoughts of ourselves and others) appears to have been crucial, along with the very large development of the frontal lobes in human brains. And I believe that the rationality of the new mind, which I discussed at the start of this chapter, is (almost) unique to human beings. Only humans live their lives by long-term goals, and only humans can engage in detailed hypothetical thinking and mental simulation of future possible worlds.

What is especially interesting is that the new mind was merely *added*: the old mind is still there and still vital to our ability to live in the world. The new mind evolved in partnership with the old, albeit a somewhat uneasy alliance. It permits us to have complex emotions, long-term goals, and the rationality of purpose that only thinking about future possibilities can bring. However, it is not really in charge. The old mind controls powerful emotions and motivations that can dominate our behaviours, most obviously in the case of anxiety and compulsive disorders. But whenever we rely on habit, intuition, and gut feelings, as we often do, the old, intuitive mind is also controlling our behaviour. This can lead us to good judgements, where we have the relevant learning from experience, and indeed much expertise is intuitive. But it can also lead us into bias and error as the discussion of the cognitive reflection test in this chapter demonstrates.

The intelligence of the old mind is universal. The ability to learn skills, perceive patterns, acquire language, and so on is roughly equal to all, except where there is a specific deficit caused by a congenital condition, or localized brain damage. By contrast, the intelligence of the new mind is quite variable across individuals. Reflective reasoning ability is strongly related to heritable IQ and working memory capacity. But as we have also seen, having a high IQ is not enough to make you a smart person and a good decision maker. You also need to have rational beliefs, justified by good evidence, and the knowledge that permits you to reason expertly in the domains of your decision making. For the kinds of problem where reflective reasoning is required, you also need to have the disposition to apply effortful reasoning, rather than to rely on intuitions and feelings. This disposition is partly a matter of personality, but also influenced by culture and context.

A key facet of human intelligence is our possession of folk psychology and a theory of mind. By assigning mental states to others; beliefs, desires, motives, intentions, and so on, we are able to understand and predict their behaviour. There is strong evidence to suggest that this facility is both innate and essentially unique to our species. Evolutionary psychologists are agreed that this development was a key factor in making our species so distinct from others. While some philosophers believe that folk psychology can form the basis for a scientific theory of mind, I, like most psychologists, find this hard to accept. It has taken us 150 years of experimental psychology, assisted recently by neuroscience, to develop the scientific understanding we have today. The great bulk of the knowledge acquired is not to be found in folk psychology, and few folk could guess the outcome of most psychological experiments. This applies also to social psychology, which deals essentially in the same concepts as folk psychology. As shown in Chapter 6, social psychological theory has moved progressively further away from folk psychology over the past 30–40 years.

The reason that it is not apparent to one and all that we have two minds is the power of this inbuilt theory of mind and behaviour. With the evolution of the reflective mind has come the *self*, the conscious person with its social identity. The narrative that defines the self is laden with self-interpretation and self-theorizing. As folk psychology is turned inwards, it provides a convincing story of behaviour controlled by conscious beliefs, desires, and intentions. Of course, the reflective mind does have access to explicit goals and intentions and when these are retrieved and processed through working memory, we experience what I am calling reflective consciousness. Hence we may carry out a volitional action with awareness that we are doing so, as when we travel to the doctor's to keep an appointment. But where our behaviour is dominated by intuitions, feelings, and habits of the old mind, as it often is, these behaviours are woven into the narrative of the self with consummate ease by our powers of confabulation. There is overwhelming psychological evidence that people do not have access to their mental processes, and frequently lack insight into the true causes of their own behaviour. And where the old mind wins out in a two minds conflict, only in extreme cases are we aware that this is happening.

So while we know that much of our behaviour is automatic and not requiring conscious effort, we still retain our illusion in our minds.

The two minds theory is, of course, a strong and controversial claim. It would be much safer simply to conduct tests of two-process theories of particular tasks, as many authors do. I have been doing that myself, as an experimental psychologist, over the past 30 years or so. But it seemed to me that the smoke of so many dual-process theories might reveal the fire of a two minds story in the human brain. In this book, I have roamed well beyond my comfort zone—the psychology of reasoning and decision making—in the quest to see whether there is a duality running through the mind as a whole. The search has taken us also into the fields of evolutionary psychology, the study of learning and memory, social psychology, consciousness studies, neurotic disorders as well as consideration of numerous neuropsychological and neuroscientific studies. It seems to me that in each of these fields, considered separately, not only is a two minds story possible to tell, but it is necessary to make good sense of the data. And when we put all of these diverse fields together, the case for two minds is very compelling indeed.

Notes and references

1 Epstein's theory has been particularly influential in social psychology. He is unusual in not only describing two distinct experiential and rational systems in the mind, but also in developing a measure of corresponding thinking styles (Epstein, Pacini, es-Raj, and Heier, 1996; Epstein and Pacini, 1999).

2 For example, Stanovich (1999, 2009b).

3 See Stanovich (2004).

4 Stanovich (2004).

5 A one-mind theory, does not mean a conscious mind theory. Although I believe that folk psychology attributes too much control to consciousness, it does not necessarily assume that the mental states that drive other people are conscious. The one-mind theory is essentially the chief executive model described in Chapter 1, in which unconscious and automatic parts are slave systems, obeying the Executive's will. The philosopher, Keith Frankish, divides the mind into personal and subpersonal components, suggesting that the folk psychology primarily deals with the personal level (Frankish, 2004, 2009).

6 For scholarly reviews and discussion of normal and pathological gambling, see Raylu and Oci (2002), Evans and Coventry (2006).

7 Reports from various web sources suggest that Las Vegas has more than three million visitors every *month*.

8 This is known as the partial reinforcement extinction effect or PREE and is covered in all standard textbooks on learning (e.g. Anderson, 2000). Its application to the persistence of gambling has been noted by many authors (e.g. Griffiths, 1995).

9 See Wagenaar (1988, Chapter 4).

10 Raylu and Oci, op. cit. p. 1023.

11 Strack and Deutsch (2004) have a dual process theory which specifically contrasts impulsive (old mind) with reflective (new mind) cognition, and have also applied this to the explanation of addictive behaviour (Deutsch and Strack, 2006).

12 For coverage of all these and their treatments, see Starcevic (2005).

13 Starcevic (2005) p. 62.

14 Butler et al. (2006).

15 For example, a spider phobic might be persuaded to sit across the room from a spider in a glass case. They sit at a distance where they can just tolerate the fear. After a while they become comfortable, and so move closer to the spider where the new fear level is now tolerable and so on. The results can be remarkable. Someone who has dreaded spiders all their life may, with a few hours of such treatment, end up holding one on their hand. Ost (1996) reports success rates of up to 80% on a 12-month follow-up of spider phobics treated in a single, three-hour group session. Needless to say, the procedure should only be carried out by skilled practioners under clinically controlled conditions.

16 For example, see Osman (2004), Keren and Schul (2009).

17 Technically, Johnson-Laird's mental models are *semantic*, whereas mine are *epistemic*. Semantic mental models represent states of affairs, and epistemic models what we believe (Evans, 2007a) . The latter, but not the former, can include such features as causal relationships and degrees of confidence. While Johnson-Laird's theory uses semantic mental models at its core, he also introduces epistemic elements with his principles of semantic and pragmatic modulation (Johnson-Laird and Byrne, 2002).

18 This is known as the conditional suppression task. The effect was originally shown by Byrne (1989).

19 Until recently, it was generally assumed that context effects in reasoning were entirely intuitive. However, they also affect the explicit, reflective reasoning that people do and the two often combine, as first shown by Verschueren et al. (2005).

20 We have recently found evidence in our own laboratory (McKenzie, Evans, and Handley, 2010) that context has much less effect on the reasoning of autistic people.

21 See Klein (1999).

22 I have termed this class of dual-process theories 'default-interventionist' and contrasted them with another type that I call 'parallel-competitive' (Evans, 2007b, 2008). A number of leading theories are of the default-interventionist type (Evans, 2006b, 2007a; Stanovich, 1999, 2009c; Kahneman and Frederick, 2002). Major theories of the parallel-competitive type include Sloman (1996) and Smith and DeCoster (2000).

23 Some experiments of this kind have been described earlier in the book. For a detailed review of this kind of research, see Evans (2007a).

24 See Thompson (2009); Shynkarkuk and Thompson (2006).

25 See especially, Stanovich (2009b, 2009c).

26 As discussed in Chapter 4, there are authors who recommend reliance on gut feelings in decision making, such as Gigerenzer (2007). For the reasons given there, I am highly sceptical of this advice.

27 See Stanovich (2009b).

28 Frederick (2005).

29 See Frankish and Evans (2009).

30 The idea of a meme was introduced by Dawkins (1976) to describe ideas that replicate themselves by analogy to genes. For recent discussions of meme theory, see Blackmore (2000) and Stanovich (2004).

Addendum

Some technical issues

In the interests of making the main text accessible to as many readers as possible, I was obliged to gloss over some technical issues and problems concerning dual-process theories. For the benefit of scholars wishing to pursue the academic literature, I will briefly summarize these issues here and point the reader towards relevant references. As this Addendum is intended for academic readers, I shall include my references within the text, in the orthodox manner.

Modes and types of processing

An important ambiguity arises, particularly in the social psychological literature, about whether theories concern two fundamentally different *types* of cognitive process, arising from distinct cognitive systems, or simply two different modes of processing. Unfortunately, the standard definitions of type 1 processes as fast, and automatic and of type 2 processes, as slow and deliberative hold some ambiguity in this respect (although not if more stringent criteria are used). As an example, one of the earliest dual-process models in the social psychological literature, Chaiken's heuristic-systematic model (Chaiken, 1980; Chen and Chaiken, 1999) distinguishes shallow from deep processing. I am inclined to view this as simply describing different modes of processing as are some other reviewers (Strack and Deutsch, 2004). On the other hand, Smith and DeCoster (2000), who most definitely propose a type distinction, feel that this theory can be incorporated within their account. This shows how ambiguous the type/mode distinction can be.

Evidence of type 1 and 2 processing provides support for two minds hypothesis, but evidence simply of two modes of processing does not. One mind could clearly apply many strategies or methods. Throughout the book, I only use dual-process research to support the two minds theory when I believe the evidence supports the type distinction. In Chapter 4, when discussing judgement and decision making, I explicitly discuss the question of whether heuristic judgements, which are often described as type 1 processes, are really type 2. The point I make is that being quick is not enough for a process to be type 1;

heuristics may be simple rules that are applied explicitly, although quickly and with little reflection. In Chapter 8, I also allude to the distinction between individual differences in cognitive ability and those in cognitive style or disposition. The disposition to adopt different styles of information processing (for example, as measured by the Need for Cognitions scale) is not in itself evidence for two minds.

Both Keith Stanovich and I have been very clear in our own writing about the type/mode distinction, although not everyone who quotes our work is as careful. I alluded to the problem in my recent review of dual process theories (Evans, 2008) and discussed it in detail in a recent chapter (Evans, 2009). Stanovich, with his psychometric approach, was clear from the start that while correlation with individual differences in intelligence provides evidence of type 2 processing, correlations with thinking dispositions do not (Stanovich, 1999). Recently, he has developed this account by pointing out that rational thinking dispositions (which I discuss in Chapter 8) are to do with methods of processing in the reflective mind, while measures of intelligence are do it with its capacity (Stanovich, 2009).

Two (or more) kinds of dual-process theories

Dual-process theories, by which I mean *type* theories, differ in their cognitive architecture, although this was not noticed until recently. I have proposed a distinction between parallel-competitive and default-interventionist theories in recent papers (Evans, 2007b, 2008), which others are now taking up and investigating (e.g. De Neys and Glumicic, 2008). The parallel theories assume that type 1 and 2 processes proceed in parallel, each having a say, with conflict detected and resolved as necessary (e.g. Sloman, 1996; Smith and DeCoster, 2000). Most theories of reasoning and decision making, however, have a sequential form (e.g. Evans, 2006b; Stanovich, 1999; Kahneman and Frederick, 2002). In the latter, it is assumed that type 1 processes provide a default mental model and or/suggested intuitive response, which may be accepted or else intervened upon by type 2 reasoning. Such intervention may lead to a different response or judgement being made.

For the sake of simplicity, I have not made much of this distinction within the main text of the book, although I do describe the case for interventionist models in Chapter 8. The evidence of two kinds of knowledge (Chapter 3), which I describe as central to the two minds hypothesis, has been claimed as evidence for parallel processing models (Smith and DeCoster, 2000) but need not be interpreted in that way. A more complex problem is whether there are type 1 processes operating within both the intuitive *and* the reflective mind (Evans, 2009). That is, processes which result directly in intuitive judgements and actions on the one hand, and those which post information into working memory for reflection on the other. I have alluded to this issue obliquely within the book but avoided tackling it head on. The reason is first that it would complicate the story too much for a book of this kind and second that there is as yet no clear consensus among theorists as to whether or not this distinction should be made. The issue of the cognitive architectures underlying dual-process theories is one that the field is only beginning to get to grips with (but see a number of contributions to the collection edited by Evans and Frankish, 2009).

Dubious and confused constructs

The list of features normally attributed to 'System' 1 and 2 processing (which I am here calling type 1 and 2) in Table 1.2 have numerous problems associated with them. Most of these are addressed directly in the book. For example, I argue in Chapter 7 that it is a mistake to consider one process conscious and the other unconscious. In Chapter 2, I say that it is better to think of the reflective mind as uniquely developed rather than uniquely present in human beings. I also comment several times that the intuitive mind, while having animal-like features, is more developed in humans. I show the problems with the fast/slow distinction (see above) and look critically at the automatic/controlled distinction (e.g. in Chapter 7), pointing out the limited form of 'control' that the reflective mind can actually exercise.

A difficulty which I have largely avoided, rather than addressed, is that assumption that many authors make that intuitive, type 1 processing leads to cognitive biases and reflective, type 2 processing to normatively correct answers. While this is common, and I understand the reason for it, it is simply wrong. I have been quite explicit about this in recent publications (Evans, 2007a, 2008) and have developed my recent accounts of cognitive biases to place equal emphasis on type 1 and 2 processing (Evans, 2006b, 2007a). While I do not discuss the issue of normative rationality very directly in the book, I never make the mistake of simply taking the correctness of a response as diagnostic of its mind of origin. I do, however, point the reader clearly to cases where either intuitive or reflective processing is more likely to be helpful to the individual.

Hostile criticisms

In this book, I have advanced the case for the two minds hypothesis, as the strongest and most interesting proposal to arise from the various dual-process theories of higher cognition. I have done so in a way which critically reformulates many of the constructs typically associated with type 1 and 2 processing, as indicated above. However, I have not directly addressed critiques which are wholly unsympathetic with the enterprise. There are a number of such hostile reviews to be found in the academic literature (e.g. Gigerenzer and Regier, 1996; Keren and Schul, 2009; Newstead, 2000; Osman, 2004; Shanks and St John, 1994). I have not addressed them here, partly because the purpose of this book was make a readable case for the apparently improbable presence of two minds in one brain, by bringing together as much supportive evidence as possible. The other reason is that I am really not very impressed with any of these critiques, none of which, in my view, has really examined carefully the wide range of evidence for dual processing, as considered in this book. However, I point the academic reader in their direction, so that they may judge for themselves the merit of these arguments.

Types, systems, and minds

The reason I have reverted to talking of type 1 and 2 processing, rather than System 1 and 2, is that there are a number of problems in a system level analysis (Evans, 2006a; Keren and Schul, 2009b). While there may be two minds responsible for type 1 and 2 processing, there clearly cannot be just two systems. Stanovich (2004) abandoned the label System 1, in favour of the term TASS, the set of autonomous subsystems. Clearly there are many different systems of an autonomous nature, even if one does not go so far as to regard the intuitive mind as entirely modular (Chapter 2). It is more tempting to think of System 2 as a single system, since type 2 processes are by their nature singular. However, the problem with this is that we then start thinking of System 2 (working memory, conscious mind) as an homunculus that can mysteriously perform multiple tasks, drawing on the vast array of cognitive functions known to correlate with working memory capacity (Barrett, Tugade, and Engle, 2004). In the book, I do not make the mistake of equating any single system with the reflective mind. I do point out that working memory is required for its function, but also that it draws upon many other resources, especially explicit knowledge systems. In my discussions of neuropsychological and neuroscientific studies, I also point out that there appear to be multiple systems in the brain for reasoning and executive function, as no particular brain regions are consistently identified across studies.

A proposal, which is very helpful, is that made recently by the philosopher Samuels (2009). He suggests that we talk of type 1 and 2 systems, which have the usual type 1 and 2 attributes. My development of this idea (Evans, 2009) is that we consider that all type 2 systems have working memory as *one* required component, whereas type 1 systems do not. The proposal of two minds, perhaps surprisingly, is less problematic than that of two systems. It is bolder, of course, because one cannot simply confine it as a two-system theory for a particular function like reasoning (Sloman, 1996) or processing social information (Chaiken, 1980). It has to range across all higher cognitive functions, as well as emotion, as this book does. But each mind can and must have multiple systems, as I indicate in the book. I am currently looking to develop the idea that the intuitive mind is comprised of type 1 systems and the reflective mind of type 2 systems.

References

Aiello, L. C. and Dunbar, R. I. M. (1993). Neocortex size, group size, and the evolution of language. *Current Anthropology, 34,* 184–193.

Alter, A. L. and Oppenheimer, D. M. (2006). From a fixation on sports to an exploration of mechanism: The past, present and future of hot hand research. *Thinking and Reasoning, 12,* 431–444.

Anderson, J. R. (2000). *Learning and Memory: an Integrated Approach.* New York: Wiley.

Andres, P. (2003). Frontal cortex as the central executive of working memory: Time to revise our view. *Cortex, 39,* 871–895.

Andrews, P. W., Gangestad, S. W., and Mattews, D. (2002). Adaptionism – how to carry out an exaptionist program. *Behavioral and Brain Sciences, 25,* 489–504.

Baars, B. (1997). *In the Theatre of Consciousness: The Workspace of the Mind.* New York: Oxford University Press.

Baddeley, A. (2007). *Working Memory, Thought and Action.* Oxford: Oxford University Press.

Ball, L. J., Lucas, E. J., Miles, J. N. V., and Gale, A. G. (2003). Inspection times and the selection task: What do eye-movements reveal about relevance effects? *Quarterly Journal of Experimental Psychology, 56A,* 1053–1077.

Barbey, A. K. and Sloman, S. A. (2007). Base-rate respect: From ecological validity to dual processes. *Behavioral and Brain Sciences, 30,* 287–292.

Bargh, J. A. (1999). The cognitive monster: The case against the controllability of automatic stereotype effects. In S.Chaiken and Y. Trope (Eds.), *Dual-process Theories in Social Psychology* (pp. 361–382). New York: The Guildford Press.

Bargh, J. A. (2005). Bypassing the will: Demystifying the nonconscious control of social behavior. In R.R.Hassin, J. S. Uleman, and J. A. Bargh (Eds.), *The New Unconscious* (pp. 37–58). Oxford: Oxford University Press.

Bargh, J. A. (2006) (Ed.) *Social Psychology and the Unconscious.* New York: Psychology Press.

Bargh, J. A. and Ferguson, M. J. (2000). Beyond behaviorism: On the automaticity of higher mental processes. *Psychological Bulletin, 126,* 925–945.

Barkow, J. H., Cosmides, L., and Tooby, J. (Eds.) (1992) *The Adapted Mind: Evolutionary Psychology and the Generation of Culture.* Oxford: Oxford University Press.

Barrett, L. F., Tugade, M. M., and Engle, R. W. (2004). Individual differences in working memory capacity and dual-process theories of the mind. *Psychological Bulletin, 130,* 553–573.

Benjamin, L. T. and Simpson, J. A. (2009). The power of the situation. *American Psychologist, 64,* 12–29.

Bennett, J. (2003). *A Philosophical Guide to Conditionals.* Oxford: Oxford University Press.

Berry, D. C. and Dienes, Z. (1993). *Implicit Learning.* Hove, UK: Erlbaum.

Betsch, T. (2008). The nature of intuition and its neglect in research on judgement and decision making. In H.Plessner, C. Betsch, and T. Betsch (Eds.), *Intuition in Judgment and Decision Making*. New York: Erlbaum.

Blackmore, S. (2000). *The Meme Machine*. Oxford: Oxford University Press.

Braine, M. D. S. and O'Brien, D. P. (1998). *(Eds) Mental Logic*. Mahwah, NJ: Lawrence Erlbaum Associates.

Bruner, J. S., Goodnow, J. J., and Austin, G. A. (1956). *A Study of Thinking*. New York: Wiley.

Buss, D. (2004). *Evolutionary Psychology: The New Science of the Mind*, 2nd ed. Needham Heights, MA: Allyn and Bacon.

Butler, A. C., Chapman, J. E., Forman, E. M., and Beck, A. T. (2006). The empirical status of cognitive-behavioral therapy: A review of meta-analyses. *Clinical Psychology Review, 26*, 17–31.

Byrne, R. M. J. (1989). Suppressing valid inferences with conditionals. *Cognition, 31*, 61–83.

Caldwell, D. F. and Burger, J. M. (1998). Personality characteristics of job applicants and success in screening interviews. *Personnel Psychology, 79*, 119–136.

Carruthers, P. (2002). The cognitive functions of language. *Behavioral and Brain Sciences, 25*, 657–719.

Carruthers, P. (2006). *The Architecture of the Mind*. Oxford: Oxford University Press.

Carruthers, P. (2009). How we know our own minds: The relationship between mindreading and metacognition. *Behavioral and Brain Sciences, 32*, 121–138.

Casscells, W., Schoenberger, A., and Graboys, T. B. (1978). Interpretation by physicians of clinical laboratory results. *New England Journal of Medicine, 299*, 999–1001.

Chaiken, S. (1980). Heuristic versus systematic information processing and the use of source versus message cues in in persuasion. *Journal of Personality and Social Psychology, 39*, 752–766.

Chaiken, S. and Trope, Y. (Eds.) (1999). *Dual-process Theories in Social Psychology*. New York: Guildford Press.

Chalmers, D. (1996). *The Conscious Mind: In Search of a Fundamental Theory*. Oxford: Oxford University Press.

Chase, W. G. and Simon, H. A. (1973). Perception in chess. *Cognitive Psychology, 4*, 55–81.

Chen, S. and Chaiken, S. (1999). The heuristic-systematic model in its broader context. In S.Chaiken and Y. Trope (Eds.), *Dual-process Theories in Social Psychology*. New York: The Guildford Press.

Chomsky, N. (1986). *Knowledge of Language: Its Nature, Origin and Use*. New York: Praeger.

Clark, A. and Chalmers, D. J. (1998). The extended mind. *Analysis, 58*, 10–23.

Colom, R., Rebollo, I., Palacios, A., Juan-Espinosa, M., and Kyllonen, P. C. (2004). Working memory is (almost) perfectly predicted by g. *Intelligence, 32*, 277–296.

Coltheart, M. (2004). Brain imaging, connectionism, and cognitive neuropsychology. *Cognitive Neuropsychology, 21*, 21–25.

Cosmides, L. (1989). The logic of social exchange: Has natural selection shaped how humans reason? *Cognition, 31*, 187–276.

Cosmides, L. and Tooby, J. (1992). Cognitive adapations for social exchange. In J.H.Barkow, L. Cosmides, and J. Tooby (Eds.), *The Adapted Mind: Evolutionary Psychology and the Generation of Culture* (pp. 163–228). New York: Oxford University Press.

Cosmides, L. and Tooby, J. (2000). Consider the source: The evolution of adaptations for decoupling and metarepresentation. In D. Sperber (Ed.), *Metarepresentations* (pp. 53–115). Oxford: Oxford University Press.

Crano, W. D. and Prislin, R. (2006). Attitudes and persuasion. *Annual Review of Psychology, 57,* 354–374.

Crano, W. D. and Prislin, R. (2008). *Attitudes and Attitude Change.* New York: Taylor and Francis.

Darwin, C. (1872). *The Expression of Emotions in Man and Animals.* London: John Murray.

Dawkins, R. (1976). *The Selfish Gene.* Oxford: Oxford University Press.

De Neys, W. (2006). Dual processing in reasoning – Two systems but one reasoner. *Psychological Science, 17,* 428–433.

De Neys, W. and Glumicic, T. (2008). Conflict monitoring in dual process theories of thinking. *Cognition, 106,* 1248–1299.

De Neys, W., Vartanian, O., and Goel, V. (2008). Smarter than we think: When our brains detect that we are biased. *Psychological Science, 19,* 483–489.

Deary, I. J. (2001). *Intelligence: A Very Short Introduction.* Oxford: Oxford University Press.

Dennett, D. (1991). *Consciousness Explained.* London: Allen Lane.

Dennett, D. (1995). *Darwin's Dangerous Idea: Evolution and the Meanings of Life.* New York: Simon and Schuster.

Deutsch, R. and Strack, F. (2006). Reflective and impulsive determinants of addictive behavior. In W.W.Reinout and A. W. Stacy (Eds.), *Handbook of Implicit Cognition and Addiction* (pp. 45–57). Thousand Oaks, CA.: Sage.

Dickens, W. T. and Flynn, J. R. (2001). Heritability estimates versus large environmental effects: The IQ paradox resolved. *Psychological Review, 108,* 346–369.

Dijksterhuis, A. (2004). Think different: The merits of unconscious thought in preference development and decision making. *Journal of Personality and Social Psychology, 87,* 586–598.

Dijksterhuis, A., Bos, M. W., Nordgren, L. F., and von Baaren, R. B. (2006). On making the right choice: The deliberation-without-attention effect. *Science, 311,* 1005–1007.

Dixon, N. F. (1971). *Subliminal Perception: The Nature of a Controversy.* London: McGraw Hill.

Dunbar, R. (2004). *The Human Story.* Chatham, Kent: Farer and Faber.

Eddy, D. M. (1982). Probabilistic reasoning in clinical medicine: Problems and opportunities. In D. Kahneman, P. Slovic, and A. Tversky (Eds.), *Judgment Under Uncertainty: Heuristics and Biases* (pp. 249–267). Cambridge: Cambridge University Press.

Edgington, D. (1995). On conditionals. *Mind, 104,* 235–329.

Edwards, W. (1954). The theory of decision making. *Psychological Bulletin, 41,* 380–417.

Edwards, W. (1961). Behavioral decision theory. *Annual Review of Psychology, 67,* 441–452.

Eichenbaum, N. J. and Cohen, N. J. (2001). *From Conditioning to Conscious Reflection: Memory Systems of the Brain.* New York: Oxford University Press.

Ellemers, N., Spears, R., and Doosje, B. (2002). Self and social identity. *Annual Review of Psychology, 53,* 161–186.

Engle, R. W. (2002). Working memory capacity as executive attention. *Current Directions in Psychological Science, 11,* 19–23.

Epstein, S. (1994). Integration of the cognitive and psychodynamic unconscious. *American Psychologist, 49,* 709–724.

Epstein, S. and Pacini, R. (1999). Some basic issues regarding dual-process theories from the perspective of cognitive-experiential theory. In S.Chaiken and Y. Trope (Eds.), *Dual-process Theories in Social Psychology* (pp. 462–482). New York: The Guildford Press.

Epstein, S., Pacini, R., es-Raj, V., and Heier, H. (1996). Individual differences in intuitive-experiential and analytic-rational thinking styles. *Journal of Personality and Social Psychology, 71,* 390–405.

Ericsson, K. A., Krampe, R. T., and Tesch-Roemer, C. (1993). The role of deliberate practice in the acquisition of expert performance. *Psychological Review, 100,* 363–406.

Evans, J. St. B. T. (1989). *Bias in Human Reasoning: Causes and Consequences.* Brighton: Erlbaum.

Evans, J. St. B. T. (1998). Matching bias in conditional reasoning: Do we understand it after 25 years? *Thinking and Reasoning, 4,* 45–82.

Evans, J. St. B. T. (2003). In two minds: Dual process accounts of reasoning. *Trends in Cognitive Sciences, 7,* 454–459.

Evans, J. St. B. T. (2005). *How to do Research: A Psychologist's Guide.* Hove, UK: Psychology Press.

Evans, J. St. B. T. (2006a). Dual system theories of cognition: some issues. Proceedings of the 28th Annual Meeting of the Cognitive Science Society, Vancouver, http://www.cogsci.rpi.edu/CSJarchive/proceedings/2006/docs/p202.pdf, pp. 202–207.

Evans, J. St. B. T. (2006b). The heuristic-analytic theory of reasoning: Extension and evaluation. *Psychonomic Bulletin and Review, 13,* 378–395.

Evans, J. St. B. T. (2007a). *Hypothetical Thinking: Dual Processes in Reasoning and Judgement.* Hove, UK: Psychology Press.

Evans, J. St. B. T. (2007b). On the resolution of conflict in dual-process theories of reasoning. *Thinking and Reasoning, 13,* 321–329.

Evans, J. St. B. T. (2008). Dual-processing accounts of reasoning, judgment and social cognition. *Annual Review of Psychology, 59,* 255–278.

Evans, J. St. B. T. (2009). How many dual-process theories do we need: One, two or many? In J.St.B.T.Evans and K. Frankish (Eds.), *In Two Minds: Dual Processes and Beyond* (pp. 31–54). Oxford: Oxford University Press.

Evans, J. St. B. T. and Ball, L. J. (2009). Do people reason on the Wason selection task: A new look at the data of Ball et al. (2003). *Quarterly Journal of Experimental Psychology, 63,* 434–441.

Evans, J. St. B. T. and Coventry, K. (2006). A dual-process approach to behavioral addiction. The case of gambling. In W.W.Reinout and A. W. Stacy (Eds.), *Handbook of Implicit Cognition and Addiction.* Thousand Oaks, CA.: Sage.

Evans, J. St. B. T. and Curtis-Holmes, J. (2005). Rapid responding increases belief bias: Evidence for the dual-process theory of reasoning. *Thinking and Reasoning, 11,* 382–389.

Evans, J. St. B. T. and Frankish, K. (Eds.) (2009). *In Two Minds: Dual Processes and Beyond.* Oxford: Oxford University Press.

Evans, J. St. B. T. and Lynch, J. S. (1973). Matching bias in the selection task. *British Journal of Psychology, 64,* 391–397.

Evans, J. St. B. T. and Over, D. E. (1996). *Rationality and Reasoning.* Hove: Psychology Press.

Evans, J. St. B. T. and Over, D. E. (2004). *If.* Oxford: Oxford University Press.

Evans, J. St. B. T. and Wason, P. C. (1976). Rationalisation in a reasoning task. *British Journal of Psychology, 63,* 205–212.

Evans, J. St. B. T., Barston, J. L., and Pollard, P. (1983). On the conflict between logic and belief in syllogistic reasoning. *Memory and Cognition, 11,* 295–306.

Evans, J. St. B. T., Handley, S., Neilens, H., Bacon, A. M., and Over, D. E. (in press). The influence of cognitive ability and instructional set on causal conditional inference. *Quarterly Journal of Experimental Psychology.*

Evans, J. St. B. T., Harries, C. H., and Dean, J. (1995). Tacit and explicit policies in general practioners' prescription of lipid lowering agents. *British Journal of General Practice, 45,* 15–18.

Evans, J. St. B. T., Handley, S. J., and Over, D. E. (2003). Conditionals and conditional probability. *Journal of Experimental Psychology: Learning Memory and Cognition, 29,* 321–355.

Evans, J. St. B. T., Handley, S., Neilens, H., and Over, D. E. (2007). Thinking about conditionals: A study of individual differences. *Memory and Cognition, 35,* 1772–1784.

Evans, J. St. B. T., Neilens, H., Handley, S., and Over, D. E. (2008). When can we say 'if'? *Cognition, 108,* 100–116.

Fellous, J.-M. and Arbib, M. A. (Eds.) (2005). *Who need emotions? The brain meets the robot.* Oxford: Oxford University Press.

Fischhoff, B. (1982). For those condemned to study the past: Heuristics and biases in hindsight. In D. Kahneman, P. Slovic, and A. Tversky (Eds.), *Judgement Under Uncertainty: Heuristics and Biases* (pp. 335–351). Cambridge: Cambridge University Press.

Fodor, J. (1983). *The Modularity of Mind.* Scranton, PA: Crowell.

Fodor, J. (2000). Why we are so good at catching cheaters? *Cognition, 75,* 29–32.

Fodor, J. (2001). *The mind doesn't work that way.* Cambridge, MA: MIT Press.

Fong, G. T., Krantz, D. H., and Nisbett, R. E. (1986). The effects of statistical training on thinking about everyday problems. *Cognitive Psychology, 18,* 253–292.

Ford, N. (1992). The AIDS awarenes and sexual behaviour of young people in the Southwest of England. *Journal of Adolescence, 15,* 413.

Forgas, J. P., Williams, K. R., and von Hippel, W. (Eds.) (2003). *Social Judgments: Implicit and Explicit Processes.* New York: Cambridge University Press.

Franco-Watkins, A. M., Derks, P. L., and Dougherty, M. (2003). Reasoning in the Monty Hall problem: Examining choice behaviour and probability judgements. *Thinking and Reasoning, 9,* 67–90.

Frankish, K. (2004). *Mind and Supermind.* Cambridge: Cambridge University Press.

Frankish, K. (2009). Systems and levels: Dual-system theories and the personal-subpersonal distinction. In J.St.B.T. Evans and K. Frankish (Eds.), *In Two Minds: Dual Processes and Beyond* (pp. 89–108). Oxford: Oxford University Press.

Frankish, K. and Evans, J. St. B. T. (2009). The duality of mind: An historical perpsective. In J.St.B.T. Evans and K. Frankish (Eds.), *In Two Minds: Dual Processes and Beyond* (pp. 1–30). Oxford: Oxford University Press.

Frederick, S. (2005). Cognitive reflection and decision making. *Journal of Economic Perspectives, 19(4),* 25–42.

Frey, M. C. (2004). Scholastic assessment or g? *Psychological Science, 15,* 373–378.

Fugelsang, J. A., Stein, C. B., Green, A. E., and Dunbar, K. N. (2004). Theory and data interactions of the scientific mind: Evidence from the molecular and cognitive laboratory. *Canadian Journal of Experimental Psychology, 58,* 86–95.

Galton, F. (1893). *Inquiries into Human Faculty and Its Development.* London: Macmillan.

Gen, M. and Cheng, R. (1997). *Genetic Algorithms and Engineering Design.* New Work: Wiley.

Gigerenzer, G. (2002). *Reckoning with Risk.* London: Penguin Books.

Gigerenzer, G. (2007). *Gut Feelings.* London: Penguin.

Gigerenzer, G. and Regier, T. (1996). How do we tell an association from a rule? Comment on Sloman (1996). *Psychological Bulletin, 119,* 23–26.

Gilinsky, A. S. and Judd, B. B. (1994). Working memory and bias in reasoning across the life-span. *Psychology and Aging, 9,* 356–371.

Gilovich, T., Griffin, D., and Kahneman, D. (2002). *Heuristics and Biases: The Psychology of Intuitive Judgement.* Cambridge: Cambridge University Press.

Gilovich, T., Vallone, R., and Tversky, A. (1985). The hot hand in basketball: On the misperception of random sequences. *Cognitive Psychology, 17,* 295–314.

Gladwell, M. (2005). *Blink.* London: Penguin.

Goel, V. (2005). Cognitive neuroscience of deductive reasoning. In K.Holyoak and R. G. Morrison (Eds.), *The Cambridge Handbook of Thinking and Reasoning* (pp. 475–492). Cambridge: Cambridge University Press.

Goel, V. (2008). Anatomy of deductive reasoning. *Trends in Cognitive Sciences, 11,* 435–441.

Goel, V. and Dolan, R. J. (2003). Explaining modulation of reasoning by belief. *Cognition, 87,* B11–B22.

Goodale, M. A. (2007). Duplex vision: separate cortical pathways for conscious perception and the control of action. In M.Velmans and S. Schneider (Eds.), *The Blackwell Companion to Consciousness* (pp. 616–627). Oxford: Blackwell.

Goodale, M. A. and Milner, A. D. (2004). *Sight Unseen: An Exploration of Conscious and Unconscious Vision.* Oxford: Oxford University Press.

Gould, S. J. (1991). Exaption: A crucial tool for evolutionary psychology. *Journal of Social Issues, 47,* 43–45.

Griffiths, M. (1995). *Adolescent Gambling.* London: Routledge.

Griggs, R. A. and Cox, J. R. (1982). The elusive thematic materials effect in the Wason selection task. *British Journal of Psychology, 73,* 407–420.

Hammond, K. R. (1996). *Human Judgment and Social Policy.* New York: Oxford University Press.

Harford, T. (2006). *The Undercover Economist.* London: Time Warner.

Harries, C., Evans, J. St. B. T., and Dennis, I. (2000). Measuring doctors' self-insight into their treatment decisions. *Journal of Applied Cognitive Psychology, 14,* 455–477.

Harries, C., Evans, J. St. B. T., Dennis, I., and Dean, J. (1996). A clinical judgement analysis of prescribing decisions in general practice. *Le Travail Humain, 59,* 87–111.

Haselager (1997). *Cognitive Science and Folk Psychology.* London: Sage.

Heller, F. H., Saltzstein, H. D., and Caspe, W. B. (1992). Heuristics in medical and non-medical decision making. *Quarterly Journal of Experimental Psychology, 44A,* 211–235.

Howcroft, D. (2001). After the goldrush: deconstructing the myths of the dot.com market. *Journal of Information Technology, 16,* 195.

Hull, C. L. (1920). Quantitative aspects of the evolution of concepts. *Psychological Mongraphs, Whole number 123.*

Humphrey, C. (1951). *Thinking: An Introduction to Its Experimental Psychology.* London: Methuen.

Izard, C. (2009). Emotion theory and research: Highlights, unanswered questions, and emerging issues. *Annual Review of Psychology, 60,* 1–25.

Johnson-Laird, P. N. and Byrne, R. M. J. (1991). *Deduction.* Hove and London: Erlbaum.

Johnson-Laird, P. N. and Byrne, R. M. J. (2002). Conditionals: a theory of meaning, pragmatics and inference. *Psychological Review, 109,* 646–678.

Johnson-Laird, P. N., Legrenzi, P., and Legrenzi, M. S. (1972). Reasoning and a sense of reality. *British Journal of Psychology, 63,* 395–400.

Jung, R. E. and Haier, R. J. (2007). The Parieto-Frontal Integration Theory (P-FIT) of intelligence: Converging neuroimaging evidence. *Behavioral and Brain Sciences, 30,* 135–154.

Kahneman, D. and Frederick, S. (2002). Representativeness revisited: Attribute substitution in intuitive judgement. In T. Gilovich, D. Griffin, and D. Kahneman (Eds.), *Heuristics and Biases: The Psychology of Intuitive Judgment* (pp. 49–81). Cambridge: Cambridge University Press.

Kahneman, D., Slovic, P., and Tversky, A. (1982). *Judgment Under Uncertainty: Heuristics and Biases.* Cambridge: Cambridge University Press.

Kahneman, D. and Tversky, A. (1973). On the psychology of prediction. *Psychological Review, 80,* 237–251.

Kahneman, D. and Tversky, A. (1979). Prospect theory: An analysis of decision under risk. *Econometrica, 47,* 263–291.

Keren, G. and Schul, Y. (2009). Two is not always better than one: A critical evaluation of two-system theories. *Perspectives on Psychological Science, 4,* 533–550.

Klauer, K. C., Musch, J., and Naumer, B. (2000). On belief bias in syllogistic reasoning. *Psychological Review, 107,* 852–884.

Klein, G. (1999). *Sources of Power.* Cambridge, MA: MIT Press.

Knowlton, B. J., Ramus, S., and Squire, L. R. (1992). Intact artificial grammar learning in amnesia. *Psychological Science, 3,* 172–179.

Kyburg, H. E. (2008). Inductive logic and inductive reasoning. In J. E. Alder and L. J. Rips (Eds.), *Reasoning: Studies of Human Inference and Its Foundations* (pp. 291–301). New York: Cambridge University Press.

Lassiter, D., Lindberg, M. J., Gonzalez-Vallejo, C., Bellezza, F. S., and Phillips, N. D. (2009). The deliberation-without-attention effect: Evidence for an artefactual interpretation. *Psychological Science, 20,* 671–675.

Lee, L. N. Y., Goodwin, G. P., and Johnson-Laird, P. N. (2008). The psychological problem of Sudoku. *Thinking and Reasoning, 14,* 342–364.

Lewicki, P. (1986). Processing information about covariations that cannot be articulated. *Journal of Experimental Psychology: Learning, Memory and Cognition, 12,* 135–146.

Libet, B. (1996). Neural processes in the production of conscious experience. In M.Velmans (Ed.), *The Science of Consciousness: Psychological, Neuropsychological and Clinical Reviews.* London: Routledge.

Lieberman, M. D. (2003). Reflective and reflexive judgment processes: A social cognitive neuroscience approach. In J.P.Forgas, K. R. Williams, and W. von Hippel (Eds.), *Social Judgments: Implicit and Explicit Processes* (pp. 44–67). New York: Cambridge University Press.

Lieberman, M. D. (2007a). Social cognitive neuroscience: A review of core processes. *Annual Review of Psychology, 58,* 259–289.

Lieberman, M. D. (2007b). The X- and C-Systems: The neural basis of automatic and controlled social cognition. In E. Harmon-Jones and P. Winkleman (Eds.), *Social Neuroscience* (pp. 290–315). New York: Guildford Press.

Lieberman, M. D. (2009). What zombies can't do: A social cognitive neuroscience approach to the irreducibility of reflective consciousness. In J.St.B.T.Evans and K. Frankish (Eds.), *In Two Minds: Dual Processes and Beyond* (pp. 293–316). Oxford: Oxford University Press.

Lord, C., Ross, L., and Lepper, M. R. (1979). Biased assimilation and attitude polarisation: The effect of prior theories on subsequently considered evidence. *Journal of Personality and Social Psychology, 37,* 2098–2109.

Lucas, E. J. and Ball, L. J. (2005). Think-aloud protocols and the selection task: Evidence for relevance effects and rationalisation processes. *Thinking and Reasoning, 11,* 35–66.

Mackintosh, N. J. (2009). *IQ and Human Intelligence.* Oxford: Oxford University Press.

Mandler, J. M. and Mandler, G. (1964). *Thinking: From Association to Gestalt.* New York: Wiley.

Manktelow, K. I. and Over, D. E. (1991). Social roles and utilities in reasoning with deontic conditionals. *Cognition, 39,* 85–105.

Manktelow, K. I. and Over, D. E. (Eds.) (1993). *Rationality: Psychological and Philosophical Perspectives.* London: Routledge.

Marcel, A. J. (1983). Conscious and unconscious perception: Experiments on visual masking and word recognition. *Cognitive Psychology, 15,* 197–203.

Matute, H., Vadillo, M. A., Vegas, S., and Blanco, F. (2007). Illusion of control in internet users and college students. *CyberPsychology and Behavior, 10,* 176–181.

McKenzie, R., Evans, J. St. B. T., and Hanoch, Y. (2010). Conditional reasoning in autism: Activation and integration of knowledge and belief. *Developmental Psychology, 46,* 391–403.

Merikle, P. M. and Reingold, E. M. (1998). On demonstrating unconscious perception. *Journal of Experimental Psychology: General, 127,* 304–310.

Michotte, A. (1962). *The Perception of Causality.* Andover, MA: Methuen.

Milgram, S. (1974). *Obedience to Authority: An Experimental View.* New York: HarperCollins.

Mithen, S. (1996). *The Prehistory of the Mind.* London: Thames and Hudson.

Myers, D. G. (2002). *Intutition: Its Powers and Perils*. New Haven, CT: Yale University Press.

Neisser, U. (1967). *Cognitive Psychology*. New York: Appleton.

Newell, B., Wong, K. W., Cheung, J., and Rakow, T. (2008). Think, blink or sleep on it? The impact of modes of thought on complex decision making. *Quarterly Journal of Experimental Psychology, 62*, 707–732.

Newman, S. D., Carpenter, P. A., Varma, S., and Just, M. A. (2003). Frontal and parietal participation in problem solving in the Tower of London: fMRI and computational modeling of planning and high-level perception. *Neuropsychologia, 41*, 1668–1682.

Newstead, S. E. (2000). Are there two different kinds of thinking? *Behavioral and Brain Sciences, 23*, 690–691.

Newstead, S. E., Handley, S. J., Harley, C., Wright, H., and Farelly, D. (2004). Individual differences in deductive reasoning. *Quarterly Journal of Experimental Psychology, 57A*, 33–60.

Nisbett, R., Peng, K., Choi, I., and Norenzayan, A. (2001). Culture and systems of thought: Holistic versus analytic cognition. *Psychological Review, 108*, 291–310.

Nisbett, R. E. and Wilson, T. D. (1977). Telling more than we can know: Verbal reports on mental processes. *Psychological Review, 84*, 231–295.

Norman, D. (1969). *Memory and Attention*. New York: Wiley.

Norman, D. and Shallice, T. (1986). Attention to action: Willed and automatic control of behavior. In R.Davidson, R. G. Schwartz, and D. Shapiro (Eds.), *Consciousness and Self-Regulation: Advances in Research and Theory* (pp. 1–18). New York: Plenum Press.

Nosek, B. A., Greenwald, A. G., and Banaji, M. (2007). The implicit association test at age 7: A methodological and conceptual review. In J.A.Bargh (Ed.), *Social Psychology and the Unconscious* (p. 11). New York: Psychology Press.

Oberauer, K. and Wilhelm, O. (2003). The meaning(s) of conditionals: Conditional probabilities, mental models and personal utilities. *Journal of Experimental Psychology: Learning, Memory and Cognition, 29*, 680–693.

Oppenheimer, D. M. (2003). Not so fast! (and not so frugal!): rethinking the recognition heuristic. *Cognition, 90*, B1–B9.

Osman, M. (2004). An evaluation of dual-process theories of reasoning. *Psychonomic Bulletin and Review, 11*, 988–1010.

Ost, L.-G. (1996). One-session group treatment of spider phobia. *Behavior Research and Therapy, 34*, 707–715.

Ostrom, T. M. and Sedikides, C. (1992). Out-group homogeneity effects in natural and minimal groups. *Psychological Bulletin, 112*, 536–552.

Over, D. E., Hadjichristidis, C., Evans, J. St. B. T., Handley, S. J., and Sloman, S. A. (2007). The probability of causal conditionals. *Cognitive Psychology, 54*, 62–97.

Petty, R. E. and Cacioppo, J. T. (1981). *Attitudes and Persuasions: Classical and Contemporary Approaches*. Dubuque, IA: William C. Brown.

Petty, R. E. and Wegener, D. T. (1999). The elaboration likelihood model: Current status and controversies. In S.Chaiken and Y. Trope (Eds.), *Dual-process Theories in Social Psychology* (pp. 41–72). New York: The Guildford Press.

Pinker, S. (1994). *The Language Instinct*. New York: Harper-Collins.

Pinker, S. (1997). *How the Mind Works*. New York: Norton.

Pinker, S. (2002). *The Blank Slate*. London: Penguin.

Pinker, S. and Bloom, P. (1990). Natural language and natural selection. *Behavioral and Brain Sciences, 13,* 707–784.

Plessner, H., Betsch, C., and Betsch, T. (Eds.) (2008). *Intuition in Judgment and Decision Making*. New York: Erlbaum.

Quattrone, G. A. and Jones, E. E. (1980). The perception of variability within in-groups and out-groups: Implications for the law of small numbers. *Journal of Personality and Social Psychology, 38,* 141–152.

Ravenscroft, I. (2005). *Philosophy of Mind: A Beginner's Guide*. Oxford: Oxford University Press.

Raylu, N. and Oci, T. P. S. (2002). Pathological gambing: A comprehensive review. *Clinical Psychology Review, 22,* 1009–1061.

Real, L. A. (1991). Animal choice behaviour and the evolution of cognitive architecture. *Science, 253,* 980–979.

Reber, A. S. (1993). *Implicit Learning and Tacit Knowledge*. Oxford: Oxford University Press.

Reeves, J. W. (1965). *Thinking about Thinking*. London: Methuen.

Rips, L. J. (1994). *The Psychology of Proof*. Cambridge, MA: MIT Press.

Roese, N. J. (2004). Twisted pair: Counterfactual thinking and hindsight bias. In N. Harvey and D. J. Koehler (Eds.), *Blackwell Handbook on Judgment and Decision Making* (pp. 258–273). Oxford: Blackwell.

Ross, L. (1977). The intuitive psychologist and his shortcomings. In L. Berkowitz (Ed.), *Advances in Experimental Social Psychology* (pp. 174–220). New York: Academic Press.

Ryle, G. (1949). *The Concept of Mind*. London: Hutchinson.

Sa, W. C., West, R. F., and Stanovich, K. E. (1999). The domain specificity and generality of belief bias: Searching for a generalizable critical thinking skill. *Journal of Educational Psychology, 91,* 497–510.

Samuels, R. (2009). The magic number two plus or minus: Some comments on dual-processing theories of cognition. In J.St.B.T. Evans and K. Frankish (Eds.), *In Two Minds: Dual Processes and Beyond*. Oxford: Oxford University Press.

Samuelson, P. (1963). Risk and uncertainty: A fallacy of large numbers. *Scientia,* 108–111.

Schaller, M. and Duncan, L. A. (2007). The behavioral immune system: Its evolution and social psychological implications. In J. P. Forgas, M. G. Hasleton, and W. von Hippel (Eds.), *Evolution and the social mind* (pp. 293–307). New York: Psychology Press.

Schneider, W. and Shiffrin, R. M. (1977). Controlled and automatic human information processing I: Detection, search and attention. *Psychological Review, 84,* 1–66.

Schwartz, B. (2004). *The Paradox of Choice*. New York: HarperCollins.

Shafir, E. (1993). Choosing versus rejecting: why some options are both better and worse than others. *Memory and Cognition, 21,* 546–556.

Shallice, T. and Warrington, E. K. (1970). Independent functioning of verbal memory stores: A neuropsychological study. *Quarterly Journal of Experimental Psychology, 22,* 261–273.

Shanks, D. R. and St John, M. F. (1994). Characteristics of dissociable human learning systems. *Behavioral and Brain Sciences, 17,* 367–447.

Sherry, D. F. and Schacter, D. L. (1987). The evolution of multiple memory systems. *Psychological Review, 94,* 439–454.

Shiffrin, R. M. and Schneider, W. (1977). Controlled and automatic human information processing II: Perceptual learning, automatic attending and a general theory. *Psychological Review, 84,* 127–189.

Shynkarkuk, J. M. and Thompson, V. A. (2006). Confidence and accuracy in deductive reasoning. *Memory and Cognition, 34,* 619–632.

Sloman, S. A. (1996). The empirical case for two systems of reasoning. *Psychological Bulletin, 119,* 3–22.

Sloman, S. A. (2005). *Causal Models.* Oxford: Oxford University Press.

Smith, E. R. and Collins, E. C. (2009). Dual-process models: A social psychological perspective. In J.St.B.T. Evans and K. Frankish (Eds.), *In Two Minds: Dual Processes and Beyond* (pp. 197–216). Oxford: Oxford University Press.

Smith, E. R. and DeCoster, J. (2000). Dual-process models in social and cognitive psychology: Conceptual integration and links to underlying memory systems. *Personality and Social Psychology Review, 4,* 108–131.

Soon, C. S., Brass, M., Heinze, H.-J., and Haynes, J.-D. (2008). Unconscious determinants of free decisions in the human brain. *Nature Neuroscience, 11,* 543–545.

Sperber, D. (2000). Metarepresentations in an evolutionary perspective. In D.Sperber (Ed.), *Metarepresentations* (pp. 117–138). Oxford: Oxford University Press.

Stanovich, K. E. (1989). Implicit philosophies of mind: The dualism scale and its relation to extrasensory perception. *The Journal of Psychology, 123,* 5–23.

Stanovich, K. E. (1999). *Who is Rational? Studies of Individual Differences in Reasoning.* Mahway, NJ: Lawrence Erlbaum Associates.

Stanovich, K. E. (2004). *The Robot's Rebellion: Finding Meaning the Age of Darwin.* Chicago, IL: Chicago University Press.

Stanovich, K. E. (2009a). Is it time for a tri-process theory? Distinguishing the reflective and the algorithmic mind. In J.St.B.T. Evans and K. Frankish (Eds.), *In Two Minds: Dual Processes and Beyond.* Oxford: Oxford University Press.

Stanovich, K. E. (2009b). The thinking that IQ tests miss. *Scientific American, November/December,* 33–39.

Stanovich, K. E. (2009c). *What Intelligence Tests Miss. The Psychology of Rational Thought.* New Haven, CT and London: Yale University Press.

Stanovich, K. E. and West, R. F. (1997). Reasoning independently of prior belief and individual dfferences in actively open-minded thinking. *Journal of Educational Psychology, 89,* 342–357.

Stanovich, K. E. and West, R. F. (1998). Cognitive ability and variation in selection task performance. *Thinking and Reasoning, 4,* 193–230.

Stanovich, K. E. and West, R. F. (2000). Individual differences in reasoning: Implications for the rationality debate? *Behavioral and Brain Sciences, 23,* 645–726.

Stanovich, K. E. and West, R. F. (2007). Natural myside bias is independent of cognitive ability. *Thinking and Reasoning, 13,* 225.

Stanovich, K. E. and West, R. F. (2008a). On the failure of cognitive ability to predict myside and one-sided thinking biases. *Thinking and Reasoning, 14,* 129–167.

Stanovich, K. E. and West, R. F. (2008b). On the relative independence of thinking biases and cognitive ability. *Journal of Personality and Social Psychology, 94,* 672–695.

Starcevic, V. (2005). *Anxiety disorders in adults*. Oxford: Oxford Univeristy Press.

Stevenson, R. J. and Over, D. E. (2001). Reasoning form uncertain premises: Effects of expertise and conversational context. *Thinking and Reasoning, 7,* 367–390.

Stewart, G. L., Dustin, S. L., Barrick, M. R., and Darnold, T. C. (2008). Exploring the handshake in employment interviews. *Journal of Applied Psychology, 93,* 1139–1146.

Strack, F. and Deutsch, R. (2004). Reflective and impulsive determinants of social behavior. *Personality and Social Psychology Review, 8,* 220–247.

Sun, R. (2001). *Duality of Mind: A Bottom-Up Approach Towards Cognition*. Hillsdale, NJ: Lawrence Erlbaum Associates.

Thompson, V. A. (2009). Dual-process theories: A metacognitive perspective. In J.St.B.T.Evans and K. Frankish (Eds.), *In Two Minds: Dual Processes and Beyond* (pp. 171–196). Oxford: Oxford University Press.

Toates, F. (2006). A model of the hierarchy of behaviour, cognition and consciousness. *Consciousness and Cognition, 15,* 75–118.

Tooby, J. and Cosmides, L. (1992). The psychological foundations of culture. In J. H. Barkow, L. Cosmides, and J. Tooby (Eds.), *The Adapted Mind: Evolutionary Psychology and the Generation of Culture* (pp. 19–136). New York: Oxford University Press.

Tsujii, T. and Watanabee, S. (2009). Neural correlates of dual-task effect on belief-bias syllogistic reasoning: A near-infrared spectroscopty study. *Brain Research, 1287,* 118–125.

Tversky, A. and Kahneman, D. (1983). Extensional vs intuitive reasoning: The conjunction fallacy in probability judgment. *Psychological Review, 90,* 293–315.

Tversky, A. and Shafir, E. (1992). The disjunction effect in choice under uncertainty. *Psychological Science, 3,* 305–309.

Uleman, J. S., Blader, S. L., and Todorov, A. (2005). Implicit impressions. In R.R.Hassin, J. S. Uleman, and J. A. Bargh (Eds.), *The New Unconscious* (pp. 362–392). New York: Oxford University Press.

Velmans, M. (2000). *Understanding Consciousness*. London: Routledge.

Verschueren, N., Schaeken, W., and d'Ydewalle, G. (2005). A dual-process specification of causal conditional reasoning. *Thinking and Reasoning, 11,* 239–278.

von Neumann, J. and Morgenstern, O. (1944). *Theory of Games and Economic Behavior*. Princeton, NJ: Princeton University Press.

Wagenaar, W. A. (1988). *Pardoxes of Gambling Behaviour*. Hove and London: Erlbaum.

Ward, J. (2006). *The Student's Guide to Cognitive Neuroscience*. Hove, UK: Psychology Press.

Wason, P. C. (1960). On the failure to eliminate hypotheses in a conceptual task. *Quarterly Journal of Experimental Psychology, 12*–40.

Wason, P. C. (1968). On the failure to eliminate hypotheses: a second look. In P.C.Wason and P. N. Johnson-Laird (Eds.), *Thinking and Reasoning* (pp. 165–174). Harmandsworth: Penguin.

Wason, P. C. and Evans, J. St. B. T. (1975). Dual processes in reasoning? *Cognition, 3,* 141–154.

Wegner, D. M. (2002). *The Illusion of Conscious Will*. Cambridge, MA: MIT books.

Weiskrantz, L. (1986). *Blindsight: a Case Study and Its Implications*. Oxford: Oxford University Press.

Whiten, A. (2000). Chimpanzee cognition and the question of mental re-representation. In D. Sperber (Ed.), *Metarepresentations*. Oxford: Oxford University Press.

Wilson, T. D. (2002). *Strangers to Ourselves*. Cambridge, MA: Belknap Press.

Wilson, T. D. and Schooler, J. W. (1991). Thinking too much: introspection can reduce the quality of preferences and decisions. *Journal of Personality and Social Psychology, 60,* 181–192.

Wilson, T. D., Lindsey, S., and Schooler, T. Y. (2000). A model of dual attitudes. *Psychological Review, 107,* 101–126.

Wittenbrink, B., Judd, C. M., and Park, B. (1997). Evidence for racial prejudice at the implicit level and its relationship with questionnarie methods. *Journal of Personality and Social Psychology, 72,* 262–274.

Zelli, A., Cervone, D., and Huesmann, L. R. (1996). Behavioral experience and social inference: Individual differences in aggressive expererience and spontaneous versus deliberative inference. *Social Cognition, 14,* 165–190.

Index

abortion 148–9
absent-mindedness 2
adaptation 23, 29, 30
addiction 7, 19, 147, 193, 195
advertising 147–8
agoraphobia 196–7, 198
AIDS awareness 146–7
amnesia 53–4
amygdala 70, 167
animal behaviour 23–4
animal cognition 39–40
animal learning 24
animal mind 23
animal rationality 188
anterior cingulate cortex 117–18
anxiety disorders 196–7
Architecture of the Mind, The (Carruthers) 42
Aristotle 9–10
art 37–8
artificial grammar 65–6
associationism 10, 11
attention 56, 117, 202–4
attention-deficit hyperactivity disorder
    (ADHD) 195
attitude 140–6
attitude change 146–50
automatic processes 8
automation 56, 201–2
availability heuristic 98

Baddeley, Alan 72
Bargh, John 145, 171
base rate fallacy 128–31
behavioural unconscious 19
behaviourism 12–14, 29
behaviour therapy 197–8
beliefs
    belief bias 114–18
    social influence 150–1
Betsch, Tilmann 97–8
bias 88–9
    belief bias 114–18
    cognitive biases 88–93, 148–9
    hindsight bias 91–2
    matching bias 124, 175
    myside bias 149
    one-sided bias 149
    outcome bias 90–1
blindsight 58–9

Blink: The Power of Thinking without Thinking
    (Gladwell) 94, 96
brain
    anatomy 44–5
    belief bias 117–18
    conscious experiences 164
    evolution 44–7
    imaging 45–6
    multiple memory systems 69–70
    size 32–3, 45
    X and C systems 179
breast cancer screening 130
Bruner, Jerome 64–5
Burt, Cyril 74

calculators 16
car driving 56
Carruthers, Peter 42, 151, 176
Cartesian Theatre 57
categorisation 64
causality 37, 101, 172–3
charity donation 84
chess playing 54–5, 107
chief executive model 3–5, 171
child custody problem 89–90
choice 175
Chomsky, Noam 54, 61
classical conditioning 12–13
cognitive-behavioural therapy (CBT) 197
cognitive biases 88–93, 148–9
cognitive feelings 7
cognitive misers 166
cognitive modules 17–18, 38–42, 61, 151
cognitive neuropsychology 45
cognitive neuroscience 45–6
cognitive psychology 2, 9, 15, 18
cognitive reflection test 206
cognitive science 15–18
cognitive therapy 198
cognitive unconscious 19
cold war 191
Coltheart, Max 45
common sense 2, 3; *see also* folk psychology
communication 35, 147–8
compulsive behaviour 7, 193
computational theory of mind 15
computer metaphor 15–18
computer programs 42–3
concept learning 64–9

conditional statements 119–22
confabulation 6, 149, 176, 210
confidence 7
conformity 150–3
conjunction fallacy 127–8
consciousness 6–8, 159
    access 174–5
    emotion and 167
    neural correlates 178–81
    phenomenal 159, 160, 161, 164, 166
    philosophy 161–5
contextualized thinking 168, 203
controlled attention 56, 117
controlled processes 8
Cosmides, Leda 39 40–1
counterexample 203
criminal justice system 130, 170
C system 179–80

Darwinian algorithm 25–9
Data, Lieutenant, 186, 187
Dawkins, Richard 26
daydreaming 10
decision making 8, 79–81, 205
    cognitive biases 88–93
    playing the markets 81–3
    rational 83–8
declarative knowledge 53
deductive reasoning 108–10
default-interventionist theories 216
Dennett, Daniel 57
Dijksterhuis, A. 96–7, 99–100
disjunction effect 93
Dixon, Norman 58
dorsal system 59
double dissociation 70
driving skill 56
dualism 3–4, 162
dual-process theories 3, 20–1, 137–8,
    216–17
Dunbar, Robert 32–3
dysrationalia 205–7

Ebbinghaus illusion 59, 60
economics 83
education system 150
emotion 18, 140, 165–6, 167–8, 186–7
empiricism 10
engineering design 26–7
environment of evolutionary
    adaptation 41, 152
episodic memory 53–4, 63
Epstein, Seymour 186–7
event handlers 43–4
evolution 24–5, 26–7, 30–8, 44–7
exclusive disjunction 64
executive functions 46
expected value 85–7
experience 110

expertise 54–5, 56, 89–90, 92, 175–6
explicit knowledge 53–7, 70, 137–8, 166,
    200–2
explicit memory 6, 54, 62, 168
eyewitness testimony 130

fear 195–9
feeling 165–9
feeling of rightness 80, 97, 205, 207
first-order intentionality 34
fluid intelligence 37
Fodor, Jerry, 38
folk psychology 2, 3, 4, 5, 32, 136, 163, 170–1,
    174, 176, 210
forecasting 80, 83
Frederick, Shane 206
free association 10
free choice 164–5
free will 170–2
Freudian theory 14–15
frontal lobes 45, 46, 47
functional magnetic resonance imaging
    (fMRI) 45–6
fundamental attribution error 32
future 191
futures market 83

Galton, Francis 11–12
gambler's fallacy 101
gambling 7, 85, 86, 192–5
game theory 83–7
general intelligence (g) 41–2, 47,
    73–5, 205–7
general intelligence (Mithen's theory) 36
genes 26
genetic algorithm 26–7
Gigerenzer, Gerd 94–5, 96, 99
Gladwell, Malcolm 94, 96
global warming 88–9, 119–20, 192
goals 177, 187–8, 190–1, 195
Goel, Vinod 117
group membership 153–5
Gut Feelings (Gigerenzer) 94, 96

habit 2, 13, 19, 62, 63, 70, 79, 80,
    161, 193
Harford, Tim 82
heuristics 95, 98–9
heuristic-systematic model 215
hindsight bias 91–2
hippocampus 69–70
HM 69
Holmes, Sherlock 108–9, 113
hot car stories 1–2
hot hand effect 101
Hull, Clark 65
hypothesis testing 44, 64–5
hypothetical thinking 34, 35,
    118, 209

'if' 118–22
'if p then q' 120
illusion of conscious intention 169–73
Illusion of Conscious Will (Wegner) 169
illusion of control 170
illusory causation 172
imageless thoughts 111
images 9–10
imagination 118–22
immune system 141
Implicit Association Test (IAT) 144–5
implicit attitudes 143–6
implicit knowledge 53–7, 137–8, 166, 200–2
implicit learning 65–7, 70
implicit memory 6, 62
impression formation 138–9
impulsivity 195, 207
inductive reasoning 108
inferior frontal cortex 117–18
information processing systems 15, 16
in-groups 153–5
inner speech 56
instinct 23–4, 188–9
instrumental rationality 187
insurance 85–6
intelligence 15, 31, 36–7, 41–2, 47, 73–5,
    148–9, 191, 205–7, 209–10
intention 8, 13, 23, 34, 169–73
intentional cognition 177
introspection 9, 11–12, 160
intuitive judgements 97–8
intuitive mind v, 5, 6, 20–1, 24, 47–8
    attitude change 146, 147, 149, 150
    attitudes and beliefs 142
    belief bias 115–16, 117, 118
    cognitive biases 88–93
    compulsive behaviour 7, 193
    conflict with reflective mind 67, 69,
        185–6, 192–9
    co-operation with reflective mind 199–207
    decision making 8, 79–80, 89–90, 92
    emotion 18, 140, 165–6, 168
    expertise 176
    fear 199
    gambling 193, 194, 195
    impression formation 138, 139
    invariance 63
    matching bias 124
    playing the markets 82–3
    power of 93–100
    prejudice 143
    probability 101, 103
    procedural knowledge 55
    rationality 84, 186, 191
    reasoning 107, 113, 125, 126–7, 128
    rule learning 65–6, 67
    social identity 155
    social judgement 146
    social psychology 137

stimulus control 44
unconscious 7, 19, 163, 168
invariance 62, 63
IQ 41, 47, 73–4, 205–7

judgements 80

Kahneman, Danny 87–8, 98
Klein, Gary 67, 92
kludges 28
'knowing that' and 'knowing how' 53–7
knowledge exchange 200–2

language 29, 31, 33, 35, 54, 61, 113–14
language acquisition device 61
learning
    animal learning 24
    language 61–2
    rules 64–9
learning devices 61
less is more 94–6, 98
Libet, B. 164
Lieberman, Matt 178, 179–80
Linda problem 127–8
linguistic intelligence 37
logic 111–14
logic puzzles 110–11
long-term memory 71
long-term store 71–2
luck 194

markets 81–3
massive modularity theory 39, 40
matching bias 124, 175
material conditional 120
materialism 4, 162
medical diagnosis 130–1
memory 6, 53–4, 168
    multiple systems 60–3, 69–70
    working memory 71–3, 74–5
mentalism 12, 13, 32
mental logic 112, 113
mental model theory 112–13, 202–3
mental pictures 9–10
mental representations 33–4
mental simulation 80
meta-representation 33–5
Milgram, Stanley 152–3
military obedience 152
mind 3
mind–body (mind–brain) problem 161–3
mindreading 31, 35, 176
mindware 82
missing link 30
Mithen, Steve 36–8
modularity 24; *see also* cognitive modules
Modularity of Mind, The (Fodor) 38
Modus Ponens 121–2
monism 4, 162

Monty Hall problem 101–3
multiple memory systems 60–3, 69–70
mutation 27–8
myside bias 149–50

naïve judgements 99
nativism 10
natural history intelligence 37
natural selection 27
need for cognition 148
neural correlates of consciousness 178–81
neural imaging 45–6
new mind v, 24, 38, 42, 44–7, 140, 163, 166,
    170, 173, 179, 181, 182, 185, 186, 188,
    189–92, 194, 196, 198, 201, 209; see also
    reflective mind
Nixon, Richard 124
no-mind hypothesis 94
Norman, Don 168
normative module 151–2
nuclear warfare 191

obedience to authority 152–3
occupation 154
old mind v, 38, 44, 48, 135, 140, 141, 151,
    165–6, 167, 170, 179, 181, 185, 188–9,
    190, 191, 192, 194, 196, 197, 198, 199,
    201, 209; see also intuitive mind
one-sided bias 149
operant conditioning 12–13, 170
opinion polls 174
outcome bias 90–1
outcome feedback 65
out-groups 153–5
Over, David 118, 176

pain avoidance 195
panic disorder 196–7, 198
parallel-competitive theories 216
parallel processing 17
partial reinforcement 193
participants in research 11
past experience 189
pathological gambling 193–5
peer groups 151
perceptual constancies 160
persuasion 146–50
PET 45, 46
phenomenal consciousness 159, 160, 161,
    164, 166
philosophy 161–5
phobias 7, 196–9
physicalism 162
piano playing 55–6
pleasure principle 167
political campaigns 148
political correctness 142–3
political polls 174

positron emission tomography 45, 46
practice 55–6
preconscious 6, 7, 55, 60, 164, 177, 202, 203
Prehistory of the Mind, The (Mithen) 36–8
prejudice 140–6
priming 143–4
probability 100–4, 127–31
problem of induction 108
procedural knowledge 53, 54–6, 62, 70
product endorsement 147
property dualism 162
prosecutor's fallacy 130
prospect theory 87–8
psychoanalysis 12, 14
psychodynamic unconscious 19
psychological immune system 141
psychological zombie 178–81
psychopaths 151

qualia 161

racial prejudice 140–2, 144
randomness 101
rational decision making 83–8
rationalisations 14
rationality 19–20, 84, 186–92
rational man 83–4
rational thinking disposition 206
reasoning 44, 64, 107, 203
    belief bias 114–18
    conditionals 121–2
    deductive and inductive 108–10
    neuroscience 117–18
    probabilities 127–31
recognition heuristic 98–9
reflective cognition 179–80
reflective consciousness 164, 178–81
reflective mind v, 5–7, 20–1, 24, 47–8, 70–1
    accident of evolution 190
    anxiety 196
    attitude change 146, 147, 148, 150
    attitudes and beliefs 140, 142
    belief bias 115, 117, 118
    cognitive biases 88–93
    confabulation 6, 149, 176, 210
    conflict with intuitive mind 67, 69, 185–6,
        192–9
    consciousness 6, 163, 168
    co-operation with intuitive mind 199–207
    decision making 8, 79, 81, 89–90, 92, 205
    emotion 167, 168
    expertise 176
    fear 199
    frontal lobes 45
    gambling 194, 195
    goals 177, 191, 195
    heuristics 98, 99
    impression formation 138

intelligence 31, 36, 47, 75, 191, 205
intention 173
invariance 63
language 31, 35
memory 54, 72, 73, 168
novel problems 44
playing the markets 82–3
probability 101, 103
procedural knowledge 55–6
rationality 84, 186
reasoning 107, 113, 122, 125, 126, 202, 203
rule learning 64–5
self 210
self-knowledge 174, 175
social influence 151
social judgement 146
social psychology 137
working memory 72, 73
reflexive cognition 179–80
rehearsal 56
reinforcement 12
relevance 202–4
religion 37–8, 154, 163
representations 15
repression 14
right inferior frontal cortex 117–18
rightness 7
risk 84, 85–6, 147
robot consciousness 162–3
Robot's Rebellion, The (Stanovich) 24–5,
    189–90
rule learning 64–9
rules of thumb 95
Ryle, Gilbert 32

sanity 151
Savant, Marilyn vos 103
scientific theories 116
second-order intentionality 34
self-consciousness 34
Selfish Gene, The (Dawkins) 26
selfish genes 26
self-knowledge 174–7
semantic memory 53–4
semantic network 143–4
serial processing 17
sexual selection 27, 28
short-term memory 71
short-term store 71–2
shuttle box 197–8
Sign of Four (Conan-Doyle) 108–9, 113
skill learning 55–6, 62, 70, 201–2
Skinner, B. F. 12, 170
snooker players 55
social desirability 142
social identity 153–5
social influence 150–3
social intelligence 31–2, 37

social psychology 9, 135–8, 200
soldiers, obedience 152
spandrels 29
specific phobias 196, 197
Sperber, Dan 35
Spock, Mr 186, 187
sponsorship 147
Stanovich, Keith 24–5, 187, 189–90, 205
stereotypes 62, 140–6
stimulus control 44, 48
stock market 82–3
stream of consciousness 163
striatum 70
structured programming 42–4
subjects in research 10–11
subliminal perception 58, 144
substance dualism 162
Sudoku 110–11
superstition 170
Swiss Army knife model 40
symbol processing 17
systematic desensitisation 198
system level analysis 218

TASS 218
technical intelligence 37
theory of mind 31–2, 34, 35, 210
thermostats 16
thinking 9–15, 165–9
Toates, Fred 48
Tooby, John 39, 40–1
Tower of London problem 46–7
traits 138
transitive relationship 111
Tversky, Amos 87–8, 98
2 4 6 problem 67–9
two minds theory v, 5–9
    conflict 67, 69, 185–6, 192–9
    consciousness 163
    co-operation 199–207
    obedience to authority 153
    rationality 19–20
    see also intuitive mind; reflective mind
type 1 and type 2 processes 3, 20, 215–16,
    217, 218–19

uncertainty 83, 84
unconscious deliberation 96–7, 100
unconscious mind 7–8, 14, 19
unconscious perception 58–9
utility 84, 85

variances 62, 63
Velmans, Max 163
ventral system 59
vision 57–60, 61–2
visual illusions 59, 61–2
visual masking 58

vividness effect 171
volitional cognition 177
voluntary cognition 177

war crimes 152
Wason selection task 122–7, 175
Wason 2 4 6 problem 67–9
Watson, J. B. 12
Wegner, Daniel 169, 172

willing 169
Wilson, Tim 96, 145
working memory 71–3, 74–5
Würzburg experiments 11

X system 179–80

zombies 178–81